A Short History of Europe

Simon Jenkins is author of bestselling *A Short History of England*, *Britain's 100 Best Railway Stations*, *England's Thousand Best Churches* and *England's Thousand Best Houses*. He is a former Editor of the *Evening Standard* and *The Times* and columnist for the *Guardian*.

A Short History of Europe

From Pericles to Putin

SIMON JENKINS

PENGUIN BOOKS

PENGUIN BOOKS

UK | USA | Canada | Ireland | Australia
India | New Zealand | South Africa

Penguin Books is part of the Penguin Random House group of companies
whose addresses can be found at global.penguinrandomhouse.com.

First published by Viking 2018
Published in Penguin Books 2019

007

Copyright © Simon Jenkins, 2018

The moral right of the author has been asserted

Map illustrations by Ian Moores

Set in 10.8/13.3 pt Dante MT Std
Typeset by Jouve (UK), Milton Keynes
Printed and bound in Great Britain by Clays Ltd, Elcograf S.p.A.

A CIP catalogue record for this book is available from the British Library

PAPERBACK ISBN: 978-0-241-35252-6

www.greenpenguin.co.uk

For Nia

Contents

Contents

Contents

List of Illustrations

Section 2

Section 3

Maps

North
Sea

*Atlantic
Ocean*

BRITANNIA

Londinium

GERMANIA
INFERIOR

PANNONIA
SUPERIOR

BELGICA

GALLIA
LUGDUNENSIS

GERMANIA
SUPERIOR

NORICUM

RAETIA

AQUITANIA

Milan

DALM

GALLIA
NARBONENSIS

ITALIA

LUSITANIA

TARRACONENSIS

CORSICA

Rome

Cordoba

SARDINIA

Pompeii

BAETICA

SICILIA

Mediterranean

Syracuse

MAURETANIA
TINGITANA

MAURETANIA
CAESARIENSIS

Carthage

AFRICA

Leptis Magna

Approximate borders of the Roman Empire
at its maximum extent

JUDAEA Roman provinces and territories

The Roman Empire,
2nd century AD

PANNONIA
INFERIOR

DACIA

Black Sea

ATIA MOESIA
SUPERIOR MOESIA INFERIOR BITHYNIA

THRACIA Byzantium CAPPADOCIA

MACEDONIA Nicaea

GALATIA PARTHIA

EPIRUS ASIA

Ephesus LYCIA CILICIA

ACHAEA Antioch

Sparta Athens SYRIA

Sea CYPRUS

CRETA

JUDAEA

Caesarea

CYRENAICA Alexandria ARABIA

AEGYPTUS

PICTS

IRISH

North
Sea

JUTES

DANES

ANGLO-
SAXONS

FRISIANS

SAXONS

BRITONS

*Atlantic
Ocean*

THURINGIANS

BRITONS

Tournai   Cologne

FRANKISH KINGDOM

Paris

BAVARIANS

Regensburg

LO

Loire

ALEMANNI

BURGUNDIAN
KINGDOM

Bordeaux

The Alps   Milan

OSTROGOTHIC
KINGDOM

SUEVI

BASQUES

Toulouse   Arles

Ravenna

Ebro

Pyrenees

VISIGOTHIC
KINGDOM

CORSICA

Rome

Toledo

SARDINIA

Naples

Cordoba

VANDAL
KINGDOM

Hippo Regius

BERBERS

Carthage

SICILY

	Germanic kingdoms and peoples *c.*525
	Eastern Roman Empire *c.*525
⊙	Late Roman imperial capitals

The Barbarian Kingdoms,
early 6th century

| 0 | 100 | 200 | 300 | 400 | 500 miles |

| 0 | 200 | 400 | 600 | 800 km |

SLAVS

Carpathian Mountains

HUNS

Dnieper

BARDS

GEPIDS

Danube

Black Sea

Adrianople

Constantinople

EASTERN ROMAN EMPIRE

Thessalonica

Tigris

Athens

Antioch

Euphrates

SYRIA

CYPRUS

CRETE

Mediterranean Sea

Ptolemais

Cyrene

CYRENAICA

Alexandria

Jerusalem

EGYPT

Nile

Red Sea

Lotharingia, 9th century

N

| 0 | 100 | 200 | 300 | 400 | 500 miles |

| 0 | 200 | 400 | 600 | 800 km |

English Channel

SAXONY

WENDS

THURINGIA

Aachen

LOTHARINGIA

FRANCONIA

BOHEMIA

BRITTANY

Paris

Verdun

Regensburg

NEUSTRIA

SWABIA

②

③

OSTMARK

Bourges

Basle

BAVARIA

①

BURGUNDY

CARINTHIA

LOMBARDY

Milan

PAPAL STATES

Pavia

AQUITAINE

PROVENCE

Adriatic Sea

SPOLETO

Rome

Mediterranean Sea

— The Empire of Charlemagne's death, 814, and under Louis the Pious (Emperor 814–40)

① The Kingdom of West Francia under Charles the Bald (843–77, Emperor 875–7)

② The Middle Kingdom of Lothair I (r. 843–55), divided between his three sons – Louis II of Italy (855–75), Lothair II (855–69), and Charles of Provence

③ The Kingdom of East Francia under Louis the German (r. 843–76)

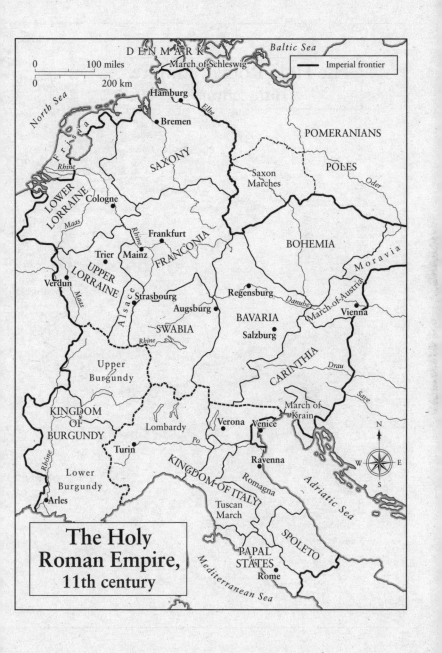

The Holy Roman Empire, 11th century

The Holy Roman Empire, 16th century

DENMAR

North Sea

Amsterdam

ENGLAND

NETHERLANDS

Bruges Antwerp

Calais

Ghent

Cologne

Brussels Liège

Arras

Mainz

Luxembourg

Trier

Paris

Metz

Strasbourg

Freibur

Seine

Loire

Dijon

FRANCHE-COMTÉ

Basel

FRANCE

Besançon

Bern

SWISS CONFEDERATI

Atlantic Ocean

Lyon

Milar

MILA

SAVOY

Avignon

Garonne

Perpignan

CORSICA

Douro

Ebro

Madrid

Barcelona

PORTUGAL

Lisbon

SPAIN

Guadalquivir

BALEARIC ISLES

SARDINIA

Cadiz

Tangier

Ceuta

Oran

Bona

European Empires, at the start of the 20th Century

0   1000   2000   3000 miles
0   2000   4000 km

NORWAY

SWEDEN

RUSSIAN EMPIRE

OTTOMAN
EMPIRE

AFGHANISTAN

CHINA

KOREA

JAPAN

Pacific Ocean

PERSIA

LIBYA

EGYPT

WEST

ARABIA

INDIA

BURMA

TAIWAN

ANGLO
EGYPTIAN
SUDAN

RIA

ABYSSINIA

UGANDA

ERITREA
SOMALILAND (Fr.)
SOMALILAND (Br.)
ITALIAN SOMALILAND
BR. EAST AFRICA
GER. EAST AFRICA
NYASALAND

SIAM

FRENCH INDOCHINA

PHILIPPINE IS.

KAISER
WILHELMSLAND

DUTCH
EAST INDIES

PAPUA

MADAGASCAR

MOZAMBIQUE

Indian Ocean

AUSTRALIA

UNION OF
SOUTH AFRICA

NEW
ZEALAND

**Europe,
at the start of
the First World War**

NORWAY

North
Sea

DENMARK
Copenhagen

Dublin

UNITED
KINGDOM

NETHERLANDS

The Hague

Elbe

Potsdam

London

BELGIUM

GERM

Thames

Brussels

Liège

English Channel

Paris

Marne

LUXEMBOURG

Rhine

Atlantic
Ocean

Loire

FRANCE

Danube

Berne

SWITZERLAND

Po

PORTUGAL

Madrid

CORSICA
(France)

Rome

Lisbon

SPAIN

SARDINIA
(Italy)

BALEARIC IS.
(Spain)

Mediterranean Sea

SPAN. MOROCCO

MOROCCO
(France)

ALGERIA
(France)

TUNISIA
(France)

Europe,
territorial changes resulting from the First World War

N
W — *E*
S

Atlantic Ocean

North Sea

NORWAY
Oslo ●

DENMARK
Copenhagen ●

①

IRISH FREE STATE
Dublin ●

UNITED KINGDOM

NETHERLANDS
The Hague ●

Elbe

Potsdam ●

GERM(Weimar)

Thames
London ●

BELGIUM
Brussels ● Liège ●

LUXEMBOURG

Paris ●
Versailles ●

Marne

Rhine

④

Danube

Munich ●

English Channel

Loire

ALSACE LORRAINE

FRANCE

SWITZERLAND
Berne ●

AU

Bordeaux ●

SOUTH TYROL

Po

KINGDOM OF THE SERBS CROATS AND SLOVENES

Marseilles ●

Madrid ●

Barcelona ●

CORSICA
(France)

Rome ●

Lisbon ●

PORTUGAL

S P A I N

● Seville

BALEARIC IS.
(Spain)

SARDINIA
(Italy)

Gibraltar (UK)
Tangier (Int.)

SPAN. MOROCCO

Mediterranean Sea

Algiers ●

MOROCCO
(France)

ALGERIA
(France)

TUNISIA
(France)

▨ territory lost by Germany	- - - - post First World War boundaries
▨ territory lost by USSR	①-④ territories returned to Germany via plebiscite
▨ Austria-Hungary in 1914	

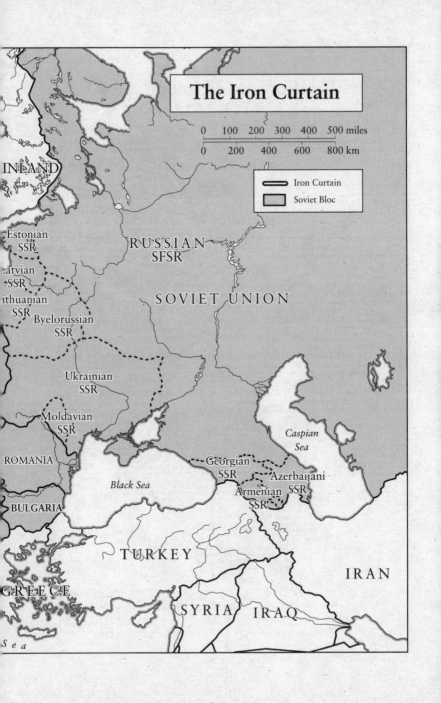

The Iron Curtain

| 0 | 100 | 200 | 300 | 400 | 500 miles |

| 0 | 200 | 400 | 600 | 800 km |

Iron Curtain

Soviet Bloc

FINLAND

Estonian
SSR

Latvian
SSR

Lithuanian
SSR

Byelorussian
SSR

Ukrainian
SSR

Moldavian
SSR

ROMANIA

BULGARIA

RUSSIAN
SFSR

SOVIET UNION

SOVIET UNION

Caspian
Sea

Black Sea

Georgian
SSR

Azerbaijani
SSR

Armenian
SSR

TURKEY

GREECE

SYRIA

IRAQ

IRAN

Sea

The European Union and NATO, 2018

0 100 200 300 400 500 miles

0   200   400   600   800 km

North Sea

NORWAY
1949

NETHERLANDS
1957 1949

BELGIUM 1957 1949

DENM
197

REPUBLIC OF IRELAND
1973

UNITED KINGDOM
(Due to leave the EU in 2019)
1973 1949

Thames

GERM
1957
1955

ICELAND
1949

English Channel

LUXEMBOURG
1957 1949

Marne

Loire

Seine

Rhine

Danube

Atlantic Ocean

FRANCE
1957 1949

Po

PORTUGAL
1986 1949

SPAIN
1986 1982

Gibraltar
(British)

Mediterranean Sea

Introduction

The cliffs of Cape St Vincent stand high and wild on the Portuguese coast, forming the south-west tip of Europe. Here we can watch the sun sink at dusk into the Atlantic, where the earliest Europeans believed they had reached the end of the world. Each night they thought they were seeing their source of heat and light extinguished by the ocean, to be reborn the following morning. I know of nowhere more conducive to such myths. Beyond these barren cliffs the viewer sees nothing but an eternity of sea. Behind is a land mass over which have rolled waves of tempestuous history.

Europe is primarily a modest peninsula off the north-west corner of Asia. It extends from the Portuguese coast north to the Arctic, south to the Mediterranean and east to the Caucasus and Ural mountains, where a rough metal sign by a road marks an arbitrary boundary. This continent has no deserts and just one notable mountain range, the Alps. Mostly it is fertile alluvial plain under a temperate sky, home to 750 million people, or more than twice the population of the USA.

Europe has no claim to pre-eminence among the world's agglomerations of peoples. Others can rival it in size, civilization and prosperity. Its emergence into imperial dominance towards the end of the second millennium was spectacular and short lived. But Europe's diversity and military supremacy, its dynamism and economic energy, its scientific prowess and cultural creativity give it a special place in human history. Even today, in a period of relative decline, it remains a magnet to refugees, migrants, scholars and travellers from across the world.

The word Europe emerged in the sixth century BC as referring to the mainland north of Greece. It has never had agreed borders. At first it was synonymous with the Roman empire and then with Christendom, both of which extended beyond the limits of present-day Europe to embrace large tracts of Asia and Africa. The eastern boundary has never been fixed but is generally accepted as the Urals, the Black Sea and the Caucasus mountains. This includes European Russia but excludes Turkey east of the Bosphorus as well as Georgia.

Any short history of this continent is essentially about its politics, the struggle of people for power over land. Hobbes declared that humans are born to perpetual conflict. Whether that conflict need be violent remains an open question, but Europe's story starts with those who were successful in battle, with the rulers rather than those they ruled. This is a narrative of power in a continent whose story, at least until recently, has been dominated by the practice of war, and therefore by the processes by which wars are prepared and concluded. Even today, Europeans seem unable to find a constitutional formula for living at peace with each other. They argue incessantly over what is meant by 'Europe'.

I am aware that history is the home to controversy. Some historians will regard a political approach to Europe's story as partial, seeing it as shutting out those who were victims of power, variously the poor, the enslaved, women, immigrants and outsiders. They all have their histories, as 'valid' as mine. So too would foreigners who lived under Europe's imperial yoke see Europe in a different light. I can only repeat that this book is about the wielding and distribution of power in the narrative of one continent. It must stand as the beginning of all other narratives.

Mine is a conventional history. I have divided Europe's story into periods. Most broadly they are the classical world, the Middle Ages, the growth of states, and the modern era. The first embraces Greece and Rome. The second covers the triumph of Christendom, first around the Mediterranean and then over northern Europe, coupled with the rise of the Holy Roman Empire and the coming of Islam to the Mediterranean basin. The third period sees the rise of nations, the wars of religion and succession, and the ideological revolutions of the eighteenth and nineteenth centuries. I end with the cataclysms of the past century, and the reconstruction of the continent we know today.

Along the way I have indicated the controversies that have dogged Europe's history, in the hope that readers may be encouraged to dig further. I am aware that views diverge over any division of Europe's story into 'ages'. They differ over the relative importance of Greece and Rome to classical culture; over the significance of Byzantium in Europe's evolution; over the impact on the continent of the Muslim invasions; over the role of the church in Europe's many conflicts, and its role in spurring, or impeding, the Renaissance and the Enlightenment. I can only nod at these differences in passing.

This is a history of Europe, not of the nations of Europe. It is an attempt to describe how a group of states, interacting with each other over time, developed a collective, continental consciousness. Geography means that some regions are more critical to that development than others, and this has guided my narrative. We shift from the eastern to the western Mediterranean, then north of the Alps to the great river basins of central Europe. France, Germany and their immediate neighbours have remained at the heart of the European story for the past millennium, and do to this day. Likewise Iberia, the British Isles, Scandinavia and eastern Europe have played more spasmodic and peripheral roles. I realize this leaves many countries out of the picture, and can seem cursory to those whose native country is omitted. My father's land of Wales does not play a role. But this is a story of Europe as a whole, not of its component parts.

My focus is chiefly on those individuals whose activities have been a part of that story and spread their influence beyond their national boundaries, leaders such as Augustus, Charlemagne, Innocent III, Charles V, Catherine the Great, Napoleon, Hitler and Gorbachev. As a student of economics, I am aware of the role of resources and money in politics, but this is not an economic history. Nor is it a cultural one. I mention Europe's rich cast-list of artists, writers and musicians, and its leading intellectual figures where I feel they illuminate the central story. Hence we meet Socrates, Aristotle, Gregory the Great, Shakespeare, Goethe, Beethoven, Hegel and Marx. They are the Greek chorus to the ever-pressing drama of these times.

Various themes surface in the course of the narrative, serving to bind it together. One is the extraordinary role of violence, and the technology of violence, in that narrative, at least until very recently. Another is the dualism of Hellenistic and Roman culture on the one hand, and Christian ethics and belief on the other. Both influences projected an external moral authority over the individual, but also stirred ideas of the individual as a force against that authority, whether embodied in church or state. Two further themes are the restless search, from the Greeks onwards, to legitimate governing power and relate it to consent, and the creative energy of trade and then of capital to drive forward the emergence of nation states. A final theme is how these forces brought the continent close to self-destruction in the twentieth century. From that crisis forged Europe's most benign legacy to the modern world, the idea of a social market economy under a democratic regime.

I have kept the narrative strictly chronological, because I believe history acquires meaning only if we can see effect following cause over time. Therefore, wherever possible I have avoided detours, backtracking or leaps forward. I have omitted anything that does not, in some sense, carry the story's central thrust while giving pen portraits of people and ideas that are important to that story. It drives towards what I hesitate to call a conclusion in the difficulties being experienced by the post-war efforts at European union.

I have long been a sceptic of the constitution and behaviour of the present European Union and its offspring the eurozone, but of the importance of its co-operative vitality I have no doubt. I have emerged from this survey with an enhanced admiration for my native continent. For all its oppressions, cruelties and ongoing mistakes, I see it as a remarkable corner of the globe, fertile in its culture and in its capacity for leadership and charity. I have learned how easily and often in the past its diplomacy has collapsed into chaos and bloodshed. I have also learned how often attempts to bond it together as one political entity have failed. Finding a balance between unity and diversity remains what it has always been, the defining challenge of European politics. I return to this theme in my epilogue.

Lastly, a note on brevity. This short book is aimed at those without the time or inclination for a longer one. I disagree with syllabuses that maintain history is better taught in depth than breadth. Depth should follow breadth, for without it history is meaningless. Without awareness of the timeline of human activity, individuals become dissociated figures on a bare stage. Those who cannot speak history to each other have nothing meaningful to say. Context – which means a sense of proportion – is everything.

I am with Cicero that 'to be ignorant of history is to be always a child', yet history as a series of random events leads to distortion and exploitation, to the weaponizing of exaggerated loyalties and long-held grievances. That is why the art of history is not just of remembering but also of knowing what to forget. It is about giving past time a plot and a narrative. That is the task that a short history should undertake.

I

Aegean Dawn – The Glory of Greece
2500–300 BC

Before the dawn: the first Europeans

It helps to be a god. As Zeus gazed along the Phoenician shore, his eye fell on a fair princess named Europa, playing on the beach. Seized with desire, he changed himself into a white bull and sauntered to her side. Entranced by the lovely creature, Europa put a garland around its neck and climbed on its back. According to the poet Ovid, the bull swam out to sea and reached the island of Crete. Here bull and princess somehow contrived to give birth to the future King Minos, stepfather of the monstrous Minotaur. From this improbable encounter was created a king, a country, a civilization and a continent.

We know little of the earliest occupants of the land to which Europa later gave her name. Prehistoric remains attest that they included both Neanderthals and Homo sapiens. Their culture embraced humans and animals, as depicted in France's Lascaux caves. Dating back some twenty millennia, these caves are still astonishing works, conveying the urge to depict reality in plastic form and hinting already at a shared humanity. At some point after the seventh millennium BC, Stone Age settlers either evolved from those crossing the Straits of Gibraltar or moved west from central Asia. They are commemorated in their henges, often gigantic structures such as England's Stonehenge, indicating a remarkable degree of social organization and engineering ability. Bone analysis shows visitors to Stonehenge travelling from as far as Switzerland. Early Europe was already bonded by travel.

Population movement greatly advanced with the discovery that tin and copper could be smelted to produce bronze. This made possible the making of utensils and the fashioning of weapons. Bronze meant trade, most easily by sea, and with it the growth of coastal settlements. Europe's interior was forested and largely impenetrable, but these settlements along rivers and coasts developed an outward-looking maritime culture, as travel by water was easier than by land.

From the fifth millennium, archaeologists have traced successive movements westwards out of Asia, the so-called Kurgan peoples from Anatolia, speaking proto-Indo-European and, from the third millennium, the incoming Celts. Trade was the lubricant of these movements. Artefacts were exchanged, from north to south and along the shores of the Baltic and North Seas and the Mediterranean. People travelled. People met. People learned.

With the late Bronze Age in the third millennium, Europe saw newcomers from two points of origin: east and south. From the east, people arrived from the Asian steppes and the Caucasus. Germanic peoples brought with them new Indo-European languages, mutating into Brythonic, Germanic, Slavonic, Greek, Italic and others. Their landlocked origins are suggested by having root words for family and farming, but none for sea and sailing. Indo-European offers a linguistic archaeology that, together with advances in the study of DNA, is constantly redefining this early period in Europe's story.

Other influences permeated the Mediterranean from further afield. By the second millennium BC, the world's most developed societies were emerging in the valleys of China's Yellow River, India's Indus and the 'fertile crescent' of the Euphrates and the Nile. Long before the stabilization of European settlement, these peoples mastered agriculture, construction, trade, art and, in Mesopotamia, writing. They developed cities and worshipped their ancestors as gods. Their buildings could be colossal. The great pyramid at Giza (*c*.2560 BC) was, at 146 metres, the highest structure on Earth, until topped by Lincoln Cathedral in the fourteenth century.

Europa's supposed son, King Minos, was regarded as founder of the Minoan empire based on Crete. It appears to have lasted at least a thousand years, from *c*.2500 to *c*.1450. Though traditionally traced to settlers from Egypt or Mesopotamia, DNA archaeology finds Minoan skeletons more closely related to ancient Greeks. They were a people who traded across the eastern Mediterranean, built palaces, settled colonies and enjoyed athletics and bull-leaping. Their lives appear to have been pacific. Despite the practice of human sacrifice, we know of no warrior caste or cult of military violence. In the murals and ceramics of Minoan Knossos we glimpse the elegant youths of Knossos leading what seems a charmed life, the first delicate link in the chain of a distinctively European culture.

The Minoan empire is thought to have declined when the island's forests, crucial to bronze production, became exhausted. Its death blows appear to have been a series of natural catastrophes, chiefly the eruption of the island of Thera, radio-carbon dated to around 1630 BC. This great catastrophe produced a tsunami that swept across the eastern Mediterranean and all but eradicated the settlements on Crete. Influence now passed north to the Achaeans of Mycenae, forerunners of the mainland Greeks.

Aegean dawn and diaspora

The Achaeans (or Mycenaeans or Danaans) came to dominate the Aegean basin from *c*.1450 to *c*.1100. They were a land-based people under monarchical rulers, whose legends, heroes and Linear B script loomed over later Greek culture. They came into conflict with the Hittites, whose occupation of Asia Minor and the Levant had long limited the northward expansion of Egypt. The Hittites were early exploiters of iron, working it into tough swords and thus more effective killing tools than clubs and stone axes. Coincidental with this period was the rise of the city of Troy, whose war with the Achaeans over the kidnap of their queen, Helen, culminated in its siege and conflagration, probably in the 1180s.

Succeeding centuries retold, and doubtless elaborated, this first recorded event in Europe's story, handed down and described by the poet Homer probably somewhere in the eighth century BC. It is a tale of tribes driven to extremes of violence and revenge by the behaviour of their neighbours. Their idols were not the static images of their ancestors. Their gods were hyperactive, anthropomorphic men and women, ready to display love, anger, jealousy and curiosity. Like humans, they schemed, argued and fought. And they backed their swords with what became Europe's most potent weapon, reason.

The so-called palace cultures of this early Greece came to an end sometime between 1200 and 1150 BC, whether through the exhaustion of woodland or natural disaster, such as volcanic eruption or plague. This period, roughly from 1100 to 900, is known as Greece's 'dark age'. It coincided with the overrunning of the Aegean basin by new intruders, Dorians in mainland Greece and Ionians on the Asia Minor coast – giving their names to styles of classical architecture. Since DNA indicates that even modern Greeks are descended from the earlier Mycenaeans, the newcomers may have conquered, but did not supplant.

As a result, the inland population dispersed from palace settlements into smaller coastal towns and villages. Here geography restricted expansion, and contact was largely by sea. This gave rise to the Greek polis, a small self-governing community that required all free citizens to participate in its defence. Such a state defined itself, said the Greek philosopher Aristotle, 'in being as far as possible composed of equals and peers', a designation that did not include women, slaves or foreigners. The growth of these maritime micro-states stirred the rudiments of individualism, self-reliance and independence that were to define the Greek view of what constitutes a human community – and ultimately a human personality.

By *c.*800 BC these city states, with perhaps a total population of some 800,000, were outgrowing the narrow shores of the Aegean. They were spreading south across the Mediterranean and north towards the Black Sea. Here they came into contact, and potential conflict, with Phoenicians from Tyre and Sidon, settling as far west as Spain. The Phoenician city of Carthage, in what is now Tunisia, was reputedly founded in 814. For their part the Greeks settled north along the Mediterranean shore, in Sicily, Italy and even France. There was sufficient integration for the Greeks to adopt the Phoenician alphabet – retaining a version of it to this day.

As many as 1,000 Greek settlements from these times have been traced across the Mediterranean, far outnumbering in size, population and luxury their places of Aegean origin. Agrigentum in Sicily and Sybaris in southern Italy became large cities, the latter prosperous enough to yield the epithet 'sybaritic'. These colonists, who spoke Greek and carried Hellenic culture to the corners of the Mediterranean, would attend the annual Pan-Hellenic Olympic games, held in Greece from 776 onwards, like Americans returning across the Atlantic to visit their European homeland.

Nowhere evokes these times as well as the ancient city of Miletus, on the Turkish coast above present-day Bodrum. It was rebuilt in 479 after its destruction by the Persians. Its grid plan lies excavated but deserted, and modern visitors can walk down paved streets, enter houses, clamber over the theatre and climb the citadel, looking out over fields towards the sea. A warm breeze blows up from the Aegean, across hillsides of exquisite beauty.

These streets would have been awash in travellers' accounts of distant places, unusual practices, creative minds and violent conflicts.

Such ideas were reflected in the lives of the gods and heroes, Aphrodite, Artemis, Hermes, Poseidon, Jason, Heracles and Theseus. Above all, the colonists were a curious people. A contemporary, Herodotus, is said to have remarked, 'Every year we send ships at great cost and danger as far as Africa, to ask "Who are you? What are your laws? What is your language?"' Why is it, he asked, 'they never send ships to ask us'? It was a question that holds within it a defining quality of later European civilization.

Persian Wars and the rise of Athens

By the seventh century BC the cities of the Greek mainland had developed new ways of governing their polis. As if by trial and error, Corinth, Sparta, Athens and other cities found how they might live together in peace. Kingdoms gave way to aristocracies, oligarchies and tyrannies. Concepts such as freedom, justice and the fair distribution of resources were debated. In 621 Draco of Athens codified a set of harsh laws, including execution 'for idleness'. Draconian laws were written, it was said, in blood not ink. They were later modified by a magistrate, Solon, who dispersed power over a propertied class of citizens. His were the first steps towards the concept of civil rights.

In 508 there was a revolt in Athens against the prevailing aristocracy, led by an elder statesman, Cleisthenes. Rather than argue about which landed family should govern and when, he proposed that the entire male citizenry of Athens should rule the city. Citizens would be known not by their family name but by their *deme* or locality. Council membership and public offices should be chosen on a rota selected by lot. Only the magistracy was restricted to qualified candidates. Misbehaving officials could be exiled for ten years by a straight popular vote, a penalty termed ostracism.

Cleisthenes' form of democracy was suited to the intimacy of the polis, rather than being mediated (and moderated) by elected representatives. Some 50,000 free male citizens would have been involved in the lottery. It was the dawn of participatory government. The venue for meetings of the Athenian council can still be seen, on the Pnyx mound beneath the Acropolis, a strangely evocative jumble of rocks, ledges and alcoves. Curiously, the only memorial to Cleisthenes I know is in the Ohio statehouse.

In the sixth century BC, Greece's stability was threatened from the east. King Cyrus of Persia (559–530) reached the shores of the Aegean in 546 and went on to occupy all of Asia Minor, including the Greek Ionian islands. In 499 the Ionian Greeks revolted against Persia and were cruelly suppressed. King Darius (520–486) sent an army to punish the Athenians for supporting the Ionians. This was defeated at the Battle of Marathon in 490, with a reported 6,400 Persian dead against 192 Athenians. News reached the city by a runner, Pheidippides, who dropped dead after announcing the victory. His run is celebrated in marathons to this day. The Persians were eventually driven off in a sea battle at Salamis in 480 and a land battle at Plataea the following year.

The Greek victories, often against overwhelming odds, have been variously attributed to superior iron weapons and to the cult of male athleticism. The Greeks fought with the discipline of men defending their homes and families. Herodotus has their general, Themistocles, pleading in his speech before Salamis for loyalty not to the polis but to 'what is noble in man's nature and predicament'. Democracy was barely a quarter of a century old, but already its appeal was to citizens fighting as individuals, for a personal as well as collective freedom from tyranny.

The Persian Wars rank among the deciding events in Europe's evolution. Had the Persians triumphed, and Greece and the Aegean basin fallen under their sovereignty, so probably would the Balkans and much of the Mediterranean. Their peoples would have been drawn to the thrones, the gods and the customs of lands to the east. Since there was as yet no concept of Europe, there might never have been cause to invent one. Even so, the Persian Wars remind us that it was from Asia that Europe was initially colonized, and from whose story it has never quite been able to detach itself.

The Golden Age of Athens

As the leading state of Greece in the Persian Wars, Athens claimed a military and cultural ascendancy that reached its peak in the Delian League (478–404). This soon became an Athenian empire, composed of some 300 tributary islands and settlements on the Aegean coastline. In 461 the city came under the leadership of a popular orator, Pericles (461–429), who secured the ostracism of his conservative opponent, Cimon. He presided over Athens throughout a third of a century of its so-called Golden Age. A cultured, ascetic, innovative man, he is said to have been susceptible only to his mistress, Aspasia. He sought peace with Persia in 449, but was constantly in conflict with the cities of the Delian League.

Pericles saw government as a web of interlocking civic and personal obligations, underpinned by an emerging rule of law. Periclean Athens blazed over the Aegean, a comet of intellectual and creative energy. The Acropolis was crowned with marble buildings. Its Parthenon temple to Athene was to become the most celebrated structure in the world, a template for (good) architects to this day. Round it were set temples to other gods, with beneath it the agora and theatre of Dionysus. These projects were financed from the Delian League, and as such were bitterly resented by its members.

To Pericles, civic life was fused with art. His friend, the sculptor Phidias, brought a new realism and grace to the previously stylized portrayal of the human form. The playwrights Sophocles, Euripides and Aeschylus analysed the emotions of love, ambition and revenge. The satirist Aristophanes made the Greeks laugh at themselves. The historian Thucydides reminded Athenians of their greatest deeds, and greatest mistakes. Hippocrates analysed disease as a natural not divine phenomenon.

The city also found room for Socrates (469–399), prophet of the concept of deliberative reasoning. To Socrates humans were free agents with wills of their own, unbounded by Promethean myths of gods and creatures. To find wisdom they needed only to open their minds to the world around them, taking other people at face value, not as the gods or society formed them. Socrates championed reason against superstition, inquiry against authority. Above all, he said, humans owed it to their nature to be curious, to inquire without inhibition.

Socrates was the master of the dialectical method, of the sceptical and challenging question. His most brilliant pupil, Plato (429–347), went on to systematize Socrates' ideas into a structure of ethical and political behaviour, governing the relations of individuals to each other and to the polis. While Plato's statist ideology is nowadays contrasted with the sovereign nobility of the individual, it was a first recorded attempt to marry justice and freedom to a citizen's obligation to society. The Athens academy, set up by Plato in 387, was home to his pupil Aristotle (384–322). It was the cradle of the European mind, evoked during the Renaissance in Raphael's great Stanza fresco in the Vatican.

The reputation of Athens was to be revived and glamorized time and again in European history. Its 'invention' of democracy proved short lived. Its intellectual and cultural legacy owed its preservation to the scribes of Alexandria and the scholars of Rome. But the achievements of the Golden Age continue to tower over all other episodes in the European narrative. I first studied it at school and it has remained a source of wonder to me ever since how this small corner of an inland sea could have produced such astonishing innovation and understanding of the human condition. The concept of European civilization without Athens is impossible to conceive.

The Peloponnesian Wars

Thucydides recorded Pericles' last three speeches as masterpieces of Greek oratory. In them (or as Thucydides recalled them) the great leader declared that the root of Athens' genius lay in tolerance. Its laws 'afford equal justice to all in their private differences . . . If a man can serve the state, he is not hindered by the obscurity of his condition. The freedom we enjoy in our government extends also to our ordinary life . . . We do not feel called upon to be angry with our neighbour for doing what he likes.' The phrases of Pericles/Thucydides have echoed down the ages, to be quoted by generations of politicians and scholars and to underpin the values that later Europeans liked to think they brought to the world.

Perhaps like those later Europeans, Pericles viewed his values selectively. They were not applied to Athens' imperial conduct of the Delian League, let alone to women or slaves. Whether it is fair to ascribe the downfall of Athenian supremacy to other Greek concepts, such as hubris and nemesis, may be moot. Pericles claimed to have 'forced every sea and land to be the highway of our daring'. Eventually this highway rebelled. Subject cities of the Delian League allied themselves to Athens' rival Sparta, whose ascetic rulers had no truck with Periclean democracy or vanity. In 431 Pericles plunged his city into what became the Peloponnesian Wars with Sparta.

They were to prove his epitaph. By 429 the greatest Athenian was dead of the plague. His war dragged on until 404, culminating in Sparta's victory and the suppression of the Delian League. The new monuments of Athens were almost razed to the ground by Spartan puritans, a fate reputedly averted only when the Athenians sang a chorus from Sophocles. While the momentum of the city's cultural life continued, the golden thread of democracy snapped, going the way its critics feared, into populism and mob rule. In 399 the Athenians decided they could not tolerate Socrates 'corrupting the minds of the young'. A corrupt jury forced him to commit suicide by drinking hemlock.

Aristotle surveyed a reputed 150 Greek constitutions, and concluded in favour of a 'structured Athenian polity', designed as a protection against raw populism. Comparing northern spirit with Asian intellect, he saw the Greeks as having both qualities. 'They have the best of political institutions,' he said. 'If they could achieve political unity they could control the rest of the world.' They could not achieve that unity. Athens allowed history to glimpse the practice of democracy, but not the means of sustaining it. That is the true art of politics, and it has eluded much of Europe, even to the present day.

The Age of Alexander

Europe's history in these early centuries is best described as under a spotlight, roving this way and that along the shores of the Mediterranean as the continent's drama unfolds. Following the decline of Athens, Greece's cities saw constant strife, sometimes against, sometimes in alliance with, the ever-menacing Persians. In 359 the kingdom of Macedon came under an ambitious king, Philip, assertively Greek and claiming descent from the Homeric Achilles. His army of pikemen, able to engage an enemy at more than arm's length, swiftly subjugated the city states of Greece. In 336 Philip was assassinated by hands unknown, and was succeeded by his twenty-year-old son, Alexander.

The youth was clearly extraordinary. He had been taught military leadership by his father, who hired Aristotle among others to tutor him in philosophy and politics. Small but charismatic, he reputedly had one blue eye and one brown, and a mesmeric hold on those he commanded. Undaunted by his youth, perhaps emboldened by it, Alexander set out to fulfil Philip's ambition to advance his empire beyond Greece into the lands held by Persia.

It was to be the most remarkable venture in the history of European conquest. Crossing Asia Minor, Alexander in 333 defeated a much larger Persian force under Darius III at the Battle of Issus. He took Darius's daughters captive and was later to marry two of them, though in the meantime he was entranced by a Bactrian princess, Roxana. Rather than simply return home with honour satisfied, Alexander now marched south to Egypt. Here his general, Ptolemy, went on to found a dynasty that was to end with Cleopatra. Ptolemy built the library at Alexandria, inventing papyrus scrolls and banning their export to the rival library of Pergamum, where costly animal parchment was still in use.

Alexander again defeated Darius and marched through Mesopotamia and across a defenceless Persia to the banks of the Indus in India. Here his generals mutinied and demanded they return home. Alexander thus had to travel back across the sands of Persia to Babylon, where in 323 he died of disease, aged just thirty-two. Everywhere he went, Alexander founded cities and colonies, many named after himself. He had crushed the greatest empire in south-west Asia. He married his troops to local women and left his commanders as local governors. But the influence of these Hellenistic colonies on the lands traversed by Alexander was not political. He left no empire.

Like most such ventures, Alexander's journey was ultimately fruitless, the expression of a gigantic vanity and greed for booty. His imperial creation was vacuous and never established a secure frontier for the Greeks in Asia Minor or Mesopotamia. It was to prove Europe's most porous boundary throughout history. But the short-lived Macedonian empire did have one lasting outcome. It entrenched Hellenistic civilization, that of Greek language and literature, across the Mediterranean. As mainland Greece fell victim to civil war, Greek traders and scholars spread out across the sea, a diaspora that historians estimate eventually numbered ten million people. The library at Alexandria became the repository and disseminator of Greece's cultural heritage.

Greece's political glory died with Alexander. But his reputation lived on, appealing to the vanity of later rulers. With his death, the window on the human spirit opened by classical Athens was to close. Our searchlight now swings west, to illuminate a city whose genius lay not in the excitement of Periclean democracy but in the potency of a militaristic republic.

2

The Ascendancy of Rome
500 BC–AD 300

The birth of the republic

If Greece was founded by a princess raped by a bull, Rome was founded by a baby suckled by a she-wolf. Somewhere in the mist of time, Romulus killed his twin Remus in an argument over where to locate the city of Rome, leaving Romulus free to choose. Many years later, at the turn of the fifth century BC, as the Athenians were ousting aristocracy in favour of democracy, the Romans ousted monarchy in favour of a republic. In 509 they exiled Tarquin the Proud, who then asked Lars Porsena of adjacent Tuscany to assist his restoration. The conflict ended in a legendary confrontation, graphically described by Macaulay in his *Lays of Ancient Rome*. Horatius' heroic defence of a bridge over the Tiber put the Tuscans to flight and came to embody military heroism. A statue of the kindly wolf is in Rome's Capitoline Museums. Once 'Etruscan', it is eleventh century.

The Romans were ancient inhabitants of Latium, the area now comprising central western Italy. Their republic was similar to Athens in that it sought to legitimize government accountability. A senate of hereditary patricians wielded executive power through two consuls, elected by free Roman citizens. Separate from it was a council of plebeians, led by tribunes who passed the council's views to the senate, not least on matters of taxation. Consuls and tribunes thus established a creative tension at the heart of the republic. As in Greece, state security required every citizen, when summoned, to serve in the army. This comprised legions of infantry, divided into units of a hundred men under centurions. They fought in disciplined phalanxes with linked shields and long spears, flanked by chariots. They were almost invincible in open battle.

The First Punic War

For two centuries republican Rome remained a city state. It did not seek to expand beyond its region, let alone imitate Athens or Macedon and embark on empire building. Only with the start of the third century did it expand across the south of Italy, where it came into conflict with Greek and Phoenician settlements along the Mediterranean coast. In 264 the Romans crossed into Sicily and challenged Carthage for control of the western sea. The Roman infantry captured Messina, but Carthage's navy remained dominant. In 241 the Romans arrived in a fleet of a hundred quinqueremes (rowing galleys) and drove the Carthaginians from the island. Thus ended the first of three Punic (or Phoenician) Wars, a fierce enmity between the two western Mediterranean powers.

In 218 a twenty-nine-year-old Carthaginian general, Hannibal, decided to attack Rome overland from Spain. He led an army through the Alps with thirty-seven battle elephants, only one of which reached Italy. The route remains a subject of scholarly debate and documentary film-making. In Italy Hannibal was able to rely, with good reason, on Rome's now subjected Italian provinces to rise up in his support. He defeated the Romans at the epic battles at Lake Trasimene in 217 and Cannae in 216, the latter being regarded as the most searing defeat in Rome's history so far, with more than 40,000 soldiers slaughtered.

Hannibal was unable to push his advantage to a conclusion. He remained penned down in the Italian countryside by the guerrilla tactics of a new Roman general, Fabius Cunctator, the 'Delayer', and never reached Rome. Another Roman general, Scipio, eventually drove the Carthaginians from Italy and finally, in 202, attacked Carthage itself. The city remained to Rome what Persia had been to Athens, an ever-present threat, yielding a jingoist slogan: *Carthago delenda est*, Carthage must be destroyed. It was, eventually, in 146.

The birth of empire

By the second century Rome's supremacy over the western Mediterranean was almost complete, and the expansion of its rule quickened. In addition to Italy, provinces were carved out of southern Spain, southern Gaul and northern Africa. To the east, a Roman force in 200 aided Athens in freeing itself from the weakening yoke of Macedon, and by 133 a new Asiatic Roman province had been created from Alexander's Pergamum. Each of these provinces had to submit to the sovereignty and taxes of Rome, receiving in return Rome's protection and citizenship for its leaders.

This Graeco-Roman ideal of citizenship under the rule of law became the glue of Rome's emergent statehood. Even as they conquered, Romans absorbed the prevailing Hellenism of the Mediterranean basin. They collected the Greeks' literature, copied their architecture and imported their sculpture. They revered the great library at Alexandria. Upper-class Romans spoke Greek and taught it to their children, much as European aristocrats were later to speak French and then English. Rome adopted Athenian philosophical fashions, such as those of the Stoics, Epicureans, Sceptics and Cynics. The orator Cicero was inspired by Greek law and the rhetoric of his Greek forebear, Demosthenes.

This was not to every taste. The self-styled patriot Cato (234–149) regarded the magnetism of Greek culture to the Romans as a 'soft' affectation. It eroded the virility of youth with the habits of a 'most wretched and unruly race'. The poet Horace wrote that 'captive Greece has made a captive of her rude conqueror'. Years later, the poet Virgil achieved a synthesis of the two cultures. He told his compatriots that the Greeks might 'draw forth living features from marble'; they might be better lawyers, astronomers and mathematicians. But these virtues depended on the freedom to act. 'You, O Romans, govern the nations with your power. Remember this. These be your arts – to impose the ways of peace.' Peace, said Virgil, began with military supremacy, so beginning a Roman stress on the virtues of warfare that lasted to the end of the empire.

Virgil's Pax Romana was based on a standing army some 125,000 strong, excluding auxiliaries. Its legions, led by patrician generals who ruled provinces with the power of warlords, were dispersed throughout the empire. While appointed by the senate, these generals grew rich on booty and taxes. This won them the often exclusive loyalty of their soldiers, but also enabled them to buy political power back in Rome. Provincial politics thus came to dominate the politics of the republic.

Matters came to a head in 133 under the tribunes Tiberius Gracchus and, later, his brother, Gaius, who sought to redistribute land to war veterans and plebeians. The Gracchi were opposed by wealthy senators, who arranged their assassination. But other politicians and former generals, such as Cinna and Sulla, took their place, testing the institutions of the republic to destruction. In 82, Sulla declared himself dictator of Rome, having introduced reforms that turned a bribed and corrupted senate into an oligarchy. A sign of the new insecurity came in 73, when gladiators near Capua staged a rebellion under their charismatic leader, Spartacus. He attracted an army of 70,000 slaves and supporters, swollen within a year to 120,000. The resulting civil war culminated in the slaves' defeat. Six thousand ghoulish crucifixions lined the roads into Rome as a deterrent to repetition.

The Roman republic was now suffering the same strains as had Athenian democracy. Personal power and ambition were corrupting its institutions and circumventing its defences. A victor in Rome's many civil wars, a soldier named Pompey, was made sole consul in 52. He had gained fame and fortune through his military successes, rewarded with three triumphal parades, in one of which he rode in a jewelled chariot, attended by wild animals and carrying a globe representing his conquests. The supposed balance of power between the senate, consuls and tribunes eventually collapsed when one man could control each in turn through public acclaim. There is no force so potent as populism.

Julius Caesar

Rome's Senatus Populusque Romanus (SPQR) had become dictatorship. Pompey was soon challenged by another returning general, Julius Caesar, member of an old Roman family. Like Pompey, he had become consul and army commander of the two provinces of Gaul, south and north of the Alps. He was thus ruler of large territories and open to consequent self-enrichment. Caesar was a brilliant soldier, ruthless, calm-headed and a literate historian of his own triumphs. His Gallic Wars (58–50) took Rome's frontier north to the English Channel and east to the Rhine. A third of Gaul's adult males were estimated (by Caesar) to have died in the process, and another third sold into slavery, much to Caesar's profit. Gaul west of the Rhine was subjected to Rome, and its leader, Vercingetorix, was sent there to be paraded in the streets and then killed.

Pompey was effectively ruler of the republic, but in 50 the senate voted that both he and Caesar disband their armies. Caesar disregarded this and in 49 he headed south from Gaul, breaking the law requiring generals to relinquish their legions on leaving command of their provinces. He theatrically 'crossed the Rubicon', the river dividing south Gaul from Rome, and entered Italy. Here he confronted the jealous Pompey, and found (and bought) support among the citizens of Rome. Pompey fled to Greece with his legions.

For two years Rome was engulfed in civil conflict. Caesar was declared dictator, testing the loyalty of such conservative republicans as Cicero, whose letters recording these times form a gripping account of first-century Rome. By 48 Caesar had chased Pompey from Greece south to Egypt and eventual assassination. On his subsequent arrival, Caesar met the twenty-one-year-old Cleopatra, co-ruler of Egypt with her brothers. She was carried into his presence wrapped in a carpet. He was smitten and she bore him a son.

Caesar now had to fight campaigns in Greece, Italy, Spain and Africa, often against mutinous armies. In early 44 he was back in Rome, showered with triumphs and honours, including that of 'perpetual' dictatorship. Money looted from the provinces was distributed to soldiers and Roman citizens. One soldier who dared protest Caesar's extravagance was killed, and his corpse nailed to the wall of the forum. All must suffer who oppose public sector vanity projects.

Rome was at Caesar's feet, but on the Ides of March 44 came nemesis. Within minutes of Caesar's arriving in the curia, he fell under a flurry of knife wounds from senatorial conspirators, including his old colleague Brutus. Reports conflict as to what were his last words, except that no one records Shakespeare's 'Et tu, Brute?' Suetonius records him saying nothing – and anyway it would have been in Greek.

The rise of Octavian Augustus

The outcome was Rome leaderless and in chaos. Finding the citizens shocked at both the fact and the manner of Caesar's death, the conspirators fled the city. Caesar's will left his putative empire to his eighteen-year-old nephew and adopted son, Octavian. A consul, Mark Antony, rashly denied the will and refused to pay Caesar's soldiers. The young Octavian summoned them to his standard, while the elderly Cicero wrote a series of lengthy speeches in his defence. Entitled the *Philippics*, they recklessly savaged Antony for everything from lust to violence, treason and greed.

Octavian, though still a teenager, acted with diplomacy. He strengthened his power base in Rome by making overtures to Antony. This reconciliation sealed the fate of Cicero, who in 43 fled Rome but was hunted down and killed, his hand and tongue pinned up in the Senate by his enemies. His epigrams remain gems of Roman letters: 'He only employs his passion, who can make no use of his reason ... Politicians are not born, they are excreted ... With a garden and a library, a man has everything he could need.'

Caesar's assassins were pursued to Greece by Octavian and Antony together, and killed after the Battle of Philippi in 42. Relations between the two leaders soon deteriorated. Antony had taken as his command the eastern empire, where he fought a series of successful campaigns to secure the frontier against Parthian (formerly Persian) aggression. He appointed Herod as king of Judaea and, in 41, followed Caesar's steps to Egypt. When he summoned Cleopatra to meet him at Tarsus in southern Turkey, she arrived not in a carpet but on her boat under a golden canopy, lying on a bed of roses. This time the result was twins, a boy and a girl, and Antony understandably reluctant to return to Rome.

When in 40 Antony did return, he sought peace by marrying Octavian's sister, but soon returned to Egypt, to Cleopatra and the production of another son. He named his earlier twins after the sun and moon and declared Cleopatra's now thirteen-year-old son by Caesar, Caesarion, king of kings. When reported back to Rome, this was understandably regarded as a fatal provocation. Octavian had by now restored his supremacy and taken the title of Caesar, with its implied divinity.

In 31, Octavian declared war on Cleopatra (as proxy for Antony), and crossed the Mediterranean to confront them. At the Battle of Actium in Greece, Antony and Cleopatra were beaten and escaped back to Alexandria. When Octavian came to capture them, Antony committed suicide, dying reputedly in Cleopatra's arms. She too died days later, probably by poisoning. Her reported death by an Egyptian cobra is thought to be a myth. With the later assistance of Shakespeare, Rome had given the world its most theatrical assassination, its most exotic love affair and its most romantic suicide.

Augustus, imperator

If any man deserves the title of founder of modern Europe, it is Octavian (Caesar Augustus). A handsome man of medium stature, intelligent, slow to anger, he was ruthless when necessary, otherwise merciful. He displayed little of the egotistical ostentation of his earlier rivals, and preserved the forms of the old republic, calling himself 'first citizen', servant of the senate and one of two consuls. None the less, in 27 he took the imperial title of Augustus, with absolute power over the senate, the administration, the courts and the army. His soldiers were well rewarded and Rome's citizens were kept content on the tribute of empire. He was in truth a tyrant.

Augustus did not create the Roman empire, which he inherited from an assemblage of territories acquired under two centuries of republicanism. He was rather its shrewd consolidator. He tidied the imperial boundaries by completing the conquest of Spain, Egypt and Syria. His one significant defeat, in AD 9, was of his general Varus at the Battle of the Teutoburg Forest in Saxony. Three entire legions were wiped out by Arminius, a Rome-trained leader of the Germanic tribes east of the Rhine. Augustus was devastated and refused to shave for months afterwards. The defeat remained on his conscience to the end.

Arminius's victory has been ranked among the decisive battles in Europe's evolution. It placed the east side of the Rhine beyond the boundary of the Roman empire, a territory now distinct from Gaul. Germans became a source of legionary recruitment, but they never came within the orbit of Roman rule or culture. The divide thus established proved to be a territorial, national and eventually psychological barrier across Europe. Arminius, Germanized as Hermann, had the misfortune to become a hero of Nazism and is consequently little celebrated today even in his own land.

Augustus was careful in his choice of aides. He relied militarily on his minister of war, Agrippa, and domestically on the able Maecenas. The latter set a rare precedent in being minister of both the interior and the arts. Under his patronage, what came to be called the Augustan age flourished. Virgil and Livy celebrated the history of the Roman state. Horace was court lyricist. Ovid, an erotic poet, evolved in his *Metamorphoses* into a writer of philosophical depth. Either his radicalism or his lascivious verse had him exiled to the Black Sea, where he became a poet of the expatriate experience: 'Our native soil draws all of us, by I know not what sweetness, and never allows us to forget.'

The culture of Hellenism remained undimmed. As the supply of Greek statuary began to run dry, patricians had it copied so well it is hard for experts to tell Greek from Roman work. Vitruvius revised the principles of Greek architecture, as cities across the empire blossomed with markets, temples and forums. Augustus claimed to have found Rome 'a city of clay and left it one of marble'. Augustan classicism became the defining style of imperial power.

With security came Rome's greatest gift to early Europe, economic prosperity. Cargo ships traversed the Mediterranean, bringing the produce of distant lands to the tables of the capital. Aqueducts supplied its baths, on a scale not to be matched until the nineteenth century. Stadia and circuses offered public entertainment, albeit with cruelty and violence. Roads were plentiful. Twenty-nine highways radiated from Rome, to become the arteries of empire, enabling legions to move to trouble spots with speed. Rome's chariot mail service could carry letters fifty miles a day. One service Rome failed to master was that of street cleaning. Streets were sewers and the source of constant complaints.

Augustus's reign lasted over forty years until his death in AD 14. The empire he founded lasted five centuries – and its Byzantine offshoot for fourteen. Despite the fondness of its rulers for the rhetoric of immortality, its greatest weakness was that it had to rely for its continuity on a mortal being. The emperor was the fount of patronage and the arbiter of life and death for millions. There was no formal succession, and no check on imperial discretion beyond assassination. Of the first twenty-three holders of the office, most died a violent death, which was often followed by a period of anarchy. They inspired Edward Gibbon's *Decline and Fall of the Roman Empire*, one of history's most beguiling classics.

Tiberius and the birth of Christianity

Augustus's stepson, Tiberius (14–37), had been a fine general, notably on the Danube frontier. But he was a gloomy and malign emperor with reputedly bizarre sexual tastes, mostly involving children. He soon abandoned Rome for his palace on Capri, where rumour spread of his vices. It was towards the end of his reign that a local governor in Judaea named Pontius Pilate executed by crucifixion an obscure Jewish teacher, Jesus of Nazareth. His crime was allegedly claiming to be the king of the Jews. His death passed unrecorded at the time.

The first of Jesus's followers to be noted was a Jewish tent-maker turned persecutor of early Christians, Saul of Tarsus. Following his conversion on the road to Damascus, Saul (later Paul) returned to Jerusalem and was in contact with the apostles Peter and James before beginning an extensive ministry across the eastern Mediterranean. The Jews were an exclusive group who did not proselytize and, as a result, were tolerated. As a Jewish sect, Christians might have stayed in Judaea. Instead they spread their faith across the eastern empire, as testified by Paul's letters. He later wrote to the Corinthians, 'If I know not the power of the voice, I shall be as a barbarian to him with whom I speak; and he that speaks, as a barbarian to me.' That voice was Greek, the language of the eastern empire and of early Christianity. In the mouths of Christian missionaries, it was to prove phenomenally appealing.

Following the death of Tiberius, emperors followed thick and fast. His immediate successor, Caligula (37–41), was noted for obscene pastimes similar to those of his predecessor. He declared himself a god and insulted the senate by proposing to make his favourite horse a consul. Murdered by his own bodyguards, he was followed by Claudius (41–54), under whom much of England was conquered, and then by Nero (54–68), who reverted to depravity, much to the subsequent delight of Hollywood. It was a sign of the growth of Christianity that Nero found it advantageous to choose Christians as scapegoats for the burning of Rome in 64, feeding them to wild beasts in the Colosseum.

Sometime after 57, Paul was arrested in Jerusalem, falsely accused of taking a non-Jew into the temple. After spending two years in prison, Paul claimed his right as a Roman citizen to trial in Rome, where he arrived in about 60 and remained, presumably awaiting trial, for some four years. The religious historian Diarmaid MacCulloch points to the importance of Paul's status as a citizen of the empire, indicating that 'the Jewish prophet, who had seized his allegiance in a vision had a message for all people, and not just the Jews'. Paul's appeal to Rome was another crucial factor in disseminating Christianity across the empire.

Paul was executed in 64 or later, possibly in the Neronian persecution. The apostle Peter also appears to have been in Rome and killed at the same time, though there is little evidence for this, and none for his founding a church or serving as its leader. Scholars regard almost everything attributed to Peter in Rome as oral tradition, and possible textual insertion. Yet the names of these two men, Paul a Greek-speaking businessman, and Peter an Aramaic-speaking fisherman, were to dominate Roman and Orthodox Christendom. In 70 the emperor Vespasian (69–79) suppressed a Jewish rebellion, culminating in the destruction of the temple in Jerusalem. The resulting exodus of Christians from the city at this time marked the emphatic separation of early Christianity from its Judaic roots.

The Antonines: empire at its zenith

Vespasian initiated the Flavian line which, followed by the Antonines, brought Rome relative stability in the second century AD. Its most notable achievements were under Trajan (98–117), when the empire reached its greatest extent, stretching from Britain in the north to Dacia and Armenia in the east. It briefly touched the shores of the Caspian Sea and embraced Syria, Mesopotamia and Mauritania. The Mediterranean was now a Roman lake, and the empire was more Asian than European. Over all this, Roman order, Roman justice and, to a degree, Roman prosperity ruled, to be admiringly charted by the historian Pliny.

Trajan was succeeded by a master-builder, Hadrian (117–38). His greatest constructs, the Pantheon in Rome (126) and Hadrian's Wall (122) in Britain, still stand, the wall a massive testament to early empire. Of all the emperors, Hadrian had the clearest concept of the extent of Roman power, and perhaps its limitations. He withdrew from some of Trajan's gains, explaining that their peoples 'must have their freedom, if we cannot give them protection'. Hadrian was one of the few emperors who stand out from Roman history as worthy of the title. His interests united the cultures of Greece and Rome. He concerned himself with the law as well as philosophy, architecture and poetry. He travelled his empire as ruler, not just conqueror. An Epicurean, he had no fear of death.

There followed the philosopher emperor Marcus Aurelius (161–80), author of a book of Stoic meditations that remains popular to this day. Like Hadrian he continued to persecute Christians, being ready to tolerate freedom of belief, but not defiance of Rome's emperors-as-gods. To supplant the emperor in this way was tantamount to treason. Romans could not see why Christians could not even nod in this direction. It was their 'obstinacy and unbending perversity' that so infuriated Pliny as governor of the Greek province of Bithynia.

These were to be regarded in retrospect as golden years. Rome under the Antonines seemed at ease with itself. It had clear boundaries, unprecedented security, freedom of travel, a common administrative language and a legal framework. Gibbon concluded that, if he had to choose a period in history 'during which the condition of the human race was most happy and prosperous', he would choose from the death of Domitian in 96 to that of Marcus Aurelius in 180. When the latter died, said a later Roman, 'our history now descends from a kingdom of gold to one of iron and rust'.

The crisis of the third century

By the third century, Rome's empire had grown unmanageably big. Its population was estimated at sixty million, with a million in Rome itself, a city of a size Europe would not see again until the nineteenth century (excepting possibly Constantinople). But its government lacked the executive sinews and the discipline of the old republic. Above all, it lacked the continuity of a legitimate succession. The practice of emperors anointing their successors by adopting them as sons ensured neither competence nor consent. Almost every succession was challenged. Rome's central government lost coherence and sense of purpose. Its ethos became one of survival.

Under the last Antonine, Commodus (180–92), Rome reverted to the narcissism and self-indulgence of Nero. By now, frontier commanders were behaving as licensed warlords, while anarchy prevailed in Rome. Commodus was eventually murdered in 192 by his mistress, Marcia, a member of the empire's burgeoning Christian community. His replacement, Septimius Severus (193–211), the first emperor to have been born in Africa, extended Rome's frontier in the east. He rebuilt the magnificent Leptis Magna in Libya, his birthplace, as well as Baalbek in what was Roman Syria.

The army remained some 400,000 strong but this meant heavy taxes, diluted loyalties and indiscipline. While the army might be strong on the frontier, it tended to weakness behind the lines. In 212, the tyrannical Caracalla (198–217) sought to curry favour – and increase revenues – by awarding Roman citizenship to all free residents of the empire. To the historian Mary Beard, this was the end of Rome as strictly an empire, by 'eroding the difference between conqueror and conquered'. Rome's domain was acquiring a hard crust but a soft centre.

During what is dubbed the 'crisis of the third century', conditions deteriorated. Emperors now tended to wear armour and be depicted as soldiers, the latter a custom retained by monarchs (including the British) to this day. In Rome, disease and famine became commonplace. Emperors were venal and idle, or at least eccentric. The literary Gordian II, who ruled for a month in 238, boasted twenty-two concubines and 62,000 books. In 268 an army of Gothic insurgents raided as far south as Athens.

As the city of Rome began a long period of decline, it attracted a close-knit network of Christian communities, pilgrims to its shrines to Peter and Paul. It remains unclear whether this alone was the cause of Rome's rise to ecclesiastical supremacy. This status was by no means preordained, as Christianity was a sect of the eastern Mediterranean, with centres in Antioch and Alexandria. The Bishop of Rome emerged only gradually as the church's father, or *papa*, while the city struggled with its eastern rivals both over primacy and over the nature of Christ's divinity. Its emergent factionalism, and later schism, was indicated as early as Paul, who in his first letter to the Corinthians pleaded, 'I beseech you, brethren . . . that you all speak the same thing and that there be no divisions among you.'

At the turn of the fourth century the emperor Diocletian (284–305) began a new phase in the empire's history. He restored to the imperial throne the competence and stability of the Antonines. He reformed the currency and the bureaucracy, and campaigned ceaselessly to secure the empire's frontiers, variously defeating Germans, Slavs, Egyptians and Persians. A religious conservative, he in 303 initiated the last systematic persecution of Christians, though the faith was sufficiently entrenched for this to be short lived.

Above all, Diocletian confronted the central weakness of all empires, its unmanageable size. In the case of Rome, he saw that a capital city long accustomed to live on the subsidies of empire was being debilitated by them. He duly divided the empire in two, east and west. He took the eastern half, based in Antioch, and appointed his commander, Maximian, to take the west. The western capital he moved from Rome north to Milan, to be closer to the legions on the frontier.

Then in 305 Diocletian did what no emperor had done before. He abdicated and retired to Split in his Dalmatian homeland. In 312 he was a rare emperor to die in his bed. His palace stands to this day, excavated in the eighteenth century, and inspiring the Georgian architecture of Robert Adam. But an empire which he had divided to keep together, now found itself divided and increasingly apart.

3

Goths, Huns and Christians
300–560

Constantine and Byzantium

From the moment of Diocletian's division of the empire, Europe moved into a state of transition. It was leaving the domain of a mostly united Mediterranean littoral centred on Rome, and approaching one whose loyalties were split between its western and eastern possessions. This gulf was long to outlast the Roman empire. There were other divisions. One was between a pagan autocracy and the authority of a new faith, Christianity. Another was between a dominant Graeco-Roman culture and the experience of peoples the Romans called 'barbarians' – not necessarily a derogatory term – living on and beyond Rome's borders.

It was symbolic of this new Europe that, when the western emperor Constantius died in 306 and was succeeded by his son, Constantine (306–37), both events occurred in York, at the empire's northern extremity. When Constantine's soldiers saluted him as the new emperor, it was not the end of the matter. He had to spend the next eighteen years fighting rivals to claim his title. Not until 324 did he win supremacy over both eastern and western thrones. He had been trained at Diocletian's eastern court and that was where Constantine's heart lay. He duly announced that he would found a new city at Byzantion, overlooking the Bosphorus. Constantinople would be the superior capital, the new Rome.

By now Constantine was a seasoned soldier and autocrat, ruthless, egotistical and duplicitous. He overcame his chief rival, Licinius, by promising him sanctuary and safe retirement before promptly having him killed. How sincere was his conversion to Christianity no one can know. What is true is that, following a battlefield 'revelation', in 313 he signed a compact granting 'both to Christians and to all others, full authority to follow whatever worship each man has desired'. His new city would, he declared, be 'a Christian city'.

Constantine soon found that asserting a faith was simpler than defining it. Already Christianity was far from united. An Alexandrian priest named Arius (*c.*250–336) said that Jesus was mortal, the agent or creation of God on Earth, and therefore subsidiary to God. That alone could explain his death. This was at odds with the Catholics, who declared the identity of a Trinity of God, Christ and what they called the Holy Spirit. To Constantine, a faith that could not agree on its core beliefs – indeed was crowded with feuding bishops – was dangerous. Within a year of consolidating power, he in 325 summoned a council to Nicaea (present İznik), to resolve the dispute.

Christianity was most strongly rooted in the eastern empire. Of 1,800 bishops, some 1,000 were in the east, and of the 318 bishops who attended Nicaea, no more than five were from the west. Equally significant, the council summons came not from any bishop but from the emperor personally. He said he would merely attend 'as a spectator and participant in those things that will be done'. Yet his biographer, Eusebius, records him saying, 'I also am a bishop, ordained by God to overlook those outside the church.' He arrived at the council, 'like some heavenly messenger of God, clothed in raiment which glittered as it were with rays of light . . . adorned with the brilliant splendour of gold and precious stones'. In the outcome, Constantine's support for the empire's Catholics was unwavering. God and Christ were 'of one substance'. This was formulated as the Nicene Creed and is used by all Christians to this day. Arianism was declared a heresy.

Constantine now had to make peace with the city of Rome,

still the emotional capital of empire. In 326 he set out with a large entourage, pausing only to kill his wife, son and nephew, for reasons that remain obscure. In Rome he was not well received by the city's careworn patricians. He appeared before them not in the military garb of a Roman imperator, but in civilian silks and with a retinue of courtiers. Nor did the custodians of the ancient temples take to his Christian enthusiasm. Rome was dilapidated, depopulated and malarial. Constantine installed a Christian governor in the city and ordered the building of two new churches, St John's by the Lateran palace and St Peter's on Vatican Hill. He left in place Diocletian's concept of a western emperor (to be based in Milan), but he affirmed the superiority of Constantinople. It was more defensible by land and sea, and held the key to trade with the Asian interior. It also lay close to the Danube frontier and the border with the Persian empire. It was close to the origins of the empire's new religion.

In 327 the emperor's mother, Helena, set off on a pilgrimage to Jerusalem. Here she fulfilled the dream of every archaeologist, 'finding' on her first day the site of Calvary and the remains of Christ's true cross buried in a cistern. She proclaimed its validity by laying other crosses on a dying woman, whom only hers cured. Helena's other souvenirs included the hatchet used to build the Ark and the basket used to feed the 5,000. The age of the fake relic had arrived. In 330, these objects were given starring roles in the dedication of Constantine's new city, just six years after it had begun construction. It had massive walls, squares and a forum, studded with porticos and carvings brought from across the empire. At its centre was a column and gilded statue to Constantine himself, portrayed as a demi-god. The emperor ordered the manufacture of fifty illuminated bibles, requiring the parchment of 5,000 cows. Byzantium, successor to the eastern Roman empire, was born.

Constantine died seven years later, in 337, being formally baptized into the Christian church on his deathbed. He left a united empire, but not a harmonious church. Nicaea did not suppress Arianism, which over the next century became the dominant faith in much of the western empire, notably among recent barbarian converts from paganism. Its hierarchy of a god in heaven and a 'son' on Earth was more appealing than the abstract theology of the Trinity. Even Eusebius, Constantine's counsellor and bishop, was an Arian.

Nor was Arianism alone. Christianity fractured, at various times, into Novatianists and Donatists, Melitians and Homoeans, Pelagians, Nestorians and Miaphysites. It disputed with dualist Manichaeans and Gnostics. Sectarianism went geographical. Alexandria quarrelled with Antioch, Rome with Carthage. The philosopher emperor Julian (361–3), who was briefly the last pagan emperor, declared that 'no wild beasts are such dangerous enemies to man as Christians are to each other'.

Constantinople grew to become the largest city in Europe, estimated at some 800,000 inhabitants. Its walls, bastions, churches and palaces far outshone those of Rome. It was located at the crossroads of Europe and Asia. But while it treasured its Hellenistic legacy, it was never able to develop the free-thinking rationalism that had once inspired the cities of the Aegean and the philosophy of Socrates and Plato. Its inhabitants were consumed by theological disputation, while suppression of dissent seemed merely to further sectarianism. One visitor to fourth-century Constantinople reported on this obsession: 'Ask a man for change, and he philosophizes about the Begotten and the Unbegotten . . . ask if your bath is ready and the attendant asserts that "the Son was made of nothing".'

Huns, Goths and Vandals

From the early 370s, just thirty years after Constantine's death, reports began arriving in Constantinople of Hun raiders (otherwise called Scythians) arriving on the banks of the Danube. They were horse-borne warriors, speaking an unknown tongue. Dark and small in stature they appeared as roaming bands of mounted archers, reputedly able to ride 1,000 miles in a month. Their clothes were stitched rat skins and they ate roots and raw meat, warmed between their thighs. Their skill at constructing siege towers and battering rams overwhelmed towns in their path. With them came a mix of nomadic and settled peoples, eager for grazing land and tribute from the territories they crossed.

Modern DNA scholarship suggests that the Hun 'invasion' was more a steady infiltration, intermarrying with local Germanic tribes, otherwise known as Goths. But the warriors in its van were like a piston forced into Europe's constricted geography. Soon they were evicting Ostrogoths and Visigoths, then Vandals and Burgundians in central Europe. Those they evicted became migrants in turn, streaming down Roman rivers and along Roman roads. This presented the empire with a double menace, from the Huns and those they forced to move. Roman soldiers, administrators and tax-gatherers withdrew into fortified citadels or fled back to Italy. The heartland of Europe emptied of defensive energy.

In 379 the eastern emperor Theodosius I (379–95) sought to reunite the empire, but it was an empire afflicted with rebellions and religious divisions. Already in 374 the governor of Milan, Ambrose, found himself acclaimed as bishop and charged with leading a campaign for the Nicene Creed against Arianism. He barricaded Milan's basilica against the western emperor, the Arian Valentinian. He even excommunicated Theodosius for ordering a gruesome massacre of 7,000 citizens of Thessalonica for killing their governor. Leaders of the Roman church were gradually assuming secular authority.

Among those uprooted by the Huns in the Balkans was a Visigoth king, Alaric. Typical of leaders within the empire, Alaric was an Arian and a trained Roman soldier, who had helped put down a rebellion of

Germanic Franks. Regarding himself as inadequately rewarded, he led his army south into Greece, sacking Athens in 395. In 401 he turned his attention to Italy, where he was disregarded by the new western emperor, Theodosius's teenage son, Honorius (393–423). In 402 Honorius decided to move his capital from Milan to the more defensible Ravenna. Alaric occupied Italy for eight years before, in 410, making a final plea to Honorius for recognition in the imperial army. Rebuffed, he marched to Rome and subjected it to three days of pillage, the first such humiliation in the city's imperial history. Despite gruesome reports of devastation, reliable sources speak of the Goths' 'remarkable clemency'. Wealth was certainly stolen, but few houses were destroyed.

By now, Gaul was in disarray as Vandals, Burgundians and others fled the Huns. In 410, as Rome was pillaged, a desperate Honorius wrote to his subjects in Britain stating that he had no legions to spare against incursion by Germanic tribes, already settled along Britain's eastern shores. They were advised to 'take steps to defend yourselves'. Angles, Jutes and Saxons took the opportunity to push westwards across Britain, gradually confining the Christian British into the western, so-called Celtic extremities. It was in these isolated communities of Wales, Cornwall and Ireland that northern Christianity was to find temporary asylum.

At the same time the Visigoths in Spain drove earlier invaders, the Vandals under their king Genseric, across the Straits of Gibraltar into north Africa. Here they moved eastwards along the coast, seizing territory that since the days of the republic had been Rome's breadbasket. In 430 Vandals besieged the town of Hippo in modern Algeria, home of the theologian and bishop St Augustine. He had studied in Carthage, taught in Milan and returned as a scholar to Hippo, applying his understanding of philosophy to his theological writings. Yet by 439 Hippo and Carthage were in the hands of Vandals, and the Mediterranean was no longer a Roman lake.

The eastern empire offered no help to the west in this crisis. It was itself divided by religious heterodoxy. Arianism had not been suppressed. A Syrian monk, Nestorius, asked how Christ could be 'eternal' and on a par with God if he so clearly lived and died a human being. A council was summoned by Theodosius II to Ephesus in 431, at which Nestorianism was anathematized and Christianity reasserted. The council abandoned any lingering tolerance and proscribed all deviation from its creed as heresy, with authorized penalties to include maiming and blinding. It dictated the terms of the Easter ritual and declared Holy Week a holiday. Further councils in 449 and 451 became ever more heated and their deliberations more obscure. At the latter, in Chalcedon, Pope Leo of Rome proposed a compromise on the 'consubstantiality' of God and Christ. A divided empire now had a fractured faith, Catholics assailed by Arians in the west and Nestorians in the east.

Attila and the end of empire

The invading Huns had in 434 acquired a charismatic leader in the pugnacious Attila (434–53). He was described as 'born into the world to shake nations, the scourge of all lands'. His rolling eyes and alarming appearance terrified all who crossed his path. Yet he was said to be 'restrained in action, mighty in counsel, gracious to suppliants and lenient to those who were received into his protection'. In 443 and again in 447, he brought his forces to the walls of Constantinople. Each time they defied him, and he was bribed to withdraw. Finally, Theodosius's militaristic successor, Marcian (450–57), refused to pay further bribes and drove the Huns from his territory.

Attila crossed Europe into Gaul, where he met a force unprecedented in the continent's history. In 451 a Roman general, Flavius Aetius, and a Visigoth king, Theodoric I, amassed an army of

Romans, Franks and Goths to confront what they saw as a collective threat. It was the first time a coalition of Roman and barbarian armies had combined to take the field against an external foe, a first 'European army'. At the Battle of the Catalaunian Plains in 451, the coalition was victorious. Attila retreated and led his battered army south into Italy. There the inhabitants of the Veneto region of north-east Italy sought refuge from him in the sparsely inhabited islands of the coastal lagoon. Venice was born. Europe has Attila to thank for its most glorious possession.

Italy was Attila's last throw. Pope Leo joined a deputation to persuade him to retreat to the Danube, and the Huns consolidated their settlement in what is now Hungary. Attila died in 453, reputedly haemorrhaging in the arms of an Ostrogoth maiden to whom he had just become 'betrothed'. Despite Attila's defeat, the Hun invasion reiterated what Alaric's more settled Goths had shown a generation before, that the new Europe was vulnerable to forces sweeping west across its central plains. Roman citizen/colonists, many half-barbarian, sought safety not in the distant hope of imperial armies but in fortified towns, where they gave allegiance to any leader who might offer them security. Empire gave way to kingdom.

Nothing could bring peace to battered Italy. In 475 a Roman official named Orestes, who had served in Attila's retinue, seized power in Ravenna and appointed his fifteen-year-old son Romulus as emperor, giving the boy the impressive name of Romulus Augustulus. There seems no limit to the agonies fathers visit on their sons. The following year the boy was ousted by a Roman soldier of Germanic origin, Flavius Odoacer, who did not bother with emperorship but took the title king of Italy with his capital in Ravenna. Accordingly, the date of 476 is generally taken as the date of the formal demise of the 'Roman empire', though a Roman empire was to continue in its Byzantine form for another millennium.

Clovis and Theodoric

The term Dark Ages to describe the three centuries between the fall of Rome and the rise of Charlemagne is now dismissed by historians of the period. But it reasonably describes a continent staggering into an uncertain future, concussed by the enormity of what was gone. In 481 a fifteen-year-old named Clovis, hewn from more resilient timber than Augustulus, emerged as leader of the Frankish Merovingian clan, in what is now Belgium. Clovis (481–511) marched his warriors across Gaul, eventually winning submission from the Rhine in the east to the Loire in the west. He then moved south to conquer the Visigoths in Aquitaine. By the turn of the sixth century he could claim overlordship from Cologne to the Pyrenees. He fixed his capital in Paris, while his name mutated into Louis, Ludwig and Lewis.

Though Clovis was pagan in origin, his subjects were mostly Arian. In *c.*492 he married a Burgundian princess, Clotilde, who, unusually for a Burgundian, was not Arian but attached to the Catholic church. She insisted that her new husband convert to Catholicism. When a tribe's faith was dictated by its leader, such conversion was critical. Had Clotilde's faith been otherwise, Christendom might have taken a very different course. From now on, and with remarkable constancy, French kings gave their religious allegiance to Rome.

At the same time, the Ostrogoths in the present-day Balkans came under the rule of Theodoric the Great. He had been raised in Constantinople as a hostage to the Ostrogoths' good behaviour, and enjoyed the patronage of the emperor Zeno. In 488 he was commanded by Zeno to return to his people and recapture Italy on behalf of the empire of the east. This required the elimination of Italy's king, Odoacer. Theodoric achieved this in 493 by inviting him to dinner and, it is said, cleaving him from the shoulder to the groin.

Clovis in Paris acknowledged Theodoric as king of Italy, sealing their treaty in 493 by giving him his sister, Audofleda, in marriage. This was despite Theodoric being a devout Arian and building an Arian basilica, St Apollinaris, which stands in Ravenna to this day as a Catholic church. Even many of its original mosaics are intact. Theodoric further strengthened his position by marrying his own daughters to leaders of the Burgundians, the Spanish Visigoths and the African Vandals. Matrimonial diplomacy was born. From this point on, Europe's political personality focused on the ever-shifting relationship between three groups of peoples in what became Italy, France and Germany, geographical terms I have so far used for convenience.

The Roman church also took a new turn. Monasteries had first been founded by the eastern church, in Egypt and elsewhere. They now appeared in the west. In *c.*500 a young priest named Benedict was so dismayed at what he regarded as the church's corruption that he retreated to an ascetic life of work and prayer. In 529 he joined a group of 'brothers' to found a monastery at Monte Cassino, south-east of Rome. Benedict's 'rule' for his monks became a key text for western monasticism, establishing an arm of Christianity that was loyal to Rome but autonomous and outside Rome's hierarchy. As such it was a safety valve for internal dissent, a 'loyal opposition'. The monastic movement swiftly spread, developing a power network of its own, a state within the state of Christendom. Benedict's monastery at Monte Cassino survived for almost a millennium and a half, until flattened by Allied bombers in 1944.

Justinian and Belisarius

Clovis and Theodoric were founding fathers of medieval Europe, dying in 511 and 526 respectively. As Greece had bequeathed its culture to Rome, so Rome bequeathed its culture to the kings and courts of what were becoming settled northern tribes. They lived in Roman cities and adopted Roman ways. They communicated with each other in Latin. But the possibly fertile fusion of northern vigour and southern culture was fragile. It depended on power, and that depended on inheritance. It could vanish if dissipated by weak heirs.

The stability implied by the alliance of Clovis and Theodoric did not survive their passing. Italy was instead traumatized by a re-emergence of the ghost of its past. The eastern empire at the start of the sixth century had been reduced to little more than the shores of the Black Sea, the Aegean and the Levant. Its court lived off the wealth of its past and the profits of trade with the Orient. In 518 Justinian, the nephew of the emperor Justin, became his adopted son and, nine years later, co-ruler and then successor (527–65). He was a competent and ambitious man, reforming the imperial administration and improving relations with the Roman church.

Justinian had shocked Constantinople by choosing as his wife an actress and reputed courtesan named Theodora, daughter of a circus performer. Justinian adored her and she became his shrewd consort – and later a feminist icon. Thanks to a contemporary historian, Procopius, Justinian and Theodora shine larger than life from this obscure period. They faced an awesome task. War with Persia had resumed and open conflict broken out in Constantinople between two factions, the blues and greens, supporters of chariot teams in the hippodrome. This culminated in 532 in riots that saw parts of the city left a gutted ruin. Justinian was prepared to flee, but Theodora urged him to stay and a loyal general, Belisarius, restored order by killing rioters by the hundred.

A reinvigorated Justinian moved to establish his authority. He made peace with the Persians and, in 532, work finally began on the city's great cathedral of Hagia Sophia, two centuries after Constantine. Justinian declared on its completion in 537, 'Solomon, I have surpassed thee.' It was the biggest and most splendid church in

Christendom, and survives (as a museum) to this day. Justinian refor-
mulated the empire's laws into the *Codex Iustinianus*, versions of
which became the standard text for law schools throughout the
Middle Ages. Drawing on Roman and Christian traditions, it recognized the idea of equality before the law, but also the exclusivity of
the Christian church.

Justinian then embarked on his greatest project, nothing less
than the reconquest for the east of the western Roman empire. By
now Italy was Ostrogoth, Africa was Vandal, Spain was Visigoth
and Gaul/France was ruled by Franks. Justinian had in Belisarius a
commander of rare talent and rarer loyalty. Gibbon portrays him as
'[of] lofty stature and majestic countenance . . . daring without
rashness, prudent without fear, slow or rapid according to the exi-
gencies of the moment'. His wife Antonina shared a theatrical
background with Theodora, and accompanied him on a lifetime of
campaigning. In 533 Justinian summoned Belisarius from the Persian Wars and dispatched him with a large army and fleet to
recapture Carthage. He returned victorious, bringing with him the
original Jewish menorah (ritual candlestick), taken from Jerusalem
by the emperor Vespasian and then from Rome by the Vandals.
Amid much ceremony, it was returned to Jerusalem.

In 535 Justinian directed Belisarius to a far greater prize, the reconquest of Italy. This again was successful, with first Naples, then Rome
and finally Ravenna falling to Constantinople. But the outcome was
not peace. For four years, the Ostrogoth leader, Witigis, fought a
guerrilla war, such that Belisarius's eventual triumph was tarnished
by ruling a devastated land. When in 540 he had to return east to fend
off another challenge from Persia, the Ostrogoths simply took back
control under a new commander, Totila.

This time an uncertain Justinian lacked the resources for an
emphatic response. Totila asked to be regarded as Justinian's subject
king of Italy, but Justinian arrogantly refused. In 552, the ageing

emperor sent a eunuch courtier, Narses, to restore the conquest, which he duly did. Spain too came briefly under the aegis of Byzantium, and Justinian was thus at last able to contemplate a 'Roman' empire revived at least round the Mediterranean. Belisarius and Justinian died within months of each other in 565, having brought to Byzantium a sort of restored self-confidence.

The cost had been dreadful. In less than half a century, Justinian had taken an Italy that Theodoric had set on the path to statehood and torn it apart. Rome's aqueducts were cut, its senate disbanded, its people reduced to plague and starvation. As Tacitus had once said (quoting a Scottish chieftain), 'They make a wasteland and they call it peace.' Within three years of Justinian's death, old factions re-emerged. Constantinople's walls could hold the capital secure, but the shrinking empire was still assailed by Persians to the east and Slavs and Bulgars to the north. The city was cut off from a distant Europe which it had just devastated and where now only the fittest would survive. Justinian's empire had been one ruler's fantasy and one general's triumph. Of the many dates offered for the Roman empire's final demise, I find the death of Justinian in 565 the most evocative.

From this point onwards, we can see the definition of Europe's outline changing. Like an amoeba, it swells to the west and shrinks from the east, where contact increases with the new empires, economies and cultures of Asia. Not since the Battle of Salamis had the concept of a 'continent' of Europe seemed so vulnerable. To the north, old Germanic tribes begin to move out of Scandinavia, to trade and often clash with neighbouring peoples, as the earlier Greeks had moved out of the Aegean. The western Mediterranean was now debilitated. Justinian's wars had left north Africa, Spain and Italy less a restored empire, more its despoiled relics. Europe was ill prepared for new invaders from the east.

4

The Age of Charlemagne
560–840

Gregory the Great

The old imperial heartland of Italy, new home to the defeated Ostrogoths, now lay open to anarchy and invasion. In 568 the Lombards, originally from Scandinavia, moved with other Germanic tribes west through the Alps in search of a new home. They seized control of Milan and Pavia and by 572 were threatening Rome. Plague had cost the city a third of an already depleted population. Close to a million had become barely 30,000. They were governed by a thirty-year-old prefect named Gregory, who soon despaired of the task and left office to found a monastery in his father's villa outside Rome. In 579 he was prevailed upon by Pope Pelagius II to go to Constantinople and plead for help against the Lombards. In this he was unsuccessful, but after his return Gregory was raised to the papacy in 590 'by acclamation'.

Since Rome had long been abandoned as a capital city, Gregory had untrammelled authority. He bribed the Lombards to leave it in peace and commenced an abusive argument with the eastern patriarch, John, for the latter's giving himself the title 'ecumenical' (or global) in 588, implying sovereignty over the western church. Never one to mince words, Gregory called John 'the fore-runner of Antichrist'.

Gregory's fourteen-year papacy (590–604) led to his being known as 'the Great'. He recast Catholic liturgy, with no reference to Constantinople. Church tradition attributes to him the beginnings of church music, introducing what became known as Gregorian chant. He demolished many of the ruins of ancient Rome as pagan distractions from pilgrim churches and shrines. The first monk to become pope, Gregory was also eager to extend Christianity through mission. Where ancient Rome had used legions to extend its command over Europe, he used abbots, priors and monks. Gregory is the first church father who emerges from this period with a distinct personality, clever, argumentative, self-confident. The historian Chris Wickham writes that, of all the personalities of the period, Gregory was one of the few 'I could imagine meeting with any real pleasure'.

In about 595 Gregory noted two blond English slaves in a Roman market, of whom he allegedly said they were *non Angli sed angeli*, not Angles but angels. Britain had been Christian under the Romans, but had mostly reverted to Anglo-Saxon paganism. Gregory commanded a Roman prior, Augustine, to travel north and bring its inhabitants back to the fold. A reluctant Augustine landed in Kent in 597, where he and forty monks swiftly converted the Kentish king, Aethelbert, with the assistance of his queen, Bertha, who was a Frankish Christian princess. Augustine's mission left Gregory delighted that 'God has brought even the ends of the Earth to the faith', but although that might have been the case in the south, in parts of the west and north inhabited by descendants of the ancient Celts, the so-called Ionan rite of St Columba remained in force. It was not until 664 that a synod at Whitby finally won England, if not all of Britain, to the Roman rite.

On the continent, the empire of Clovis had disintegrated on his death. Under Frankish custom, property was divided among male heirs, rather than left to an eldest son. Such partible inheritance might suit a migratory tribe, dividing the spoils of conquest between kinsmen, but it was disastrous to the cohesion of an emergent state, dependent on the security and continuity of a hierarchy of nobles, merchants and farmers. The winner from partigeniture was the church. Bishops and abbots negotiated legal sanctuary and immunity from taxes and military service. They enjoyed increasing wealth and spiritual power over the souls of men. They offered rulers a corps of trained administrators and diplomats. Above all they represented continuity with the past, sustaining a tenuous link with the tradition of classical learning. Hence by the time of Gregory's death in 604, a new empire was emerging from the ruins of the old, that of the church of Rome. In its grandeur and discipline, and in its capacity to inspire loyalty, it was for a time that empire's worthy successor.

Persia and Islam

At the turn of the seventh century it was Constantinople's turn to face an existential threat. The emperor Heraclius (610–41) was under pressure from Slav, Bulgar and Avar forces to the north, and from a recuperated Persian empire to the east. The Persians advanced across Syria, seizing Jerusalem in 614 and cutting Constantinople's grain supply. They finally reached the city's walls, where Gibbon claims they were offered 'a thousand silk robes, a thousand horses and a thousand virgins', of which the city apparently had an inexhaustible supply. Heraclius eventually repulsed the Persians in a daring winter campaign, driving them deep into Mesopotamia and defeating them at the Battle of Nineveh in 627.

For the eastern empire it was a short-lived victory, as it left a weakened Persia vulnerable to a new force out of Arabia of unprecedented potency. In 632, the death in Medina of the prophet Mohammad unleashed a burst of expansionist zeal. Mounted Arab armies overran Mesopotamia, entered Syria and took Damascus in 635. Egypt fell next, and Alexandria was taken in 642. North Africa followed. As if overnight, a Christendom that had embraced the Mediterranean,

Black and Caspian seas, and reached the banks of the Nile and the Tigris, did so no more. The great cities of antiquity – Antioch, Damascus, Alexandria and Carthage – passed to Islam, taking with them roughly a third of Christendom's population. Nothing in Europe's history so emphatically altered and fixed the concept of its eastern boundary with Asia.

Christianity was ill equipped to meet this crisis. The faith of the eastern empire was immersed in theological schism and persecution. Provinces lived in fear of heresy and excommunication as Heraclius had sought to impose Orthodox belief on his war-weary people. The Muslim advance was initially tolerant. It was not seeking mass conversion, only submission and tribute. In his study of the Silk Roads, the historian Peter Frankopan stresses the sympathy with which early Islam treated the faiths of the near east. 'The message was inclusive and familiar, and seemed to draw the sting out of the fractious arguments that had set Christians on edge.'

As a result, the expansion of Islam out of Mesopotamia found widespread support among Jews and dissident Christians in the newly conquered territories. Pockets of Christian worship remained throughout the Middle East into modern times. Alexandria retained its status as a centre of both Hellenistic and Christian culture. Egypt's Copts lived without being castigated as heretics. The Muslim conquests of the seventh century were, in almost all cases, never to revert to Christianity. That faith was now to enjoy only a distant, sometimes violent, relationship with the land of its birth.

Charles Martel and Pepin the Short

In France a new Frankish leader, Pepin of Herstal (687–714), began to reassemble Clovis's domain. In 687 he gained power over northern France and went on to subdue Burgundy and Aquitaine, as well as lands along the Rhine. His son, Charles Martel (714–41), pushed north into Frisia and the Low Countries. To the south Martel reached the borders of Lombard Italy. But his greatest challenge was in the west. In 711 an Umayyad army in Africa reached the Straits of Gibraltar, finally crossing into Spain. By 719 Muslims were in command of all of Iberia except the Basque lands. They then crossed the Pyrenees, reaching as far into France as the Garonne and the Rhône. In the east, Umayyad forces were also attacking Constantinople, where in 718 they were narrowly repulsed by Leo III. They moved on into the Balkans.

This was the most serious incursion into the European land mass since the demise of Rome. Christendom faced not just a conquering army but a faith that was both united and yet tolerant of the beliefs of its conquered peoples. After a series of advances into and retreats from the south of France, in 732 an army under Abdul Rahman crossed from Spain into Gascony and the heart of Frankish territory. Martel summoned troops from across his domain and confronted Rahman at the Battle of Poitiers (or Tours). Here the Umayyad army was conclusively defeated.

The importance of the victory to the fate of medieval Europe is much debated. The threat was clearly real. Arabs had overrun Spain, were facing Italy from north Africa and had Constantinople and the Balkans in their sights. Gibbon concluded that without Martel's achievement at Poitiers, Oxford would have been teaching the Koran. Kenneth Clark agreed that, without Martel, 'western civilization might never have existed . . . we survived by the skin of our teeth'. One of the pleasures of counter-factual history is that its practitioners can endlessly disagree, some now treating Poitiers as no more than a gigantic raid. As it was, retaliatory Frankish expeditions soon recovered parts of north and west Spain, while the Umayyad empire gave way to over-extension and fragmentation. A Berber revolt of 741 was followed in 750 by the overthrow of the Umayyads in Iraq by the Abbasids. Islam became as divided and argumentative as had been Christendom. Had it won at Poitiers, it is doubtful it could have held Europe for long.

Despite these divisions, Islam proved remarkably tenacious in Spain. Cordoba declared itself an independent emirate in 756 and survived as such into the thirteenth century, while Granada did not fall to Castile until the fifteenth. Cordoba grew to up to 500,000 inhabitants. Its markets were celebrated, its religious life tolerant and its streets famed for their arcaded courts, cool fountains and nocturnal lighting. One ruler, Al-Hakam II (961–76), kept a male harem and a Christian concubine, building a library to rival Alexandria's. He appears in few histories of Europe.

Martel died in 741. His son, Pepin the Short (751–68), sustained his father's domain but with a significant departure. He was officially no more than a Frankish warlord, a so-called 'mayor of the palace' (after major domo), and he craved papal coronation. At the time, Pope Stephen II in Rome needed a different sort of help. In 751 a Lombard army had seized Ravenna and demanded exorbitant tribute from Rome. Stephen did something no pope had done before. He left Italy and travelled north to Pepin's court outside Paris. The offer was simple. Stephen would anoint Pepin king of the Franks and 'Patrician of the Romans' if, in return, Pepin would intervene to prevent a Lombard attack on Rome.

The deal was honoured on both sides. Stephen crowned Pepin in Reims in 754, together with his sons Carloman and Charles (the future Charlemagne). In return, Pepin invaded Italy and forced the Lombards to surrender Ravenna to the pope. They also had to surrender a strip of territory across Italy as far as Rome. These 'Papal States' brought the papacy both revenue and a buffer zone against Lombard aggression. They were known as the Donation of Pepin. Since the gift was of land still claimed by the eastern empire, its disposal by Pepin was outlawed by Constantinople. This gave rise to a celebrated forgery, of the 'Donation of Constantine', a supposed fourth-century document indicating that Constantine had given imperial lands in Italy to the church of Rome. Either way, the donation further cemented the alliance between France and Rome.

Charlemagne

In 768 Pepin split his kingdom between his two sons, who immediately quarrelled. We know only that within three years Carloman was dead, according to rumour, of a bad nosebleed. Charles then seized from Carloman's young sons their half of France and combined it with his own inheritance, mostly in modern Belgium and Germany. Charles the Great (768–814) was, for those times, a giant of over six feet, heavily bearded, and wearing a sheepskin tunic and cross-gartered leggings. He styled himself a Frankish king, with eighteen children by ten wives and concubines (the numbers vary).

Almost throughout his reign, Charlemagne was fighting, pushing outwards the Frankish borders set by Clovis, Martel and Pepin. He conquered pagan Saxony and Catholic Bavaria to the east and Catalonia to the south. In 774 he invaded Italy and made himself king of the Lombards. Other Germanic tribes beyond the Elbe, unconquered since the days of Rome, paid obeisance to Charlemagne, though many remained pagan. The sacred groves of Odin (or Wotan) still cast their spell, as they continued to do over Scandinavia. While France and Italy developed variants of the Latin tongue, the German Franks continued to speak Charlemagne's native version of Dutch or Old High German.

Charlemagne sought to make his capital of Aachen a northern Rome. He modelled his palatine chapel on St Vitale in Ravenna, and begged the pope for mosaics from Ravenna to adorn it. He saw learning as part of his status as a Christian king. He could speak Latin, though he never mastered the art of writing. Pre-eminent among his scholars was an amiable English monk, Alcuin from York (735–804), where the library was reputedly the finest in northern Europe. Alcuin became head of Aachen's palace school and the king's spiritual adviser, presiding over what came to be known as the Carolingian renaissance.

In 800 Charlemagne travelled to Rome to defend Leo III against charges of simony and adultery concocted by his enemies. At a Christmas ceremony in 800, Leo rewarded him with a Mass in St Peter's and the title 'emperor', conscious that this Frankish monarch might prove a more reliable ally than distant Constantinople. Charlemagne worried that the title would infuriate the eastern emperor, but he accepted it and boasted 'imperator' on his coinage.

Thus was born what became the Holy Roman Empire, a feature of Europe's political geography until its dismantling under Napoleon in 1806. Its heartland was the German-speaking areas of central Europe – indeed its full title was 'Holy Roman Empire of the German nation'. It had no capital, no army and no revenue, and was later ridiculed by Voltaire as 'not holy, nor Roman, nor an empire'. Yet the title of emperor was valued by its holders for its grandeur, and by the papacy for the power implied by conferring it. Strong emperors exploited loyalty to the imperial title to raise armies, weak ones had to concede 'autonomy' to its subordinate rulers. The very fact of its existence impeded the unification of both Germany and Italy until well into the nineteenth century. Even today, its loose-knit confederacy is evoked by champions of a devolved and localized European union.

The Treaty of Verdun

With the eastern empire now reduced to Asia Minor and its Mediterranean outposts, Charlemagne, as secular head of western

Christendom, was the first figure since the Roman emperors to bestride at least the heart of Europe. As such he became an icon of the early European Union. But as with the Merovingians so with the Carolingians: no empire was safer than the calibre of its succession. When Charlemagne died in 814 at the age of seventy-two his court went into deep mourning, and was understandably nervous. The curse of partigeniture soon settled over it. Charlemagne's heir, Louis the Pious (814–40) divided his domain in turn among his three sons, who on his death resorted to three years of fratricidal war. This culminated in 843 in the Treaty of Verdun, in which they agreed to partition their grandfather's empire between them. No treaty was more significant in the early history of Europe.

The partition of Verdun saw the lands west of the Loire/Rhône go to Charles the Bald. Those to the east of the Rhine went to Louis the German. Thus were created the first precursors of today's France and Germany. Between these two lands ran territory to be ruled by Louis's eldest son, Lothair. This comprised a series of unrelated territories south from the Rhine basin through what is now Belgium, Alsace, Lorraine, Burgundy and Savoy, into Charlemagne's kingdom of Lombardy. Initially called Lotharingia, it included Charlemagne's capital at Aachen, and carried with it the title of emperor. While France and Germany went their distinctive ways, and with their own languages, Lotharingia acquired neither a stable boundary nor an identity. It would fragment into kingdoms, principalities and bishoprics, some no more than a few miles wide. But its cities grew to become the richest in Europe, from Antwerp and Ghent in the north to Genoa and Milan in the south. Mastery of them and of the fertile lands round them was bitterly contested, and became the flashpoint for Europe's most savage wars.

5

The New Europeans
840–1100

The Vikings are coming

With Charlemagne gone, the concentration of power on which his empire relied went into decline. Towards the end of his life, he was told that a band of 'Northmen' had been driven away from a local harbour. The chronicle records him as not rejoicing but gazing out to sea, 'overwhelmed with sorrow as I look forward, and see what evils [the Northmen] will bring upon my offspring and their people'. The Vikings had come. So named from the creeks or 'viks' in which they lived, they were outgrowing their fjords and cramped settlements and learning of riches that lay over the seas. They sought new lands to exploit and old wealth to plunder.

The Vikings travelled in long, shallow-bottomed boats with carved prows, oars and sails, an advance on any Europe had seen before. They were not wide-bellied to carry cargo, like the ships of the Mediterranean, but narrow for warrior oarsmen. They could cut through heavy seas at speed and yet drew no more than two or three feet for travel up rivers. They could thus carry their fighters along the shallowest of inland waterways.

The so-called Viking 'swarmings' were unlike Charlemagne's land-based power. They were marauders rather than occupiers of land. They wanted treasure, and showed no conscience or restraint in getting it, killing or enslaving anyone unfortunate enough to encounter them. They first attacked monasteries, as these were undefended and usually wealthy. Vulnerable Lindisfarne off the Northumberland coast was devastated in 793, Iona in Scotland successively from 795. Other Vikings went east, penetrating the inland rivers of Russia, the Dnieper, the Don and the Volga. They reached as far south as the Caspian and Black seas, overwhelming the indigenous Slavs and selling them as slaves (the word derived from Slav) in the markets of Crimea. By the 840s riverside trading settlements had been established and by the 860s the Swedish warlord Rurik had founded colonies at Novgorod and Kiev. His follower Oleg formed the empire of Kievan Rus'. In 860, 200 'Russian' ships arrived outside Constantinople and devastated its surroundings, though the siege of the city was unsuccessful.

Though recent historians have sought to 'humanize' the vikings, the reality was that nothing so terrified ninth-century Europe as the sight of a longship sliding ashore on a river bank. The raids spread round the mainland coast. Paris was sacked in 845, the people of Nantes were massacred in 843 and Hamburg and Bordeaux were put to the sword. Initially the victims could save themselves with payments of gold and silver, hence the term Danegeld, but soon the Vikings formed trading posts and sought new homes. They began to settle.

In 865 a Danish fleet landed in East Anglia and the chronicle records 'a great army' coming ashore, followed in due course by cargo ships bringing wives and cattle. This invasion was halted in 878 by Alfred, king of Wessex (871–99), at the Battle of Edington in Wiltshire. He drove the Danes from southern England and persuaded their leader, Guthrum, to be baptized a Christian. But Alfred was king only of Wessex. The invaders were left undisturbed in their so-called Danelaw, covering eastern England from London north to York. This third of England remained in Danish hands for half a century.

With the passage of time, Vikings integrated with local populations and adopted local languages. They brought a new commercial energy to the coast of Europe, from the North and Baltic seas to the

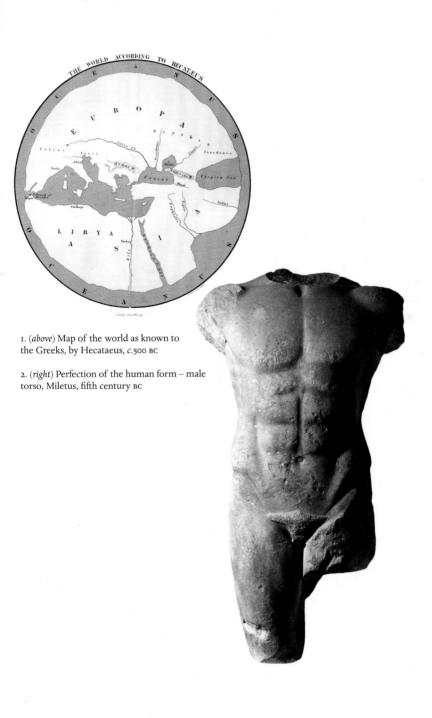

1. (*above*) Map of the world as known to the Greeks, by Hecataeus, *c*.500 BC

2. (*right*) Perfection of the human form – male torso, Miletus, fifth century BC

3. (*right*) Pericles, presiding figure of Athenian ascendancy, *c.*430 BC

4. (*below*) Symbol of Athens' golden age – Acropolis, with Parthenon temple

5. Carthaginian coin, possibly of Hannibal and elephant

6. Perhaps the first portrayal of Christ, as a shepherd, from the Roman catacombs, third century

7. Hub of empire – ruins of the
Roman Forum in the eighteenth
century, by Piranesi

8. Constantine the Great, the
first Christian emperor, 306–37

9. Meeting of Pope Leo, attended by angels and apostles, and Attila the Hun, 452

10/11. The empire's last gasp – Justinian (*left*) and his wife Theodora, Ravenna mosaic, *c.*547

12. (*right*) Charlemagne, King of Franks and first Holy Roman Emperor, 768–814

13. (*below*) Islam's European splendour – the Great Mosque in Cordoba

14. Death of Harold of England at Hastings, 1066, from the Bayeux tapestry

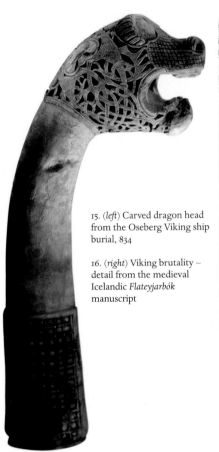

15. (*left*) Carved dragon head from the Oseberg Viking ship burial, 834

16. (*right*) Viking brutality – detail from the medieval Icelandic *Flateyjarbók* manuscript

17. (*top*) First Crusade assault on Jerusalem, 1099

18. (*above left*) Church versus state – Becket arguing with Henry II

19. (*right*) Church triumphant – Pope Innocent III

trading routes of the northern arc through Russia. By the end of the tenth century they had expanded across the then warmer north Atlantic and settled in Iceland. Here in 930 they founded the Althing, Europe's oldest continuous parliament. In c.1000, Leif Ericsson sailed beyond Greenland and founded a short-lived settlement at L'Anse aux Meadows on the northern tip of Newfoundland, thereby 'discovering' America. In just two centuries, Scandinavian tribes had thrown round Europe a girdle of enterprise. A mobile and aggressive dynamic was injected into Europe's history.

The Magyars and Otto the Great

As the Vikings started to settle and form colonies, a new migration began from the Ural mountains. The Magyars were first reported in the Crimean peninsula in 860. They came, like the Huns, as mounted warriors, eager for plunder and land. They reached Orléans in France and as far south as Rome. In 910 they defeated a German army, and in 924 devastated Provence. As the Vikings were unstoppable at sea, so the Magyars seemed unstoppable on land. After they had marauded across central Europe for some years, they were confronted by another of the dominant personalities of medieval Europe, Otto the Great of Saxony (936–73), ruler by inheritance of both Germany and Lotharingia. In 955 he assembled an alliance of German duchies to face the Magyars at the Battle of Lechfeld in Bavaria. Otto's mail-clad cavalry overwhelmed a much larger force of Magyars, and the latter retreated to settle, to this day, in Hungary.

Otto, often seen as the first leader of today's Germany, showed how crucial to the security of Europe was a strong personality able to attract military support. He reasserted imperial sovereignty in northern Italy and was formally crowned Holy Roman Emperor in Rome in 962. He reached 'tributary' treaties with Poland and Bohemia. He also reasserted Charlemagne's supremacy of monarchy over the Roman church. No pope could take office, he said, without swearing allegiance to the emperor. But he also proved vulnerable to his predecessor's love of Rome. He moved his court to Italy and married his son to a Byzantine princess, in hope of better relations with Constantinople. Pope and emperor cohabiting in the one city did not prove a success, if only because, as John Julius Norwich put it, 'Otto considered the pope as little more than his chaplain.'

By the end of the tenth century, most but not all of what is now eastern Europe had been brought within the Catholic rite. Ten years after Otto's death in 973, compulsory Christianization led to an uprising of pagan Slavs known as Wends living east of the Elbe. A series of 'marches' were established, fixing the eastern boundary of the Holy Roman Empire, roughly on the line of that river. Paganism survived among the Wends for another two centuries. The boundary later separated the Germany of the Holy Roman Empire (and of West and East Germany) from Saxony and Prussia.

Vladimir and the rise of Russia

By now King Vladimir of Kievan Rus' (980–1015), who claimed descent from the Viking Rurik, was sovereign over Slav peoples stretching from the Baltic to the Black Sea. Eager to modernize his realm, he in 987 sent emissaries to advise which faith would best suit his people. As a result, Vladimir rejected the Bulgars' Islam as 'having only sorrow and a great stench', and for opposing alcohol, 'the joy of all Rus''. Judaism was rejected as having lost its capital, Jerusalem, and thus its god. German Christianity was 'just churches of no beauty'. But Constantinople greeted the emissaries with a royal welcome, leaving them 'not knowing whether we are in heaven or on earth'. The dazzling salesmanship succeeded, though

Vladimir's choice of Byzantine Orthodoxy was probably a foregone conclusion.

A year later, in 988, Vladimir married Anna, sister of the emperor Basil II of Constantinople, and brought Russia into the Byzantine church. He led the entire population of Kiev into the river for baptism. Byzantine craftsmen were hired to build churches, including the Church of Tithes in Kiev, making the onion dome a signature Russian style. He also sent his best Varangian (Viking) warriors as permanent bodyguards for the Constantinople court. These contacts greatly improved trade in the region, with Constantinople soon rivalling Baghdad as a focus of Silk Road commerce. A Viking colony has even been found on the shores of the Persian Gulf, while Sweden was an early user of oriental silk. Vladimir wisely saw Russia as a natural ally of Constantinople and later Russians dreamt of Moscow as the 'third Rome'.

The Northmen come of age

Vladimir's cousins back in Scandinavia were proving no less enterprising. In 876 a warlord called Rollo, believed to have come from Denmark, raided deep into France and seized the city of Rouen. In 911 the French king, Charles the Simple, finally told him he could keep Rouen and its surroundings, if in return he defended his realm from further raids. He also demanded that Rollo kiss Charles's foot. Legend has the bodyguard of a reluctant Rollo, a giant of a man, grabbing the proffered foot and raising it to his mouth, tipping Charles to the ground. More diplomatically, Rollo married Popa of Bayeux and founded what became the dukedom of the Northmen, or Normandy.

The Vikings were no less active across the North Sea. The English kingdom of Wessex, which by now had recaptured much of the Danelaw, was in 1015 invaded by a force of 200 ships under the Danish leader Cnut, son of Sweyn Forkbeard and Sigrid the Haughty. This was a full-scale conquest, albeit of lands in which many Danes had already become assimilated. A contemporary history records that 'in this great expedition there was present no slave, no man freed from slavery, no low-born man, no man weakened by age; for all were nobles'. England's King Ethelred and his Anglo-Saxons were no match for the newcomers, who swept the country from Wessex north to York in 1017. Cnut married Ethelred's Norman widow, Emma, and by 1028 had expanded his domain to embrace Norway and part of Sweden. For a quarter of a century, England was thus part of a Scandinavian empire. The devout Cnut visited Rome and dispatched an army of missionaries to Christianize his Scandinavian domain.

Other Normans ventured south round the coast of western Europe and into the Mediterranean as far as Italy. Here they established a strong foothold through Robert Guiscard (1015–85), eventually Duke of Apulia and Calabria. Led by his brother, Roger, the Normans defeated the Muslim Saracens in Sicily, where to this day churches and castles are adorned with Norman motifs. By the twelfth century, all southern Italy had been united into the Kingdom of Sicily, an entrepôt of Norman, Italian and north African cultures.

The Great Schism

In Rome, the papacy was drifting far from Gregory the Great's ideal ruler of a new European establishment. Popes became corrupt and often incompetent, in ambivalent and frequently hostile dealings with Otto's descendants in Germany. Regular attempts at reconciliation with Byzantium had been made by Charlemagne and Otto, but without success. Just as westerners saw Byzantines as debauched and enfeebled, so Byzantines regarded westerners as upstart barbarians.

The dispute between eastern and western churches had long been both theological and political. While Frankish monarchs had finally seen Arianism off-stage, new disputes emerged within Christianity. Did the Holy Spirit proceed from the Father through the Son, or from the Father *and* the Son? The latter, so-called *filioque* clause implied an equal rather than sequential role for Christ. To the uninitiated, it was arguing over angels on pin-heads, yet it divided empires. Of immediate concern was whether Rome or Constantinople enjoyed supremacy in regulating church dogma and organization. Rome was hostile to Byzantium's bouts of iconoclasm, which occurred in 730–87 and 815–43, rooted in the Old Testament prohibition of 'graven images or any likeness of anything'. These periods led to the destruction of what had been a vast treasury of Byzantine art, leaving church interiors stripped to the bare bricks still seen in older Orthodox places of worship to this day.

In 1053 Pope Leo IX accused his opposite number, the Patriarch of Constantinople, of 'unexampled presumption and unbelievable effrontery . . . You place your mouth in heaven while your tongue, going through the world, strives with human arguments and conjectures to undermine and subvert the ancient faith.' A year later, efforts at compromise ended with abuse hurled at Rome's emissaries on a visit to Hagia Sophia in Constantinople. Exasperated, the emissaries laid a papal bull of excommunication on the high altar, shook the dust of the church from their shoes and retreated to their ships. The patriarch excommunicated them in turn. The Christian church was in formal schism, a schism that remains unresolved to this day.

William's conquest of England

Rome badly needed friends, of whom the most obvious were the emergent Normans. Those in Normandy were naturalized as French, speaking the language, evolving knightly traditions and paying token homage to Clovis's dynasty in Paris. Their society was ordered on feudal lines, in which land belonged to the duke as sovereign over barons, knights and serfs. The tenancy of land was paid for in taxes and military service in time of war. Only the church, in buildings of ever grander 'Romanesque' splendour, enjoyed financial liberty and relative autonomy.

In 1066 the succession to the English throne passed controversially from Edward the Confessor to Harold, Earl of Wessex. The succession of Harold, himself an Anglo-Dane, was challenged by not one but two rivals, Norway's Harald Hardrada and William Duke of Normandy. The latter claimed, with some plausibility, a formal promise of the crown by the dead Edward, who was a distant relative. Hardrada struck first, invading Northumbria and seizing York. But he was defeated and driven off by Harold at the Battle of Stamford Bridge in September 1066.

After weeks of delay, William of Normandy landed in what was then Kent and confronted Harold at the Battle of Hastings on 14 October 1066. Here the disciplined Norman cavalry won a crushing victory. Harold was killed and, within a year, England was under William's control. Despite brief resistance in East Anglia and the north, England proved as susceptible to conquest by Normans as it had by Danes. The conquest was celebrated in narrative form in a tapestry seventy metres long, made in England but displayed in Normandy at Bayeux.

William the Conqueror (1066–87) was crowned on Christmas Day, not in the Saxon capital of Winchester but at Westminster, Edward's Anglo-Norman abbey outside London. Though the language of England was Anglo-Saxon and of its administration Latin, England's court under Edward was already speaking and legislating in French. While the Norman conquest is traditionally portrayed as France against England, it was as much a personal struggle between two Viking descendants, an event in European as much as English history.

The nature of William's conquest was unlike any other. His expedition had been opposed by his barons as a private venture, outside the requirements of feudal loyalty, but he gained legitimation for it from Pope Alexander II, who sent him a ring and papal standard. He said he would not just win the submission of the English but also grant his supporters the entire wealth of Anglo-Saxon England, civil and ecclesiastical. He would plunder England on a massive scale.

William was as good as his word. Within five years, an astonishing ninety-five per cent of England south of Northumbria was in Norman hands, a quarter of it passing to the church. This financed probably the greatest building programme to be undertaken anywhere in pre-nineteenth century Europe. The Normans demolished and replaced nearly every Saxon cathedral and abbey, and built a network of castles and fortified towns. In 1086 a land census, the Domesday Book, was drawn up on a scale not seen elsewhere in Europe until the fifteenth century. Within a generation, taxes were being collected, registered and audited by clerks on an exchequer board. Justice was administered by sheriffs and judges through assize courts. The Normans were no longer wild northern raiders. Though England and, eventually, Wales and Ireland were notionally colonies of Normandy, they became a centralized nation state in embryo. A century earlier, England had been part of a Scandinavian empire. In 1066 it was betrothed to continental Europe.

Henry IV's investiture controversy

On one matter William never deviated. He knew how much his conquest had owed to Rome, which also approved his reform of the dysfunctional Anglo-Saxon church. He rewarded the Norman church with cathedrals, abbeys and, above all, land, but this in turn assailed the church with pressures created by its burgeoning role in the secular life of Europe. As its spiritual empire grew, it became embroiled with local rulers and inevitably conflicted with them. Since bishoprics and their revenues were a source of local patronage, it was a matter of dispute as to whom this patronage belonged. Who in truth was the Holy Roman Emperor?

The monastic movement was now a major force within the church, and one over which Rome could exercise little regular control. Even the ascetic Benedictines had fallen prey to comfort and corruption. The result was the emergence of new monastic orders, the Cluniacs (910) and the Cistercians (1098), which were to become both popular and a source of ecclesiastical power. They were builders on an imperial scale. The twelfth-century Cluniacs of Burgundy boasted a phenomenal 10,000 monks spread across 1,450 monasteries from England to Poland and Palestine. The abbey at Cluny itself was the greatest church in western Christendom, until the rebuilding of St Peter's in Rome in the sixteenth and seventeenth centuries.

In 1073 a Tuscan Cluniac named Hildebrand was elected pope, taking the name and ambitions of Gregory the Great, his sixth-century predecessor. As Gregory VII (1073–85), Hildebrand two years later formulated a statement of policy, *Dictatus papae*, that was bold to the point of megalomania. It stipulated the absolute supremacy, secular as well as religious, of the Roman church. The pope could depose emperors, appoint and transfer bishops, and ordain priests. Priests were to be celibate. Princes should kiss the feet of the pope. Should there be any doubt, 'the Roman church has never erred nor, as witness the Scripture, will it ever do so'. Gregory saw himself as the successor not just of Charlemagne but of imperial Rome: *Quibus imperavit Augustus, imperavit Christus*, where

Augustus ruled, Christ ruled. Should anyone disagree, excommunication would follow.

Germany's new king and Holy Roman Emperor, Henry IV (1056–1106), certainly did not agree. He had grown from infant king to headstrong but shrewd ruler. He spent much of his reign fighting Saxons and pagan Slavs across the Elbe border, but his most persistent foe was Gregory. The pope's *Dictatus* on the appointment of bishops was a direct assault on Henry's patronage and authority. In 1076, he summoned a diet of his local bishops and formally declared Gregory deposed.

Thus began the 'investiture controversy', a euphemism for what became an often bloody conflict between the papacy and the heirs to Charlemagne's empire. German kings did not automatically inherit their crowns, but were chosen by a college of princes and bishops, known as 'electors'. Succession was usually but not always based on family inheritance, influenced by merit and corruption. This in turn enabled Gregory to exploit opposition to Henry among his electors, princes and dukes, backed by the threat of excommunication. He condemned Henry's 'unheard of arrogance', and absolved 'all Christians from the bond of the oath they have made to him'.

Many of Henry's supporters were unnerved by this and demanded he seek forgiveness from Gregory, then lodging at Canossa in Emilia. In 1077 Henry capitulated. The celebrated 'walk to Canossa' saw him travel to Italy and prostrate himself outside Gregory's castle, 'standing barefoot in the snow and clothed in the woollen robe of the penitent'. He stood for three days and nights 'moaning, weeping and craving pardon'. Eventually, Gregory gave in and allowed him communion. 'Going to Canossa' remains a German expression for extreme repentance.

For a man like Henry, such humiliation would not go unavenged. In 1080 he duly raised an army and returned to Rome, where he appointed an anti-pope and toppled Gregory. Gregory pleaded for help from his Norman neighbour, Robert Guiscard of Sicily, who obliged in 1084 by sacking Rome, destroying many of its buildings and slaughtering many of its citizens. Henry retreated and Gregory was restored, but Rome never forgave the pope the manner of his return. He died the following year, a broken man.

Henry's reign survived another two decades, but the investiture controversy outlived him. A compromise settlement was reached in a concordat at Worms in 1122, whereby church appointments could be made by monarchs, but 'bishops' were formally 'invested', or installed by the pope with appropriate insignia. It was a compromise in which the church's lack of worldly power was evident. Worms acknowledged the sovereignty of secular rule, and was a building block in the emergence of states. Henry's challenge to Rome led Luther to hail him as 'the first Protestant'.

6

The Church Militant
1100–1215

The first crusade

In 1095, the emperor in Constantinople, Alexios Komnenos, approached the pope in Rome, Urban II, with a plea to heal the now forty-year-old Great Schism. He was desperate. It was the eastern empire, not Rome, that now faced a 'barbarian' threat, from the new rulers of Persia and Turkey, the Seljuks. They had shrivelled his empire to just Greece and a northern strip of Asia Minor. Pilgrims were being massacred in Jerusalem, and Alexios needed soldiers. It is not known if Urban mentioned how often similar pleas to the east from his predecessors in Rome had gone unanswered. The balance of power in Christendom had clearly shifted.

Urban was a politician. He saw the request as an opportunity to carry forward Gregory VII's vision of the papacy as a pan-European force. Preaching in November 1095 in Clermont in France, he responded to Alexios by summoning all Christendom to a crusade. It would save Byzantium and liberate Christian Jerusalem from infidel occupation. Petty squabbles over investiture should be set aside in a war of faith. 'Let those who have been fighting against their own brothers and relations,' said Urban, 'now rightfully fight the barbarians. Let those who were hired for a few pieces of silver win their eternal reward.' The slogan, said Urban, was *Deus vult*, God wills it.

This was a venture on a different scale from the coalitions

summoned to confront Huns, Umayyads or Magyars. Christendom's elites were being invited to put aside their local rivalries and gather under the church in a collective cause. Urban linked his call to the cult of knightly enterprise and chivalric glory. Warriors for Christ should rise above feuding and banditry, and aspire to honour, godliness and comradeship. They responded with enthusiasm, encouraged by a papal pardon for all their sins.

In 1096 at least four crusader armies set off across Europe. First to leave was a chaotic 'People's Crusade' under a charismatic French evangelist, Peter the Hermit. He led an estimated 15,000 variously adventurous and starving peasants, with little idea of where they were going or what to do. On the way Peter's crusaders and other hangers-on killed thousands of Jews in the Rhineland, possibly a quarter of those in the region. They went on to inflict similar pogroms in Hungary, largely in a quest for food. Disoriented survivors eventually arrived in Constantinople, where they again raided the countryside for supplies. A dismayed Alexios pushed them south, where in October the remnants were massacred in an ambush by the Turks. They were heard of no more.

The other armies, from France, Flanders, Germany and Italy travelled more comfortably by sea, some 35,000 assembling outside Constantinople in 1097. Their motives have been much debated, a mix of adventurism, hope of gain and genuine piety. As the crusaders marched south they were debilitated by heat, disease and disagreement. They captured Nicaea and Antioch, and entered Jerusalem in 1099. Here they perpetrated another mass killing, this time of the city's Muslim population, and held the Jews for ransom. By then, barely 12,000 crusaders remained. Jerusalem was garrisoned and four Christian settlements were formed, including a 'kingdom' of Jerusalem. Coastal trading colonies were established. All were clearly vulnerable to Seljuk counter-attack.

The second crusade

For half a century this early venture in European imperialism re-opened the Levant to Christian pilgrimage. Such were its dangers that two orders of knights, the Hospitallers and Templars, were formed in Jerusalem. The first was to care for the health and welfare of pilgrims, the second, based on the site of Solomon's temple, was military, to defend pilgrims on the road up from the coast. The orders soon acquired the sponsorship of the Roman church – in effect as lay monastics. They also acquired wealthy backers and a secretive and glamorous mystique. Both survived the crusaders' later expulsion from the Holy City. The Templars became so rich as to suffer French government confiscation in the fourteenth century, while the Hospitallers (later of Malta) remain as a provider of St John ambulances to this day.

The papacy could launch a crusade, but it could not sustain one. In 1144 the first colony, at Edessa, was overrun by the Seljuks, and the rest were threatened. The following year a second crusade was summoned by Pope Eugenius III, promoted with 'the splendid bargain' of copious indulgences in the afterlife. Their champion was a firebrand Cistercian, Bernard of Clairvaux, who claimed to be so good at recruiting that wherever he went 'you will afterwards scarcely find one man to every seven women'. The kings of both France and Germany promised armies, which they would personally lead. For good measure, crusades were also declared against pagan Slavs and Muslim Saracens (or Moors) in Spain.

This second crusade left in 1147 and proved a fiasco. After arriving in the Levant, where the crusaders found Jerusalem to be safely Christian, they tried and failed to capture Damascus. They suffered numerous defeats at the hands of the Turks, fell to infighting and retreated home. The Iberian crusade was more fruitful. By now roughly half the peninsula – León, Aragon and Castile – had returned to Christianity in the so-called *reconquista*. The south, on the other hand, had prospered under the sometimes tolerant regime of the caliphs, with Muslims, Jews and Christians coexisting. English knights on their way to the Mediterranean landed at Oporto, where they agreed at least to help King Afonso of Portugal recapture Lisbon in 1147, a victory hailed as the sole success of the second crusade.

Henry II and Becket

Five years later, an eighteen-year-old prince from Anjou named Henry Plantagenet, son and heir of Matilda of England, paid homage at the French court in Paris. He was a stocky, red-haired youth, with a piercing stare and bursting with virility. He soon infatuated the thirty-year-old former queen, Eleanor of Aquitaine, who ruled most of south-west France and had led her own army to the second crusade. Her marriage to Louis VII of France, whom she derided as 'not a king but a monk', had ended in annulment. Two months later, amid a scandal that mesmerized Europe, she married Henry, who proceeded to mount the English throne as Henry II (1154–89). Their joint domains embraced not just England but more of France than did those of Louis. The couple held an empire from the Cheviots to the Pyrenees.

In 1164 Henry revived the investiture controversy by promulgating his Constitutions of Clarendon, declaring his power over the English church and bringing to a head a running dispute with Thomas Becket, his former friend and now Archbishop of Canterbury. Becket, echoing Gregory VII, threatened to excommunicate his own king for making appointments behind Becket's back, including the naming his own successor. By 1170 relations were so bad that Henry, dining in France, said words, variously translated but to the effect of 'Who will rid me of this turbulent priest?' Four knights sailed for England, found Becket and murdered him in Canterbury Cathedral.

The horror of the deed, not least the abuse of sanctuary, scandalized Europe, and Henry was unable to escape responsibility. Like Henry IV at Canossa, he was forced to humiliate himself in penance. He showered privileges on the church and instigated a frenzy of cathedral and monastery rebuilding. Pilgrims from across Europe flocked to Becket's miracle-rich shrine at Canterbury, where the cathedral was expanded and redesigned in the new French 'gothic' style. Becket's cult was celebrated until the English Reformation.

Barbarossa and the third crusade

Henry's contemporary, Frederick 'Barbarossa', ruler of Germany (1152–90), was a different character, a calm, intelligent and handsome knight in the crusader tradition. Named for his red beard, he came to the German throne as the son of a peacemaking marriage between the rival Hohenstaufen and Welf clans. Replicated in Italy as Ghibellines and Guelphs, they backed respectively the Holy Roman Empire and the pope. Their enmity was often bitter, memorialized by Shakespeare as the Montagues and Capulets in *Romeo and Juliet*.

Barbarossa set about retrieving for the Holy Roman Empire the authority diminished by Henry IV's investiture dispute with Gregory. This meant securing the loyalty of Germany's myriad pocket rulers, as well as risking a revival of the dispute itself. When in 1155 Barbarossa arrived at Rome to be crowned Holy Roman Emperor by Pope Hadrian, argument immediately arose over who should kiss whose feet and lead whose horse into Rome. The new emperor succeeded in making his territories cohere sufficiently to raise and equip an army. But the contradiction between autonomy and kingship within the Holy Roman Empire was growing ever more insistent.

Barbarossa's independent-minded German states and his dissident Italian ones put his authority always under threat. To the east, he had to fight his neighbour, Henry the Lion of Saxony. In Italy he fought five campaigns against the cities of the north, with Milan in frequent revolt. The papacy was factionalized, forcing Barbarossa to take sides and at one point declare an anti-pope. In 1176 he was heavily defeated at the Battle of Legnano by an alliance of Venice, Lombardy and Sicily, leading to another imperial penance before the pope. It might be concluded that, if Barbarossa's talents could not hold together a Holy Roman Empire, the concept was inherently dysfunctional.

These disputes were interrupted when, in 1187, a new Muslim leader in the Levant, a Kurd named Saladin, virtually wiped out all Christian presence in the Holy Land at the Battle of Hattin. Jerusalem reverted to Muslim rule. This traumatic event galvanized Europe to a third crusade. Three monarchs stepped forward, Barbarossa himself, Philip II of France (1180–1223) and Henry of England's son Richard the Lionheart (1189–99). In 1189 all three left for the Holy Land. The German contingent went overland, to be joined by the Hungarians. The other monarchs went more comfortably, 'first-class' by sea.

On their way to Syria, disaster struck. The one commander who might have brought the expedition success, Barbarossa, was drowned crossing a Turkish river, weighed down by his armour. His dismayed troops tried to pickle his body and bury it in Jerusalem, failing in both respects. The remainder of the third crusade was a repeat of the second. England's Richard, who displayed much skill on the battlefield, succeeded in the siege of Acre in 1191, which remained in Christian hands for another century, but he could not recapture

Jerusalem. Eventually he could do no more than secure from Saladin a promise to admit Christian pilgrims to the holy places. After three years of defeat and disease, the crusaders headed for home.

Innocent III and the fourth crusade

If the crusades achieved anything, they produced in the emergent nations of Europe a sense of common purpose. Widely differing peoples, used only to fighting each other, congregated and co-operated under the aegis of the church. As such, the sponsors of the crusades, successive popes, emerged strengthened even by their failure. The papal authority formulated under Gregory the Great and Gregory VII now reached its peak under Innocent III (1198–1216). He came to office at the unusually young age of thirty-eight, when two powerful kings, England's Henry II and Germany's Barbarossa, were both dead and their states weakened by succession disputes. Innocent called himself Vicar of Christ and, in 1202, tried to play the crusade card, to recapture Jerusalem.

This time Europe's monarchs did not respond. Innocent's fourth crusade was a disaster. Short of money, he tried to levy possibly Europe's first income tax, wisely confined to the clergy. This proved impossible to collect. The crusade was then hijacked by the Venetians, who had money but were reluctant to damage their Levantine trade with the Turks. They cared little for Jerusalem, but with the help of Norman mercenaries they were happy to evict 'the Greeks', as they called them, from Constantinople. A crusader force duly set sail in 1202, first besieging Venice's rival city of Zara in Croatia and then diverting to Constantinople, to help restore a deposed emperor to the throne in return for a large reward.

The plan went awry. The reward was not delivered and, in retaliation, the crusaders in April 1204 undermined and scaled the city walls and stormed inside. A French nobleman present recorded that they 'could never have imagined so fine a place in all the world, high walls, lofty towers, rich palaces and tall churches . . . there was no man so brave that his flesh did not shudder'. The crusaders then subjected this paragon of a city to days of pillage and destruction. Priests were murdered, icons smashed, towers toppled, nuns raped and half the city set on fire. What was still the greatest city in Christendom was stripped of its treasures. The Count of Flanders was made new eastern emperor, and a Venetian nobleman was made patriarch. The Great Schism was notionally in abeyance, and Constantinople was declared a Latin city.

The fourth crusade seemed a throwback to a time of Viking banditry. It was a reminder that the dominant concern in the eastern Mediterranean was less events in Rome and more trading opportunities eastwards – irrespective of who might from time to time be in occupation of the holy places. The merchants of Genoa and Venice, always competitive with each other, did not reduce their reach but extended it, with Constantinople as their new base.

When reports of the city's sacking reached Rome, Innocent despaired. He excommunicated the crusaders, crying that 'swords supposed to be used against infidels now drip with Christian blood'. The crusaders had 'spared neither religion, nor age, nor sex. They have committed incest, adultery, and fornication before the eyes of men.' The accusation of incest was puzzling, but the Byzantine view of the west as inhabited by thugs and barbarians was vindicated. The Venetians remained in Constantinople for half a century, stealing its magnificent quadriga of horses (which had originally come from Rome) to adorn the cathedral of St Mark's. Not until 1261 were the Byzantines able to return to their city and repair the damage – though they never recovered the horses.

Despite this reverse, Innocent grew in self-confidence. In 1209 he excommunicated King John of England (1199–1216) for rejecting his nominee as Archbishop of Canterbury, placing the entire English church under interdict. John capitulated and made England technically a fiefdom of the papacy. Also in 1209, Innocent declared another crusade, for the suppression not of Muslims but of the Albigensian Cathars in south-west France. A new order, the Dominicans, was founded to confront their heresy, which held there to be a worldly dualism of good and evil, with humans free to achieve salvation by their asceticism.

For some forty years, the Cathars held out against both the pope and the French monarchy, including investigators who were precursors of the Inquisition. In 1244 the Cathars' hilltop fortress of Montségur was finally captured, and over 200 of their leaders roasted on an enormous pyre. It remains a grimly evocative site to this day. Both the church's obsessive persecution of the Cathars and their supposed treasure, have fascinated historians and novelists ever since.

Fourth Lateran Council versus Magna Carta

Innocent's power resulted in large part from the feuds and consequent weakness of Europe's monarchies at the turn of the thirteenth century. Tension came to a head in 1214 when a territorial dispute over the city of St Omer, on the old Lotharingian border, gave a foretaste of struggles to come. The Count of Flanders formed an alliance with John of England and the Holy Roman Emperor Otto IV in northern Germany. Against them was Philip II of France (1180–1223), whose claim to St Omer was contested, but supported *in absentia* by Otto's twenty-year-old rival for the imperial crown, Frederick of Sicily (later Frederick II). The two sides met at the Battle of Bouvines in 1214, where Philip was victorious.

The battle was a disaster for England's John, who had to accept the loss of the Angevin empire bequeathed him by his father, Henry

II, and his mother, Eleanor, including all of Normandy and Brittany. For his part, Philip could now consider himself truly king of most of France. England subsided into civil war between John and his barons. A year later, in 1215, an accumulation of grievances saw him forced to sign a charter in a meadow at Runnymede outside Windsor. It asserted the rights of his barons, and in some respects of all free men, against the judicial and executive authority of the monarch. It made the king concede that taxes could not be levied without the consent of a royal council of twenty-five barons. He also had to agree that 'to no one will we sell, to no one will we deny or delay, right or justice'. Every man should have the benefit of 'the lawful judgment of his equals [and] the law of the land'. It was a rudimentary declaration of the equality of all men before the law. It made no mention of women.

As soon as he had he signed the charter (later called Magna Carta) John repudiated it. His new feudal lord, Innocent III, added an edict that it was 'shameful, base, illegal and unjust'. The infuriated barons displayed their contempt for Rome by inviting the heir to the French throne, the future Louis VIII, to invade England, topple John and become their king. Louis invaded in 1216, occupying the Tower of London. He was forced to withdraw after John died later that year, and French forces were defeated at Lincoln and at sea off Dover by those fighting on behalf of John's son, the nine-year-old Henry III (1216–72), to be crowned king in Gloucester. He ruled initially under the protection of the elderly Sir William Marshal, a celebrated warrior, said to have 'worsted' 500 knights in tournaments.

As for Innocent, he staged a climax to his extraordinary career. In 1213 he had summoned 1,500 delegates to a Fourth Lateran Council in Rome. They gathered to discuss, or at least acclaim, his personal vision of a church dominant and intolerant, but also reformed and disciplined. The council restored papal supremacy over civil authority and the clergy. It asserted transubstantiation, that bread and water became Christ's flesh and blood during the Eucharist. It proscribed Jews as second-class citizens, and called for the eradication of heretics. The council also took time to put an end to such judicially primitive practices as trial by combat and ordeal.

The Fourth Lateran's decrees were promulgated in 1216, a year after England's Magna Carta. In the light of subsequent history, these two documents tower over the dawn of the thirteenth century. Innocent's decrees were autocratic and superstitious, defining an empire of faith under the authority of a single man in matters both religious and secular. It was an empire of a reborn Rome, a constitution for all of Christendom.

Magna Carta began with an acknowledgement of the church, but it could hardly have been more different. It was secular, practical, individualist and appealing to all under the king. While it largely reflected the particular balance of power in thirteenth-century England, it came to be seen as a founding text of civil liberty and thus proof of English exceptionalism. It is on any showing a very different view of medieval society from that of Innocent III. As Kipling was to write: 'And still when mob or Monarch lays / Too rude a hand on English ways, / The whisper wakes, the shudder plays, / Across the reeds at Runnymede.'

7

The Rise of States
1215–1400

Frederick II

Innocent III intended Christian Europe to be an empire of the spirit under his command. But though Europe might devote its soul to the service of one master, the church, its body was in the service of others, kings and emperors. Between them, at least in central Europe, there stretched the tenuous bridge of the Holy Roman Empire. When Innocent's Fourth Lateran Council turned briefly to secular matters, it acknowledged the twenty-two-year-old Frederick II of Germany as Holy Roman Emperor (1220–50). It is hard to believe the delegates knew the man they were honouring.

Frederick, like his grandfather Barbarossa, was a comet that flashed bright across the medieval sky, leaving barely a trace behind. Though a German, he was born in 1194 in Apulia in Italy, where his forty-year-old mother gave birth to him in public in a town square, to counter any doubts over his maternity. He was of German and Sicilian blood, and Palermo remained his favoured home. He became king of Germany at the age of two and of Sicily at three. For good measure, Innocent III was his guardian.

The young man grew up strong, intelligent and his own man in all things. He spoke six languages – Latin, Greek, French, German, Arabic and Sicilian – and kept a cultured court in Palermo. He was also a religious eccentric, an Epicurean with little time for the papacy and its voluminous edicts. He wrote a book on falconry, kept a menagerie and experimented on humans, such as locking away infants before they learned to talk, to see 'what language was spoken in the Garden of Eden'. Frederick was in every way an 'alternative' monarch. He was constantly at odds with popes, one of whom called him 'the beast that comes up from the sea'. In 1239 he was excommunicated for not completing a crusade, and then again for doing so when excommunicate. This crusade, the sixth, was the most successful since the first, and saw Frederick briefly installed as king of Jerusalem. He did not reject Christianity as such but rather the church – which called him an Antichrist – and he died a Cistercian monk. He chose Muslims as bodyguards, so they would be immune from excommunication if needed to defend him from papal assassins.

Though Frederick's flamboyance had him nicknamed, with a touch of irony, *stupor mundi*, the wonder of the world, his career was consumed by the same task as his grandfather, that of holding together the fragmented outer fringes of his empire. In 1226 he issued the Golden Bull of Rimini, authorizing the Prussian order of Teutonic Knights to protect the frontier with Poland. Originally formed to aid pilgrims in Jerusalem, the knights were drawn from the Hansa merchants of Lübeck and Bremen and created a military-religious state in what became East Prussia. There were other German settlements across east Europe, on the Volga and in the Saxon lands of Transylvania, relics of which survive today. In 1231 Frederick agreed the Privilege of Worms, granting yet more autonomy to the rulers of Germany's many statelets. But Frederick also had to acknowledge the fixation of his predecessors with the empire's Italian territories, leading to campaigns that were complex and indecisive. Had German king/emperors confined their attention to (present-day) Germany, Europe's history would have taken a very different turn.

The Golden Horde

While Frederick alternately fought and freed his subjects, Europe faced yet another invasion from the east. In 1240 the lands beyond the Danube suffered a reprise of the Hun and Magyar incursions. The Mongol 'Lord of the Earth', Genghis Khan (ruled 1206–27), father of a reputed 2,000 children, turned from his conquest of China to send horsemen 4,000 miles across Asia towards Europe. When Genghis died in 1227, his successor Ögedei ordered Batu Khan, leader of his western army, to send a 'Golden Horde' across the Volga and reach 'the Great Sea', the Atlantic.

Batu invaded in 1236, sweeping aside every force that tried to stop him. In 1240 he sacked the Russian city of Kiev. A year later he defeated a mostly Polish army in a battle at Legnica, while another army crushed the Hungarians and reached the Danube. Hungarian pleas to Frederick for help fell on a deaf ear; he merely ordered the reinforcement of fortifications along the Bohemian–Austrian border. At its greatest extent the Mongol empire stretched from the China Sea to the walls of Prague, one of the most extensive land empires ever created.

The Mongols, later known to the Europeans as Tartars, did not intend to settle. They were tolerant of religions and eager only for tribute, taking a terrible toll on those who refused. Entire cities might be slaughtered to deter others. But the Tartars opened a new age in east–west contact and trade. European caravans were allowed on the Silk Road and priests and scholars reached deep into China. The historian Daniel Boorstin, an admirer of the Tartars, credited the Golden Horde with a 'military genius, personal courage, administrative versatility and cultural tolerance unequalled by any European line of hereditary rulers'.

The Tartar advance ceased with Ögedei's death in 1241 and the abrupt withdrawal of the Golden Horde to Mongolia to await his successor. Later incursions never extended its domain, though the Tartar yoke continued to exact tribute from Russians into the fifteenth century. Russia, however, was traumatized by its new vulnerability to invasion. Kiev never recovered its ancient pre-eminence, and Novgorod and Moscow became Russia's chief cities.

To Russia's west, the Swedes and Teutonic Knights used the Mongol opportunity to extend eastwards. A Prussian force campaigned in 1242 to convert Russian Christians to Catholicism. With the Tartars still on the Danube, the Russian king, Alexander Nevsky (1236–63), had to confront the Prussians on what is now the Estonian border. In the 'Battle on the Ice' he drove them back across a frozen lake. The scale and significance of this battle are nowadays doubted, but Nevsky entered Russian legend as saviour of his people. The battle was celebrated in Eisenstein's epic film re-enactment.

Henry III and the birth of Parliament

Europe had showed no defensive coherence in the face of the Mongols. Countries were yet to evolve political or military institutions to supply continuous leadership, and there were few leaders with the power or charisma to fashion alliances. The church could unite but, as the crusades had shown, it could not fight or hold land. Frederick II's dream of a transcontinental empire from Sicily to the North Sea evaporated in 1250 when he died. Pope Innocent IV and his allies took control of southern Italy and tried to expel Frederick's son, Manfred, from Sicily. In 1254, he even offered the Sicilian crown to Henry III of England (1216–72), if he would pay the cost of Manfred's expulsion. Henry initially agreed, eager to pose as a new-style European monarch. He had a forceful French wife, Eleanor of Provence, and an enthusiasm for the flamboyant ('decorated' or traceried) style of French architecture, which he employed for his lavishly rebuilt Westminster Abbey. His one handicap was a shortage of money.

Just as a medieval monarch could fight only with the soldiers he could levy from his supporters, so he could spend only such money as he could extort from rents and general taxation. Magna Carta made it plain to Henry's father, John, that such taxation would be forthcoming only in return for consent from a royal council. This was reinforced in 1259 by the Provisions of Westminster. The king had to summon and consult a 'parliament' of barons and others. When Henry sought what was, in effect, permission for his Italian venture, it was denied.

Opposition to Henry was led by his brother-in-law, the French-born Simon de Montfort, Earl of Leicester. As relations worsened between the king and his barons, de Montfort raised the banner of revolt, eventually taking Henry prisoner at the Battle of Lewes in 1264. De Montfort then summoned the barons, bishops, county knights and, for the first time, civic burgesses, to meet at Westminster. It was the first time such a body had met without royal summons, in effect claiming sovereign power over the king. It met from January to March 1265, and proved too argumentative to survive. It broke up in disarray.

The barons divided for and against de Montfort, who was eventually defeated and killed at the Battle of Evesham. Henry was succeeded by his son, Edward I (1272–1307), a warrior king who fought to extend his sovereignty over Wales and Scotland. But Edward was careful to bring requests for taxation to a series of parliaments. Thus a potent concept was born. State power resided not in the will of a monarch but in a compact between him and a council of at least his more important subjects, discussing the affairs of state as they chose. The ghost of Cleisthenes flitted over Westminster, as it had through the reeds at Runnymede. De Montfort's assembly was not the only one in Europe – Spain had its Cortes and France its Parlement – but it was the first to develop effective power over the executive, largely because England's monarchs were perpetually in need of money for wars.

Boniface and the Avignon papacy

By the turn of the fourteenth century, Europe's economy was delivering new sources of wealth. In the Low Countries and Italy, the merchants of Antwerp and Ghent, Genoa, Milan and Venice were prospering, mostly from the north–south trade in cloth and the east–west trade in silks and spices. They built their own fleets, and Lombard financiers, first in Siena and then the Medici of Florence, developed skills in the handling and lending of money (hence London's Lombard Street). As the wealth of England's sheep-laden uplands emboldened England's barons and burgesses under Henry III, so across Europe money rivalled religion as an engine of power.

In France and Italy, money bred artistic patronage and confidence in new forms of culture. Northern Italy produced masters of late-medieval literature and art, the poet Dante (1265–1321) and the romanticist Petrarch (1304–74). Finding inspiration in the rediscovery of Cicero, Petrarch wrote that 'after the darkness has been dispelled, our grandsons will be able to walk back into the pure radiance of the past', that of classical civilization. This concept of going back gave rise to what was to be called the Renaissance. The painter Giotto (1267–1337) turned away from the Byzantine style of his master Cimabue and, in Padua's Arena chapel, produced in 1305 the first masterpiece of a new naturalism, a 'Proto-Renaissance'.

Little of this as yet touched Rome, already shorn of the authority and discipline ordained by Innocent III. In 1294 Boniface VIII (1294–1303) stretched papal autocracy to the limit, calling crusades and excommunicating his enemies as if these were mere orders of the day. He called a crusade against his clan rivals in Rome, the Colonna family. He declared 1300 a 'holy year' to attract pilgrims to St Peter's, and sold indulgences in the afterlife to anyone who came. Half a million people did so. Dante placed Boniface in the eighth circle of hell, and compared the pilgrim crowds of 1300 to a procession through Inferno. Today's summer tourists might sympathize.

Boniface then forbade all Catholic churches and priests to pay taxes to any monarch without his express consent. In 1302 he declared it 'necessary to salvation that every human be subject to the Roman pontiff', a statement flung in the face of rulers across Christendom. Even the French, long trusted allies of the papacy, found this too much. France was under Philip IV 'the Fair' (1285–1314), determined to raise his country from its patchwork of semi-autonomous dukedoms. Provinces that had previously paid notional homage to Paris were now to be governed by royal agents, bailiffs and senechals. Paris became a true capital and seat of Philip's authority. He allowed no echo of England's bargain between monarchy and Parliament.

Philip not only rejected Boniface's bull, he went further. In 1303 he sent agents to aid the Colonna family and kidnap the sixty-eight-year-old pope, charging him with a spectacular list of crimes, including murder, heresy, blasphemy, sodomy, simony and, for good measure, sorcery. Boniface escaped and soon died, but in 1305 Philip secured a French pope, the Gascon Clement V (1305–14), who wisely thought it best not to visit Rome. He settled first in Poitiers, and then comfortably in the Sicilian-owned enclave of Avignon, reputedly to be close to his mistress, the Countess of Perigord. Thus began in 1309 the (first) Avignon papacy, encompassing sixty-seven years and seven pontiffs.

Pope Clement was a creature of the French king, but he was barely an improvement on Boniface. From Avignon he proceeded to excommunicate one Italian city after another. He declared a crusade against Venice and even suggested Venetians captured abroad be sold into slavery. An Italian cardinal declared, 'The ship of Peter is shaken by the waves, the fisherman's net is broken.' Avignon was 'the mother of fornication, lust and drunkenness, full of abomination and filth'. The medieval church loved tabloid prose.

Philip was desperately short of money. In 1306 he imitated Edward I of England, who in 1290 had expelled virtually all of England's Jews and seized their wealth. The victims found asylum in the Netherlands and Poland. Philip was also in debt to the Knights Templar. In 1307 he induced Clement to disband the entire order, arrest its members and torture them into confessing heresy and immorality. Their estates passed to the Hospitallers, but the rest of their wealth went to Philip. For good measure, the Lombard bankers also were expelled. Not for the first time, or last, European monarchy was to prove the enemy of enterprise.

The Hundred Years War

France had little chance to benefit from Philip's firm hand on power. After his death in 1314 it was cursed by a disputed succession. Three royal sons and one grandson all died without male heirs – though one, Louis X, lived long enough to invent 'real' (or royal) tennis. However, Philip's daughter, Isabella, wife, widow and probable murderer of England's Edward II, was very much alive. So too was her teenage son, Edward III (1327–77). Under English law, the French crown now passed to her and then to him. Under French Salic law, forbidding female inheritance, it passed to the more distant House of Valois, to Philip VI. Though Isabella did not herself claim the throne, her son most certainly did. In 1330 the eighteen-year-old boy fully assumed his throne when he and a group of friends removed his regents, toppling his mother and butchering her lover, Roger Mortimer.

Both English and French aristocrats schooled their sons to regard war as a glamorous knightly adventure. Awash in Arthurian legend, Edward and his friends would dress in antique clothes, with himself as Sir Lancelot and his (forgiven) mother as Guinevere. Days were passed with jousting in the lists. The French chronicler Froissart wrote that 'the English will never love and honour their king unless he be victorious and a lover of arms and war against their neighbours'. Two of Europe's richest and most united countries would now torment each other for over a century to satisfy the lust of their young for honour in battle.

The Hundred Years War was fought almost entirely on French soil. Apart from his claim to the French throne, Edward's initial cause in 1337 was a French threat to the Flanders ports and thus to England's wool trade. First blood went to England in 1340 at the naval Battle of Sluys, off Belgium. It saw 20,000 Frenchmen killed, mostly shot with arrows when floundering in the sea. It was said that so many died that even the fish in the Channel spoke French. This freed the Flemish ports and should have removed the bone of contention.

Instead Edward continued to campaign, invading France and pressing on towards Paris to claim his crown. The Battle of Crécy in 1346 saw a decisive turn in military technology. French knights found their lavish armour ineffective against English (and Welsh) archers, using longbows of unprecedented drawing power and reloading speed. Lines of French mounted knights fell under clouds of missiles. Horses were brought down and their riders, near immobile in heavy armour, were bludgeoned to death on the ground. It was said that more than 12,000 French died, against just a hundred English.

Despite this victory, Edward was forced to withdraw when his army was hit by the occupational hazard of French wars: dysentery.

He turned back to besiege Calais, where six starving burghers came out to offer their lives if their citizens would be spared. Edward's French wife, Philippa, pleaded for them, and they were taken hostage instead, to be memorialized in a nineteenth-century sculpture by Rodin. The Calais wool staple, or market, remained in English hands for two centuries.

The war took on a nightmarish quality. English troops arrived annually to mount raids of plunder, known as *chevauchées*, horse charges, which involved them living off the local subsistence-farming inhabitants. Northern France was devastated. Europe in the early fourteenth century was entering a period of extended cooling from the 1320s onwards, sometimes called a 'little ice age'. There were exceptionally cold winters and famine on all sides. Yet for Edward's barons and their French opposite numbers, the war was like a seasonal diversion, celebrated by Edward inventing the chivalric Order of the Garter in 1348.

The Black Death and Wycliffe

That same year, Europe was in the grip of an affliction thought to have originated in the east and deadlier than any Tartar horde. The Black Death was a plague allegedly carried by fleas on the back of rats – though this is challenged by claimants for anthrax and pneumonia. As much as a third of the world's population died and, in a Europe already weakened by famine, possibly more. The catastrophe evoked desperate responses. It was attributed to God's vengeance on a sinful world, to be blamed on a corrupt papacy, a venal church and, if available, the Jews. In 1349, 2,000 Jews in Strasbourg were massacred overnight. Thousands more fled east, to find a welcome in the tolerant Poland of Casimir the Great (1333–70).

Nothing could impede Edward's war. In the 1350s he sent his

sons, the Black Prince and John of Gaunt, on regular campaigns of slaughter and pillage through plague-ravaged central France. This culminated in 1356 in the Battle of Poitiers, where, as at Crécy, English archers overwhelmed the French cavalry. The French king was captured and imprisoned for ransom. Despite this, Edward lacked the resources to move on to Paris, let alone capture it. Conditions forced him to retreat, and in 1360 sign the Treaty of Brétigny (or Calais). This acknowledged the loss of Normandy and Anjou, conceded by John after Bouvines, though Edward was able to reassert English sovereignty over Aquitaine to the south.

Brétigny ended an era when England's governing class still looked across the Channel to its ancestral roots. Though for three centuries it had resided in England, the English court had spoken French and adopted French manners and dress. Its architecture had taken its lead from France, and clergy and scholars had moved easily back and forth to Normandy. From 1362 all legal and parliamentary documents were to be in English. Easy intercourse across the Channel ceased. Pilgrims went to Becket's shrine at Canterbury rather than to Rome. A new English style of gothic architecture arrived – elegant, lofty and later called 'Perpendicular' – manifest in the Crécy window of Gloucester Cathedral, still considered the largest expanse of gothic glass in existence. Three centuries after the Norman conquest, England regained its sovereignty.

The Black Death drastically altered the terms of trade between master and worker. Attempts to pass laws to stop artisans from moving and bidding up their wages failed. Landowners began to enclose their land and specialize in cash crops. A subsistence rural economy gradually turned into a monetary one. Living standards and productivity rose, while rents from property fell. Wool became as critical to late-medieval England as oil was to twentieth-century Arabia. A golden sheep adorned the London staple, later the stock exchange, and the Lord Chancellor sat in Parliament on a woolsack.

English ships traded with Flanders and with the Hanseatic League. The North Sea was the new Mediterranean.

The England that recovered its prosperity after the Black Death was best captured in Chaucer's epic poem *The Canterbury Tales* (c.1387). It could hardly be more distant in content and spirit from Dante's *Inferno* of half a century before. Not for Chaucer the mythology of heaven and hell, or the gloomy imaginings of a superstitious church. His characters, men and women, were worldly, cynical, humorous and curious. Above all they showed no respect for the established church or state. Chaucer's pilgrims were harbingers of an English Renaissance and perhaps of an English Reformation.

The French war had inclined the English to treat the Avignon papacy as a poodle of their enemy. Loyalty to the Christian faith was one thing, to the Roman/Avignon church quite another. The nature of worship also changed. Over the fourteenth century the focus of church services moved west from the chancel and its Mass chanted in Latin behind a rood screen. Worshippers were welcomed to airy naves lit by Perpendicular windows, where the Bible message was interpreted from pulpits in English by itinerant preachers.

Chief among these was an Oxford theologian of Yorkshire descent, John Wycliffe (1320–84), who launched himself on the church in the 1370s. He attacked ecclesiastical self-indulgence and corruption. He criticized icons, monasticism, transubstantiation and the veneration of saints. His writings, in Latin and English, sought an end to church hierarchy and its replacement by 'poor priests'. As Wycliffe and others began to translate the New Testament into English, his preachers, known as Lollards, were commanded 'to pick out such sharp sentences of holy scriptures . . . to maintain their sect and lore against the ordinance of holy Church'.

Much has been made of Wycliffe as a forefather of the Reformation. But he was always a Catholic and regarded himself as a critic rather than an apostate. At the peak of his popularity, he was said to enjoy the support of half the population of England, though his followers were almost all in the south and east. More crucially, he had sympathizers at Edward's court, including no less a figure than the king's son, John of Gaunt.

Any hope that Brétigny might have ended the French war was shattered by the ageing Edward III's refusal to accept its settlement. In the 1370s he sent Gaunt and the Black Prince back to ravage Gascony and Aquitaine, but now the French, under the leadership of Charles V, avoided battles. They let the English soldiers wander the wastes of central France, increasingly hungry and crippled by disease. When in 1376 the dying Edward summoned Parliament to ask for more money, it called a halt.

Edward's successor, Richard II (1377–99), had little interest in war with France. Instead in 1381 he had to confront an unprecedented crisis, a peasants' revolt against the imposition of a poll tax, levied by the king to circumvent Parliament's fiscal parsimony. The revolt was soon suppressed, but similar revolts in France arose from the same cause, that of a workforce shrunk by the Black Death, its survivors liberated by the laws of supply and demand to revalue their labour. The plague changed fundamentally Europe's structure of power. It led to a rapid decline in serfdom, at least in the west – it often became more severe in the east to prevent labour migration.

The western schism

In France peace could not come soon enough. In 1376, Pope Gregory XI in Avignon decided that his place was in Rome, and declared he would take the papacy back to its proper home. But he died soon afterwards and his successor, Urban VI, was immediately disputed. The clergy still comfortable in Avignon rejected Urban for being a

Neapolitan and in 1378 acknowledged a French claimant, Clement VII, still in Avignon. Thus there were now two popes. A Christendom that had already split, west from east, was further divided by what became known as the 'western schism'. This one lasted from 1378 to 1417.

The criticisms of the church voiced by Wycliffe in England began to echo across northern Europe. They were heard particularly in Bohemia, now the largest component of the Holy Roman Empire. Its king, Charles IV (1346–78), became emperor and extended Bohemia's overlordship from the Baltic to the Danube. He attracted to Prague German merchants and scholars, and won favour across Germany by his Golden Bull of 1356, rendering Frederick II's light imperial touch even lighter. He formally stated that 'Roman emperors' should not interfere with 'the liberties, jurisdictions, rights, honours or dominions of the ecclesiastical and secular prince electors'. He also proposed that these electors should be just seven in number, four princes and three bishops. They alone would choose the German king, and thus the Holy Roman Emperor.

In 1402 Wycliffe's teachings against the church were brought from Oxford to Charles's new university of Prague, where they were translated and read from the pulpit by a theologian, Jan Hus (1372–1415). 'O Wycliffe, Wycliffe,' he declared, 'you will trouble the hearts of many.' It was an understatement. The message of a personal faith in the biblical Christ, with the church as an elitist and corrupt institution, was a spark that lit a fire of rebellion. The particular bone of contention was indulgences.

Throughout Christendom, the church was regarded as custodian of the hereafter. Whatever one's sins in this life, salvation in the next was a matter on which believers tended to defer to the church. Portrayals of heaven, hell, saints, angels and demons were on all sides, with the church going beyond traditional concepts of sin, penance and atonement to claim that it alone could rescue the faithful, for a fee. To Hus this concept of payment for the 'relief of souls' was quack religion. He said, 'One pays for confession, for Mass, for the sacrament, for indulgences, for churching a woman, for a blessing, for burials, for funeral services and prayers. The very last penny which an old woman has hidden in her bundle . . . will not be saved. The villainous priest will grab it.'

Hus's revisionism was not universally popular. His university suffered a mass defection of German scholars to Leipzig. But the church's leadership of Christendom was now under systematic attack. For centuries it had been held together by a continent-wide fraternity of priests, scholars, monks and devotees. Reformers could found a new monastic order, with the pope's blessing. The church was rich without equal, and claimed possession of the minds of men and women across the Christian world. Now that world was again shrinking. In 1389 Ottoman Turks defeated Slavic Serbs at the Battle of Kosovo and penetrated far to the west of Constantinople, deep into Balkan Europe. At home, schism, faction and corruption were costing the church loyalty and consent. Hus might prove more than a passing sore.

8

The Death of Byzantium
1400–1500

Sigismund: the end of the Avignon papacy

The church was aware of its critics. In 1409 a grand council of bishops assembled at Pisa. The purpose was to resolve the western schism, now thirty-one years old, and confront the challenge of Hussitism. The council was drastic. On the schism, it deposed both Roman and Avignon popes as 'heretics and schismatics', and appointed a third of its own, Alexander V. Since the other two refused to step down, the schism was resolved by having not two popes but three. When Alexander promptly died, the council elected John XXIII (1410–15), a cardinal and alleged local bandit said to have 'seduced two hundred matrons, widows and virgins' along with 'an alarming number of nuns'. At his first synod, John was distracted by a demented owl that kept flying into his face, understandably seen as a bad omen.

At this crucial moment there arrived onstage an able monarch, Sigismund, newly enthroned king of Germany, soon to be king of Bohemia and later Holy Roman Emperor. He committed all and sundry to ending the Avignon schism and appeasing the Hussites, possibly by persuading the church to accept reform. In 1414 he proposed a new council at Constance in Switzerland, to be attended by 700 divines from across Europe. Hus was personally invited, on a safe-conduct pledge from Sigismund himself. It was a moment when, under new leadership, the Roman church seemed to be girding itself to accept what many knew it needed, the setting of its decrepit house in order.

As soon as the council opened in 1415, disaster struck. Sigismund was away and the council began its proceedings by ceremonially burning Hus at the stake as a heretic. This breach of safe passage ignited fierce anti-papal feeling across Bohemia, forcing thousands of German Catholics to flee Prague. A Hussite rising led to fifteen years of Hussite Wars (1419–34), including five crusades, with a Catholic coalition fighting Bohemian forces under an able general, Jan Žižka. They culminated in a compromise that Bohemia would submit to Rome but be allowed its Hussite faith. Prague was rightly to proclaim itself the cradle of the Protestant Reformation.

Back at Constance, deliberation descended into farce. Pope John was hounded from the council and sought sanctuary, disguised as a stable boy with gold ducats sewn into his coat, with the Duke of Burgundy. The council tried him in his absence. Gibbon delightedly noted, 'The most scandalous charges were suppressed . . . the Vicar of Christ was only accused of piracy, murder, rape, sodomy and incest.' He was later classified as an anti-pope and was lucky to die in his own bed, his tomb to be sculpted by Donatello.

In 1417 Sigismund's council concluded its three years of lakeside sojourn by achieving its chief purpose. It deposed two more popes, and crowned as a third a cardinal from Rome's powerful Colonna family, Martin V. His orders were to return to Rome, re-establish the papacy and report back. The Avignon schism ended.

Constance had made a significant reform. Martin was now the council's servant, an innovation referred to as 'conciliarism'. Apart from being a nod towards institutional democracy, this tore up the thesis, sustained from Gregory the Great to Innocent III, that the pope had an exclusive line to God. That conduit was now through the church's council. Its authority came 'immediately from Christ; everyone of every rank and condition, including the Pope himself, is bound to obey [the council] in matters concerning the faith, the abolition of schism and the reformation of the Church of God'. It was the papacy itself that first adopted the word reformation.

Agincourt: England's victory, England's defeat

No sooner had the Roman church apparently found order than France reverted to anarchy. Its throne was occupied by Charles VI the Mad (1380–1422), but his regency was contested by two wings of the Valois dynasty, Louis of Orléans and John of Burgundy. Orléans was the senior line, but the dukedom of Burgundy, stretching from the Low Countries to the Rhône, was among the richest provinces in Europe. The merchants of Bruges and Antwerp now outstripped those of northern Italy in wealth. In 1412 the Duc de Berry commissioned a magnificent work of late-gothic art, the *Très Riches Heures*, and by the 1420s, Jan van Eyck and Rogier van der Weyden were producing paintings of intense naturalness and power.

What might have been a simple war of French succession was complicated by the decision of a new English king, Henry V (1413–22), to resume Edward III's claim to the French throne. It was a calculated and cynical gesture to aid his legitimacy, given his father Henry IV's usurpation and probable murder of Richard II. Prior to his departure for France, Henry in 1415 built himself a magnificent chapel in Westminster Abbey, asserting his pre-eminence by elbowing aside the tombs of his Plantagenet predecessors. Once across the Channel he allied himself to the Burgundians and confronted the French king and the Orléanists on the battlefield of Agincourt. The French cavalry again ignored the lesson of previous defeats. Henry's archers repeated the massacres of Crécy and Poitiers. Some 30,000 French were overwhelmed by just 12,000 English. Agincourt was greeted with euphoria in England – and later dramatized by Shakespeare in *Henry V*.

It took another five years for Henry finally to conquer French forces in northern France. At the Treaty of Troyes in 1420, Charles declared Henry V his successor as king of France, and in December Henry became the first English king to enter Paris. There he married Charles the Mad's daughter Catherine. The couple gave birth to a son, the future Henry VI of England, who inherited his maternal grandfather's mental weakness. Henry's own succession was not put to the test as he died of dysentery two years later. Charles died at the same time, leaving the baby Henry to inherit both thrones. His claim to that of France was immediately contested by the dauphin, Charles.

War drearily resumed, dragging on until, in 1429, an incident occurred in the French camp, during the English siege of Orléans. A seventeen-year-old peasant girl named Joan of Arc (d'Arc was her father's surname) was smuggled into the dauphin's presence, possibly by scheming courtiers. With a charismatic personality, she claimed to have heard voices commanding her to lead the French in triumph to Reims. Believing her to be a saint and dressing her in armour, a reinspired French army broke the English siege and accepted Joan's advice to march on Reims. Here Charles VII was crowned as anointed king of France (1422–61). Joan was later captured by the Burgundians, and handed over to the English, who tried and burned her as an agent of the devil. She was later made a saint.

In 1435 Burgundy switched sides and joined Charles's cause, a defection that was enough to end England's hope of ruling France. Two decades later, in 1453, at the Battle of Castillon near Bordeaux, France used gunpowder to fire cannonballs at the English archers and overwhelm them. England was finally driven out of France, left with sovereignty only over the port of Calais. A century of conflict had dribbled away in failure. English history tends to forget Castillon, remembering only Agincourt.

An end to the Great Schism

The task facing the new pope, Martin, on returning to Rome in 1420 was near impossible. The city had fallen into dereliction. Its population was a mere 25,000 and wolves roamed the streets. The contrast was stark with the booming mercantile cities of northern Italy, their palaces now filling with the artists of the early Renaissance. Florence was embarking on its golden age, under successive members of the Medici family. Likewise the Sforzas of Milan and the doges of Venice were enthusiastic patrons. On arriving in Rome, Martin did his best to compete. He summoned Pisanello, Gentile da Fabriano and Masaccio to adorn new palaces and churches.

In 1431 a new council assembled in Basel to discuss the authority of the papacy, but Martin was now dead and few attended. His successor, Eugenius IV (1431–47), disregarded the council altogether, summoning a new one for 1438 in Ferrara, later moved to Florence. This was to discuss a possible end to the Great Schism with Constantinople and other matters of reform. Since some delegates refused to move from Basel, there were now two councils, and once again two popes.

All this was transformed by the arrival in Ferrara of the leaders from Byzantium – including the eastern emperor and the Patriarch of Constantinople – pleading for an end to schism and, more urgently, for help against the Ottoman Turks. The Byzantines brought some 700 retainers, many of whom clearly had no intention of returning home. The gout-ridden emperor had to be carried in a chair, his attendants mesmerizing the gathering by their long robes and great beards. Negotiations moved slowly. There were initial arguments over primacy, and whether proceedings should be in Latin or Greek. The delegates then plunged into the *filioque* dispute that had cursed the initial schism in 1054, whether Christ was on the same plane as God or somehow subordinate. At this point the Patriarch of Constantinople collapsed and died.

Eventually a Decree of Union was agreed, almost entirely on Rome's terms, and Eugenius was able to return to Rome in 1443 as triumphant head of an ostensibly united Christendom. For good measure, the rump Basel council was excommunicated. When the Byzantine delegates returned to Constantinople, they were denounced as traitors, but the city had little time for events in distant Italy. With Bulgars and Ottomans at its gates, all it craved was western ships on the horizon. In 1443 a Hungarian and Balkan army was indeed formed to confront the Turks, led by a Hungarian general, John Hunyadi, largely at his own expense. But though Hunyadi advanced successfully down the Danube, the unity of his army soon disintegrated, and he was defeated by the Ottomans at the Battle of Varna. Rome felt it had honoured its pledge.

Within four years Eugenius was dead, to be succeeded by Nicholas V (1447–55). He was intellectually sophisticated and sought in his short reign to restore Rome's dignity and that of the papacy, earning him the title of first Renaissance prelate. The walls of the city were rebuilt, as was its principal aqueduct delivering water into what is now the Trevi fountain. Nicholas planned the rebuilding of St Peter's in the classical style by Leon Battista Alberti. He welcomed scholars from the east, and was said to be acquainted 'with all philosophers, historians, poets, cosmographers and theologians'. The Vatican amassed the greatest classical library since Alexandria, 'for the common convenience of the learned, a library of all books both in Latin and in Greek'.

The year 1450 was ordered to be a jubilee, with promises of indulgences that drew 100,000 pilgrims to Rome. Two years later the Habsburg king of Germany, Frederick III, ruler by marriage of Austria, Hungary and Burgundy, revived the lapsed tradition of coronation in Rome as Holy Roman Emperor. He travelled from

Austria in state with 2,000 attendants. He also married Eleanor, daughter of the king of Portugal, who became his empress. A great beauty, she had turned down an offer of marriage to the dauphin of France as that would make her only a queen and she wanted to be an empress. For a brief period, the Holy Roman Empire was looking at once holy, Roman and imperial. The Habsburgs were to honour that loyalty to Rome for three and a half centuries.

The fall of Constantinople

Festivity was short-lived. As Rome celebrated the reunion of Christianity, Constantinople's demise was at hand. In 1453 the twenty-one-year-old Ottoman Sultan Mehmed II (1451–81) laid siege to the city, hauling his ships overland to the Bosphorus and circumventing part of the Byzantine defences. Siege engines were wheeled into place and an assault commenced on the once invincible walls. Mehmed deployed the one weapon to which they were now vulnerable, cannons, including a twenty-six-foot monster that could fire a shot a mile. Ambassadors pleaded with the emperor Constantine XI to surrender the city, as there was no sight of a Roman rescue and Mehmed had promised no plunder and safe conduct. Inexplicably, Constantine refused. Mehmed's army duly entered the city at midnight on 29 May, and subjected it to three days of rape and pillage. Mehmed set up his throne under the great dome of Hagia Sophia, which remains today as a museum.

An offshoot of the Roman empire that had outlived it for a thousand years met an abrupt end. The Roman and Hellenistic tradition of which it had been custodian would henceforth live in exile, in the cities of north Africa or reborn in Renaissance Rome. Athens fell to Mehmed in 1458 and the rest of Greece in 1460. The Aegean had long ceased to be at Europe's heart, but it was now an Ottoman lake.

Byzantium's most passionate champion, Steven Runciman, ended his obituary, 'A civilisation was wiped out irrevocably. It had left a glorious legacy in learning and in art; it had raised whole countries from barbarism and had given refinement to others . . . The quick brilliance, the interest and the aestheticism of the Greek, the proud stability and the administrative competence of the Roman, the transcendental intensity of the Christian from the East, welded together in a fluid sensitive mass, were put now to sleep.'

Byzantium's curse had once been its strength, its location at Europe's extremity. It was no longer able to exploit its position as commercial and cultural entrepôt between west and east. Italian merchants had come to dominate this trade, notably since the fourth crusade. Even its modern eulogist, Bettany Hughes, admits that Constantine's great city was always 'both ours and others' . . . [it] is not where East meets West, but where East and West look hard and longingly at one another'. News of the collapse of its old rival traumatized Rome. Christendom had suffered a setback at the very moment of its reconciliation. A familiar rival had vanished, a part of Rome's ancestral soul had been destroyed.

Not everyone cried. As Christian refugees fled Constantinople with their libraries and other treasures, the boats that brought them westwards returned east with Genoese and Venetian merchants, eager to talk trade with the triumphant Mehmed. A Genoese deal with Mehmed was dated just two days after the sack. The cities of northern Italy now entered a period of great splendour. Mantua saw the flowering of Mantegna's genius (1431–1506), while Venice's glories were celebrated by Giovanni Bellini (1430–1516) and Vittore Carpaccio (1465–1520), the latter with a vividness and humour that evoke the colourful company of his times, as the Brueghel family were later to do in the Netherlands.

Pope Nicholas tried to rouse enthusiasm for a new crusade against Mehmed but found no takers. The fall of Byzantium confirmed

Rome's status as spiritual capital of Christendom. Under Eugenius and Nicholas, the papacy had reasserted its primacy over the conciliarists of Constance and Basel. Church reform had flowered but was allowed to lapse. Sixtus IV (1471–84) was a pope in a new league. He outstripped his predecessors in nepotism – appointing teenage 'nephews' as cardinals – and was their equal in extravagance. The High Renaissance arrived in Rome in earnest. Sixtus replaced medieval lanes with avenues. He trebled the size of the Vatican library. The Sistine Chapel, named after him, was decorated by Botticelli, Ghirlandaio, Perugino and other artists lent by the Medici of Florence. The discovery in c.1480 of the remains of Nero's Domus Aurea was a sensation to artists, who were lowered into its long-hidden chambers to marvel at the classical murals.

Russia and a Third Rome

The fall of Byzantium opened the plains of south-eastern Europe to Ottoman expansion and created a new balance of power in the region. The kingdom of Poland-Lithuania had been united in 1386, with the conversion to Catholicism of Europe's last pagan realm, Lithuania. But it was not until the epic Battle of Tannenberg (or Grunwald) in 1410 that the aggressive stance of the Prussian Teutonic knights was finally halted. Baltic trade now expanded rapidly, and Poland-Lithuania briefly became the largest state by area in Europe, reaching from the Baltic to the Black Sea. Beyond it, as if beyond the European pale, ancient Russia still struggled as an Orthodox land, sandwiched between Catholic Poland-Lithuania to the west, the Tartars to the east and the Ottomans to the south.

With the reign of Ivan the Great (1462–1505), Moscow was finally able to gather up what Russian historians called the 'assembly of the Russian lands'. Novgorod was brought under Moscow's heel by

Ivan in 1478. He then revived Vladimir's dream of becoming master of eastern Christendom, and of Moscow becoming 'the new Rome', a post left vacant by the fall of Constantinople. In 1472 Ivan married Zoe Palaiologina, niece of the last Byzantine emperor, who encouraged him to make his city like old Constantinople in every respect. He invited foreign architects to rebuild the Kremlin and erect churches across his land. He adopted the imperial two-headed eagle as his emblem. Even his title of tsar was a corruption of Caesar.

In 1476 Ivan stopped paying tribute to the Tartar khans. Four years later he defied a retaliatory attack in the 'great stand on the Ugra River', when a Tartar army gazed at Ivan's assembled forces and decided to turn away. It did not come back. Of Christendom's eastern bastions, Constantinople had fallen but Moscow survived. Trade continued to flow along the great Russian rivers, north to the Hanseatic ports of the Baltic and south to the Black Sea. But Russia did not flirt with the Renaissance, let alone with the forces of religious reform surging through the German-speaking lands. The khans of Tartary had left a mark on Russia. It became a standard dictum of Russian leadership that an empire so extensive and so disparate needed rule by a single unchallenged leader and a strong central authority. It was a dictum later tsars would test to destruction.

9

Renaissance and Reformation
1450–1525

The new learning

The Renaissance and the Reformation were processes as well as periods. The one was essentially aesthetic and intellectual, its impact initially confined to centres of wealth and learning. In the short term it had little impact on the narrative of European power. The other was theological and ecclesiastical, and its impact soon became political. Together they stand like two portals marking the exit from the Middle Ages and from a millennium in which the way Europeans viewed the world had been conditioned primarily by their faith, under the tutelage of the church.

As we have seen, the Italian Renaissance was stimulated by Petrarch's 'walk back into the pure radiance of the past'. Poets, painters and sculptors had since the fourteenth century found inspiration in the writings and artefacts of Greece and Rome. Scholars reworked the humanism of the classics, reviving the concept of a morality that emerged from the thoughts and actions of individuals, rather than from the supernatural. To this was added an interest, borrowed from Aristotle and taken up by Augustine, in the free will of the individual. In northern Europe, the Dutch scholar Erasmus (1469–1536) subjected the words of the Bible to textual analysis, the better to comprehend his faith. England's Sir Thomas More (1478–1535) satirized the states of modern Europe and described a proto-communist land of Utopia, based in part on Plato.

This opening of the mind stimulated a scientific revolution, initially a rediscovery of the mathematics, astronomy and geography of the ancients, Aristotle, Ptolemy and Pythagoras. The medieval *mappa mundi* had portrayed the Earth as flat and surrounded by metaphorical dragons. Although most scholars now accepted its spherical form, they still placed the planet at the centre of the universe while map-makers placed Jerusalem at the centre of the known world. In 1543 a Pole, Nicolaus Copernicus (1473–1543), announced that the Earth went round the sun, to the dismay and disbelief of the church. Though the church was not hostile to these movements, it saw itself losing its licence over knowledge. In 1455 a revolution in communication had come. A German, Johannes Gutenberg (*c.*1400–1468) in Mainz, produced a Bible using lines of moveable metal type held in a frame and printed from it. Writers could now more easily disseminate their views, not least on matters of faith, across borders and into courts, colleges and churches, by-passing costly manuscripts.

In the practical world of navigation, the lateen sail enabled ocean-going ships to voyage into the wind. This was to the age of discovery what the longship had been to the Vikings. It offered a new freedom of the high seas, and a broadening of the concept of an outside world. Europe's awareness of the Orient had been fragmentary, reliant on the tales of the Venetian Marco Polo (1254–1324), and the accounts of returning traders and sailors. Europeans became increasingly conscious that other civilizations to the east might have more to contribute to humanity than exotic silks and spices. Their cultures merited study. The elaborate design of the fourteenth-century porch of St Mary Redcliffe in Bristol is traceable to Isfahan in Persia.

While the impact of the Renaissance was gradual, the impact of the Reformation was immediate. As the teachings of Wycliffe and Hus gained currency, their supporters looked beyond theologians to ask how much they could know for sure about the world about them. A new discipline of reasoning took hold in centres of learning in England, France, the Low Countries and Germany. As individuals argued, so they formed into groups, factions and parties, creating divisions that would be exploited as yet another round in Europe's timeless dynastic struggles began in earnest.

Isabella, Ferdinand and Columbus

In the 1420s, Portugal's Prince Henry 'the Navigator' began to dispatch ships down the African coastline, eager to find a trade route to India that avoided the risks and costs of crossing Arabia. Henry himself never travelled, living as a virtual hermit in Sagres, on his country's southern tip. There he studied his maps and awaited the return of his captains, each year bringing back tales of new lands. By the 1450s Henry was sending fleets to the Azores, Madeira, the Canaries, Guinea and Senegal. In 1456 the Cape Verde Peninsula, market for buying quantities of gold, was reached. Suddenly Europe's western boundary of the Atlantic seemed permeable. To Daniel Boorstin, Henry's enterprise was the true Renaissance, 'an adventure of the mind, a thrust of someone's imagination ... The pioneer explorer was one lonely man, thinking.'

In Spain, only Granada was still in Muslim hands. Cordoba had been conquered by Castile in 1236, but Granada survived as a trading centre and haven for refugees from religious intolerance. In 1469, Castile was joined to its neighbour Aragon through the marriage of Isabella of Castile (lived 1451–1504) to Ferdinand (lived 1452–1516), heir to the throne of Aragon. Both were still in their teens, but soon became rulers of their respective countries, and from 1479 joint rulers of both. They together forged a new state and founded a dynasty that was to bring the Holy Roman Empire to its apotheosis.

Ferdinand was an assiduous soldier and administrator, Isabella was forceful and fanatically pious. She determined to ban all other faiths and sects from Spain. In 1478 her Dominican confessor, Torquemada, persuaded her that the conversion of Jews in formerly Moorish Andalusia was insufficiently rigorous, and she in turn persuaded Pope Sixtus to initiate an 'inquiry' into these conversions. This became the Spanish Inquisition, led by Torquemada from 1483 to 1498. John Julius Norwich reflects on the irony that 'the originator of one of the most beautiful buildings in the world [the Sistine Chapel] should also have been the inspiration for one of its most odious institutions'.

Spain now saw a campaign of conversion, expulsion or execution, first of Jews then of Muslims. Evidence would be collected of suspect practices by supposed converts, with tortures and burnings at the stake. This was despite pressure from the pope for tolerance, reflected in allowing appeals to Rome against the Inquisition. These were ignored by Torquemada. Then in 1492 came the annus mirabilis of the so-called dual monarchy. After a ten-year campaign, Ferdinand captured Granada and the last emir handed over the keys to the Alhambra palace.

Ferdinand offered the Moors freedom of movement and religion, and instantly reneged on his promise. The Alhambra Decree of 1492 demanded the conversion or expulsion of all non-Catholics from Granada, as from the rest of Spain. Some 40,000 Jews converted and more than 100,000 fled into exile, most of them initially to Portugal. The great library of Granada, some 5,000 Islamic books, went up in flames. It is believed that 2,000 Jews died at the Inquisition's hands.

A newly emboldened Spain now found itself in open rivalry with Portugal. In 1488 a Portuguese sea captain, Bartolomeu Dias, had rounded the Cape of Good Hope and realized the prospect of a new sea route to the Orient. Portuguese trading posts sprang up along this coast. Within a decade another Portuguese, Vasco da Gama, had reached India, and the Arab monopoly on Europe's commerce with the Orient was broken.

Spain decided to compete. In 1492 Isabella and Ferdinand celebrated the fall of Granada by supporting the project of a Genovese admiral, Christopher Columbus, to find an alternative route to the Orient to Portugal's by sailing west across the Atlantic. It was a measure of how little European science had advanced in a millennium that Columbus relied on the second-century Ptolemy's calculation of the Earth's circumference (at three-quarters of its actual length). He assumed that he would reach China in three months. He even took with him a Chinese interpreter. If Columbus's crew had known how far China really was, they would never have set sail.

Columbus's return from the Caribbean stirred a frenzy of exploration, part commercial, part nationalist, part missionary. As early as 1494 the monarchs of Portugal and Spain averted conflict between themselves by agreeing the Treaty of Tordesillas, mediated by the pope. This divided the 'New World' either side of a line of longitude 1,100 miles west of Cape Verde, with the lands to its west going to Spain and to its east, that is Africa, to Portugal. The line was later found to slice into the shore of South America, which became Portuguese Brazil and speaks Portuguese to this day.

The Medici, Savonarola and the Borgia papacy

The year 1492 also saw the death of the Florentine banker and Renaissance grandee Lorenzo de' Medici 'the Magnificent'. He had been moneylender to all Europe and even to the Ottoman sultans. He was a bastion of its emerging capitalist economy and patron of the masters of the High Renaissance, Sandro Botticelli (1445–1510), Domenico Ghirlandaio (1449–94), Michelangelo (1475–1564) and Leonardo da Vinci (1452–1519). Of these, Leonardo was the quintessential product of the Renaissance, self-educated and self-made. He was, above all, insatiably curious about the workings of nature and humanity. He was the perfect foil for Lorenzo, not just a grandee but an artist, poet, bibliophile and civic leader. The bulk of Lorenzo's fortune went on art and charity, since 'I consider that it gave great honour to our State . . . to have money well-expended'. One ancient custom the Medici were unable to avoid was the bequest of an incompetent heir.

Two years after Lorenzo's death, the Medici family was expelled from Florence in an uprising led by a friar, Girolamo Savonarola. He preached hellfire and the damnation of sinners, outdoing Hus in accusing the papal church of every kind of corruption. From 1494 to 1498 he ruled Florence as a 'popular republic'. The papacy was 'a prostitute sitting on the throne of Solomon'. Savonarola instituted a 'bonfire of the vanities', committing hundreds of Renaissance treasures to the flames. The Virgin, he said, 'seems dressed as a whore'. After four years, the same mob that had welcomed Savonarola overthrew him, and he was burned alive as a heretic.

The papacy was now in the hands of a family that made the Medici look like saints, the Borgias. The second Borgia pope, Alexander VI, arrived in office in 1492 as father of eight children (by three women), five of whom he made cardinals. He celebrated with a bullfight in front of St Peter's. One of his sons, Cesare, became a legend of dissolution and hooliganism. Disfigured by the syphilis brought back to Europe by sailors from America – a return for the diseases they had taken there – Cesare was beyond any law. His sister, Lucretia, was married three times, two husbands being killed by her jealous brother. The Venetian ambassador wrote that 'every night four or five men are discovered assassinated, bishops, prelates and others. All Rome trembles for fear of being murdered.' Cesare lost power only when Alexander died in 1503, going into exile in Spain and dying there four years later, aged just thirty-one.

To northern Europe, tales of the Borgia papacy fused with those of the Spanish Inquisition to indicate a church with little claim to respect. The reformism of the Council of Constance had vanished.

The church's maltreatment of fellow humans in the name of Christ was reminiscent of the sadism of ancient Rome, or at least reflected that of secular authorities at the time. Nor could Protestants claim any special sanctity, retaliating by torturing and burning Catholics, from Elizabethan England to seventeenth-century Switzerland. Amid such instability, the age bred its own political philosopher, Niccolò Machiavelli (1469–1527), a perceptive student of the acquisition of power in times of turbulence. Though portrayed as a political cynic, he was in truth the reverse, an observant realist who saw that only through security could a moral prince gain influence over the conduct of affairs.

The rise of the dynasts: Spain and Austria

In Spain, the ageing Isabella and Ferdinand had other concerns, primarily those of succession. Never in western Europe's history was that question so critical. The continent was cohering into three centres of political power: Spain with its outreach across the Atlantic, France fearing encirclement within its historical borders, and the unstable Holy Roman Empire, embracing Germany and the ever-reluctant Italy. After the death of Isabella's only son, her surviving daughters would marry variously: two to the king of Portugal and one, Catherine, to a prince and then a king of England. Another, Joan the Mad, was to marry Philip the Handsome, Habsburg son of the Holy Roman Emperor Maximilian I (1493–1519). These marriages would furnish the architecture of European power into the eighteenth century.

Catherine of Aragon (1485–1536) was beautiful and intelligent. The English king Henry VII was the Tudor Lancastrian victor over the Yorkist Richard III in England's dynastic Wars of the Roses. Sensitive to the accusation of usurpation and desperate for status,

Henry in 1488 engaged his son Arthur to the three-year-old Catherine, who was finally dispatched to England in 1501 at the age of sixteen. They married, but Arthur died soon afterwards, the match allegedly unconsummated. Catherine remained in England and went on to marry Arthur's younger brother Henry, who had in 1509 taken the throne as Henry VIII. The marriage was initially happy and Catherine was a popular and lively consort, friend of Erasmus and More. Her crucial failing was not to bear Henry a son.

Her sister Joan's fate was no less vexed. Her father-in-law, Maximilian, was king of Austria and Germany and Holy Roman Emperor from 1493. He was notional ruler of much of Italy and, by marrying Mary of Burgundy, ruler also of Burgundy and Flanders. To this estate he added his talents at matrimonial diplomacy. One daughter was betrothed, at the age of three, to the dauphin of France. Others were married to rulers of Bohemia and Hungary. The marriage of his Italian niece to Sigismund I of Poland expedited a Polish renaissance. No heiress in Europe was said to be safe from a Habsburg ring. 'Let others wage war,' it was said of Maximilian, 'but thou, O happy Austria, marry; for those kingdoms which Mars gives to others, Venus gives to thee.'

The strategy was not always successful. France bitterly contested Maximilian's marital claim to Burgundy. In 1499 the Swabian Wars also lost the empire its hold on the Alpine cantons of Switzerland. Despite later marrying a Sforza of Milan, Maximilian was no more successful than his predecessors in securing his sovereignty in Italy. None the less, as Joan's Spanish siblings died, her own inheritance grew until it embraced all of Spain and its overseas empire.

Then came catastrophe. When Joan's mother, Isabella, died in 1504, her father, Ferdinand, promptly had his daughter declared insane. Rumour held that she was not insane, but was showing un-Catholic allegiances. She was incarcerated for the rest of her life in Valladolid. Then in 1506 Philip, her husband, also died, leaving her with two sons and four daughters. Her eldest son, Charles, would thus inherit both her Spanish empire and the Habsburg empire from Maximilian, who was still alive.

On Ferdinand's death in 1516, the sixteen-year-old Charles assumed the Spanish throne. Since he spoke only French and Flemish, he was told he had to learn Spanish to rule in Madrid. As heir through his dead father to his grandfather, Maximilian, he would assume the crowns of Germany and Austria, but one other title was at issue, that of Holy Roman Emperor. This depended on the decision of the seven electors. The elderly Maximilian now had to ensure their votes. This in turn meant fending off a challenge from France's new king, Francis I, who was spending enormous sums on bribing the electors. Maximilian would have to out-bribe him.

Imperial politics became fiendish. The electors included a German aristocrat, Albrecht of Brandenburg, who in 1518 was sufficiently eager for Maximilian's bribe to have acquired his electorship through buying a cardinal's hat from Pope Leo X. Leo's church was close to bankruptcy through the expense of rebuilding St Peter's and of Raphael's decoration of the Vatican rooms. Leo agreed with Albrecht to share Maximilian's bribe. Jacob Fugger, banker of Augsburg and the Medicis' successor as one of the richest men of all time, was on hand to lend money as required. The security for any loans embraced contracts for selling papal indulgences in Germany.

Maximilian was successful, and he died in 1519 with Charles's inheritance safe. At the age of nineteen, the young man took the imperial throne as Charles V (1519–56). His combined empire was unprecedented, stretching in various forms from the Polish border across central and western Europe (other than France) to Spain, and across to the New World. To the north it was bounded by the Baltic Sea, to the south by the Mediterranean. All this passed under the absolute power of a feeble and unprepossessing youth.

Martin Luther and the Diet of Worms

The marketing of indulgences to repay the Fugger loans became fanatical. Leo stipulated that they could be bought not only by sinners but as gifts for sinners. They could be bought on behalf of dead relatives, claimed to be at that very moment suffering agonies in purgatory for want of such purchase. Indulgence 'futures' could even be bought as insurance, by the living for sins not yet committed. Scenes of the fate awaiting sinners in the afterlife were horrifically portrayed by the Dutch painter Hieronymus Bosch. The remission of sins became salesmanship on an industrial scale.

This was all too much for one plain-speaking German friar and son of a mine-owner, Martin Luther. He visited Rome and was shocked by what he saw. He returned to Germany to contemplate, as many others had done, the present state of the institutional church and its relationship to his faith. In particular, he waged war on indulgences, inveighing against money being extorted from worshippers as if 'the soul flies out of purgatory the moment money tinkles in the box'. In 1517 Luther drew up ninety-five theses 'for discussion' – whether he pinned them to a Wittenberg church door is now doubted.

Luther appealed to the spirit of Wycliffe and Hus, asserting that faith was a personal relationship between man and God. It did not require the intercession of Catholic priests or obscurantist dogmas, let alone the terrorizing of the poor into parting with their savings. Salvation was not a purchasable reward, but God's gift of love. Luther was a deeply thoughtful man, but also brash and unsubtle, certainly no tolerant compromiser. He declared the papacy 'to be more corrupt than Babylon and Sodom'. He hated Jews, and later found himself in conflict with other reformers, notably his early hero, Erasmus. While Erasmus remained committed to reforming the church from within, Luther would have none of it. Erasmus said of Luther, 'I laid an egg. Luther hatched a bird of quite different species.' Luther ended by calling Erasmus a 'viper, liar, the very mouth and organ of Satan'.

Many German rulers could see political advantage in Luther's stance. The church's landed wealth was detested by aristocrats, merchants and populace alike, and was vulnerable to seizure. The church hit back. In 1521 a diet, or legislative assembly, was assembled at Worms, chaired by Charles V and with Luther present. Charles declared that 'a single monk, led astray by private judgment, has set himself against the faith held by all Christians for a thousand years and more. He impudently concludes that all Christians up till now have erred.' Charles said he would stake his body and soul on opposing him.

Luther replied with his famous declaration of dissent: *Hier stehe ich. Ich kann nicht anders*, Here I stand, I can do no other. Despite an imperial guarantee of safe conduct, he recalled Hus's fate in 1415 and decided it was best to flee, to find sanctuary in The Wartburg with the Elector of Saxony. With the assistance of the artists Lucas Cranach and Albrecht Dürer, he proceeded to publish illustrated essays defiant of the church. The Reformation spawned a publishing empire.

A quieter theologian than Luther might have been able to unite the German-speaking world against Rome, or at least direct it towards tolerance and reform. Luther was a political conservative. When in 1525 the German peasantry rose against their landlords, he supported their suppression, declaring that everyone 'stab, smite and slay . . . the thievish, murderous hordes of peasants'. He campaigned against other Reformers, the Anabaptists, Ulrich Zwingli's Protestants of Zurich and Calvin's dissenters of Geneva. He derided Copernicus's thesis that the Earth went round the sun as the work of 'an upstart astrologer . . . this fool'.

Germany now split roughly north and south, for and against Luther's Reformation. First to join his cause in 1525 were the Teutonic knights of Prussia. The northern Netherlands, north Germany and Prussia did so too. Charles's Habsburg lands, together with Austria, Hungary and Flanders, remained loyal to Rome. The Holy Roman Empire was thus divided, and the devotion of the Habsburgs to Catholicism was to keep it so for more than three centuries.

Charles V proved a more substantial figure than had at first seemed likely. He was uncharismatic and cautious, with a keen conscience and a shrewd head. But his empire encircled and overshadowed Europe's most populous country, France, ruled at the time by a flamboyant Francis I (1515–47), defeated by Charles for the Holy Roman emperorship. At the same time, the throne of England was occupied by the young Henry VIII (1509–47), whose wife Catherine was Charles's aunt. These three princes, Charles, Francis and Henry, were to bring down the curtain on medieval Europe. They did so with Luther's words pounding in the background from Gutenberg's presses.

10

Wars of the Princes
1525–1560

Henry VIII of England

The rulers of medieval Europe acquired legitimacy through force of arms. A weakling inheritor would be challenged by a stronger one or by no inheritor at all. For their subjects what mattered was one thing, security, and they would support any ruler who could deliver it. One country whose security was aided by geography was England. As Shakespeare's John of Gaunt remarked, England was 'set in a silver sea / Which serves it in the office of a wall / Or as a moat defensive to a house'. Invading armies did not undermine England's domestic order or its economy. Its civil wars were brief and, apart from the Wars of the Roses massacre at Towton in 1461 (when 28,000 are reported to have died), its casualties were relatively few. England's wars were mostly fought overseas. There was thus little to intrude on the annual harvest and the conduct of trade, lubricated by the gods of wool.

Henry VIII had arrived on the English throne in 1509 at the age of seventeen. He was intelligent and energetic, benefiting from a full treasury left by his father, Henry VII, and an able counsellor in Thomas Wolsey, who rose swiftly to be a cardinal and his chancellor. For the first decade of his reign, Henry delegated the business of government to Wolsey while he enjoyed himself. Wolsey was an ambitious diplomat on the European stage. After conducting a desultory war with France, he in 1520 engineered a spectacular meeting between Henry and Francis I, still smarting from his loss of the Holy Roman emperorship to Charles V the year before.

The French monarch was, for those days, remarkably tall – over six feet. He had an unusually long nose and was dubbed *le grand nez*. He was extrovert, fond of hunting, jousting, women and lavish clothes. His cloaks of ermine were trimmed with gold and heron feathers. Unlike Henry, he was neither learned nor shrewd. His vanity inclined him to travel the country with 10,000 attendants, and fornicate with his mistress in front of his wife. He enticed Leonardo da Vinci to his burgeoning court and built Europe's most flamboyant Renaissance palace at Fontainebleau.

Wolsey's location for the meeting with Henry was outside England's remaining toehold in France, Calais. The Field of the Cloth of Gold was an event of extreme extravagance. Henry brought a retinue of 5,000, in addition to 6,000 workmen to build his camp. Not all went well. Henry challenged Francis to a joust, which was mercifully replaced by a wrestling match that Henry, to his fury, lost. The feasting and the entertainment were stupendous, an exercise in competitive vanity, pomp without circumstance.

Henry got on well with Francis, but over time he became more attached to the unflamboyant Charles V, whom he met more quietly on two occasions. To ingratiate himself with Rome, Henry in 1521 penned a careful defence of the Catholic church and its Seven Sacraments against Lutheranism. He won for the English crown the papal accolade of *fidei defensor* (defender of the faith). It was the last sign of concord between England and the Holy See, one that still adorns British coins as FD.

Francis of France; Charles of Spain

No such concord existed between Francis and Charles. The French king saw it as his mission to avenge the defeats his predecessors had suffered at the hands of the Holy Roman Empire in Italy. Wars in Italy became to Francis what wars in France had been to Edward III. They were displays of aggrandizement, revenge and knightly glory. Battle followed battle, mostly involving French cavalry against German and Spanish infantry, with the French almost always losing. The hapless citizens of northern Italy scarcely knew, from one year to the next, who was their current master.

A climax was reached at the Battle of Pavia in 1525, where the firepower of Charles's artillery and hand-held guns proved as effective against the French as had England's longbows at Agincourt. Disaster struck when Francis's horse was shot from under him and he was taken prisoner. Held captive for a year, he was forced to renounce all claims to Naples, Milan and Burgundy, a humiliating agreement on which he soon reneged. The victory brought Charles little peace. Francis schemed relentlessly against him, an ally to any enemy of Charles, be it a German prince, a problematic pope, or even the Ottoman empire.

That empire's young sultan, the twenty-six-year-old Suleiman the Magnificent (1520–66), deserves to rank as fourth of the sixteenth-century princes of Europe. Though no friend of Christendom, he was in many respects a Renaissance prince. He reformed Ottoman education, law and government, his celebrated maxim being that 'a king's greatest treasure is a wise vizier'. His court was civilized and his capital, Constantinople, a worthy successor to its Byzantine forebear. He was, in other words, a player on a corner of the European stage where, since the demise of the crusades and the fall of Constantinople, he had clearly indicated an ambition to expand and conquer. Europe's powers seemed prepared to accept his presence, insofar as he did not venture further west. Gone was the crusader zest for conquest and conversion. Constantinople was later seen as an important bulwark against Russian aggrandizement.

Suleiman acknowledged no such limit on his ambitions. In 1521 he besieged and captured the Serbian city of Belgrade on the Danube. A year later he built a new port for his navy in Asia Minor and, after a five-month siege, captured the Knights of St John's fortress of Rhodes. The knights re-settled in Malta, on the payment to Spain of an annual rent of a single 'Maltese falcon'. Charles's cousin, Louis II (1516–26), of the Polish Jagiellonian dynasty, was married to a Habsburg and was left, at the age of just twenty, with inadequate forces to defend the empire's eastern flank. In 1526 Suleiman, equipped with modern cannon and muskets, met Louis's sword-wielding troops at the Battle of Mohács and destroyed them, killing Louis and wiping out the Hungarian nobility.

The opportunistic Francis encouraged Suleiman to resume his advance on Charles's capital, Vienna. For a devout Catholic, this was a spectacular betrayal of Christendom, dubbed by Francis's enemies the 'impious alliance'. In 1526 Suleiman had pressed on to take Buda and occupied much of Hungary, putting him within striking distance of the Holy Roman Empire's capital. Here Suleiman paused, as if not knowing what to do next.

That same year, Charles fell in love with Isabella, daughter of the king of Portugal. At the wedding, the emperor was so ecstatic he stepped in front of a matador at the celebratory bullfight and personally killed the bull. The happiness evaporated a year later with an atrocity committed by Charles's army fighting Francis – then allied to the pope – in Italy. Among his troops were German mercenaries, who assaulted Rome and went on a rampage. Not a street was left undamaged; thousands were killed and their bodies thrown into the Tiber. Raphael's tapestries were torn from the Vatican walls and the Sistine Chapel was coated in graffiti. Three-quarters of the city's population fled, leaving a mere 10,000 behind.

The horrors unleashed on the holy city in his name remained on Charles's conscience for the rest of his life. Luther was characteristically cynical. He remarked that 'Christ reigns in such a way that the emperor who persecutes Luther for the pope is forced to destroy the pope for Luther'. Luther soon gained another ally. In 1528 Pope Clement was languishing in Orvieto, effectively a prisoner of Charles's army, where he received petitioners from England's Wolsey, requesting permission for Henry VIII to divorce Charles's aunt, Catherine of Aragon. He needed a son, and had fallen in love with Anne Boleyn. The English monarch was a Catholic but he needed a favour from the pope. Clement dared not comply with so glaring an insult to his captor's aunt, and he refused, precipitating a constitutional crisis in England.

Charles had better news elsewhere. Suleiman's army in Hungary was far from home, with poor lines of communication. When, in the spring of 1529, the long-anticipated advance on Vienna began, Suleiman found himself vulnerable to Austrian counter-attack and eventual repulse. The city did not fall, and the failure of the siege of Vienna brought the Ottoman advance into Europe to a halt. At the same time, Charles's empire was greatly expanding into the New World. Cortés took the decisive step in moving Spain's presence on to the continental landmass, conquering the Aztec empire in modern Mexico. From there, Spanish power spread.

The Diet of Augsburg and Counter-reformation

To Charles, Germany was always the challenge. Desperate to prevent Lutheranism from sapping the unity of his empire, he in 1530 summoned a diet at Augsburg to seek some accord between the Lutheran north and the Catholic south. The Lutherans presented him with the so-called Confession of Augsburg, a statement of faith prepared by Luther himself and his associate, Philip Melanchthon. It was implacable. It rejected the centrality of the Roman church in the Christian faith and declared, 'We are wholly reliant on Jesus

Christ for reconciliation with God.' The church and its priests should take their lead from the Bible alone, not from Rome.

Theology rarely admits to compromise, and Charles could not accept so bald a confession. Augsburg led to the formation in 1531 of the Schmalkaldic League of Protestant states, a defensive alliance to counter any military action that might be taken against them by Charles and the Holy Roman Empire. It included Saxony, Hesse, Frankfurt, Augsburg and Pomerania. Brandenburg later joined. Lutheranism was acquiring a political colouring, relying heavily on the constitutional autonomy of German states ordained by Barbarossa and Frederick II. The Augsburg Confession soon embraced Prussia, Sweden, Denmark, the Netherlands and most of Switzerland. As for France, Francis was always happy to give tacit support to any alliance that might embarrass Charles.

England did not join Augsburg, but it hardly needed to. Furious at the pope's refusal to grant him a divorce, Henry by the 1534 Act of Supremacy put himself in the pope's place as head of the English church. He seized its extensive monastic and other properties, either keeping them for himself or distributing them to England's rising mercantile class. It was England's greatest redistribution of wealth since the Norman conquest. Henry did not subscribe to the Schmalkaldic League. His was to be a strictly English Reformation.

In Switzerland Protestantism took a more fundamentalist turn. In the 1520s Zurich had come under the influence of Zwingli, but in 1536 a French scholar from Picardy named John Calvin arrived in Geneva. His doctrine was rigorous, holding that the saved were predestined by God at conception. Asceticism was a necessity, with most entertainment, music and good living banned. Voltaire said that Calvin opened the gates of the convents, but only 'to turn all society into a convent'. Calvin was intolerant, even advocating the execution of Catholics. He became the inspiration of French Protestantism under the Huguenot banner, and of puritan nonconformity in Scotland and much of England. Geneva became a refuge for Protestant exiles from across Europe, notably Huguenots from France and followers of John Knox from Scotland.

The Catholic church could not ignore this challenge. Rome was now recovering from its sack by Charles's troops. Pope Paul III (1534–49) was a bold reformer and patron of Michelangelo, having him rebuild the ancient Campidoglio piazza on the Capitoline hill, overlooking the old forum, and later design a new dome for St Peter's. In 1536, six years after Augsburg, Paul commissioned a report on ecclesiastical abuses, cataloguing them in language worthy of Hus and Luther. It blamed the spread of the Protestant Reformation squarely on the church and its curia. However, the church reacted to such self-criticism not with reform but with enhanced missionary zeal. In 1540 Paul blessed a Basque monk, Ignatius Loyola, as head of the Society of Jesus, or Jesuits, a new monastic order based in Spain.

The Jesuits were to be the church's elite force in the fight against Protestantism. These 'Spanish priests' fanned out across the capitals of Europe, owing loyalty to none but the pope. They concentrated on indoctrinating the young, founding seminaries and taking control of university faculties. Jesuits conveyed a simple message: obey Rome. They were particularly successful in central Europe, where they took Austria and Poland by storm, though Hussite Bohemia was resistant. Poland was to remain one of the most loyally Catholic states of Europe.

The Council of Trent

In 1545 Pope Paul summoned a council to Trent in northern Italy to address the Reformation head-on and to attempt to repair the damage of Augsburg fifteen years before. Again a church council could not bring itself to contemplate doctrinal compromise or reform. The edicts of the Fourth Lateran were reaffirmed, in direct refutation of Luther's Augsburg Confession. No quarter was given to Luther, then at the end of his life. The Council of Trent remains the basis of Catholic doctrine to this day. By facing intransigence with intransigence, it made virtually certain what was to be the most gruesome confrontation so far in Europe's violent history.

The Counter-Reformation under Paul's leadership reinvigorated the church. It took religious doctrine into the realms of Mannerist art and Baroque architecture. It deplored artistic nudity and the arousal of 'carnal desire', encouraging the depiction of suffering and agony, often in the presence of the Virgin Mary. Artists such as Titian, Tintoretto, Annibale Carracci and El Greco answered the call. Huge canvases were crowded with movement and emotion, most impressively in Venice's Scuola di San Rocco series by Tintoretto.

Charles V became a proselytizer for Trent. He travelled to Germany to confront his Lutheran subjects and, when they pleaded their autonomy under the Holy Roman Empire, he ordained that faith overruled such refinements. In 1547 he returned with a Spanish army, confronting the Schmalkaldic League at the Battle of Mühlberg. The league was temporarily crushed, but not Protestantism. Charles had broken explicit guarantees of self-government given to his northern peoples by his imperial predecessors. To Protestants, he was recasting the empire as a tyranny of the mind and soul.

Peace of Augsburg and the death of Charles

Argument continued until 1555 when, back again at Augsburg, an exhausted Charles left his younger brother Ferdinand to seek a final compromise with the German Protestants. Ferdinand indeed achieved a breakthrough, in fact a virtual capitulation. It was agreed that in future a state's religious affiliation would be decided on the principle of *cuius regio, eius religio*, whoever governs a country determines its faith. This meant that Roman Catholicism could not be enforced on the Lutherans of north Germany and their neighbouring states, within or outside the empire. There was even a licence granted to individuals and cities to disagree with the religion of their ruler. The decree reflected Ferdinand's private Protestant sympathies, and is believed to have echoed those of Charles's imprisoned mother, Joan the Mad. It was an extraordinary moment of tolerance and sanity.

That his brother should have made such a concession appalled the ailing Charles. In 1556, though aged only fifty-five, he was rid-dled with gout. He travelled to his Flemish capital, Brussels, and before a gathering in its palace, passed the throne of Spain to his twenty-eight-year-old son, Philip II (1556–98). All reports are of a desperate scene. Philip, whose father had married him to England's Catholic monarch Mary I in 1554, looked unimpressive. His meagre stature and ugly 'Habsburg' lip and protruding jaw were com-pounded by his habit of looking at the ground when he (rarely) spoke. Charles finished his abdication speech and sank back in his chair weeping. Philip could speak neither French nor Flemish and mumbled a few inaudible words in Spanish, before leaving a bishop to continue for him. He was to be Europe's fate.

Charles retired to a monastery in Extremadura, his retinue reduced from 762 to 150. Two years later, in 1558, he died, and Philip began the colossal Escorial palace outside Madrid as his father's mausoleum and memorial. It became a psychological prison for successive Span-ish rulers. Charles had begun his reign an unprepossessing monarch, yet he kept his own country of Spain at peace, while containing the French and Ottoman incursions on his inherited empire. He was one of only a handful of rulers given the chance to 'unite Europe'. The irony was that, had his brother Ferdinand lived long enough to entrench the Peace of Augsburg, he might have achieved such a goal.

As for the succession, Charles understood as had Diocletian that such vast territories were beyond the power of one man to rule. Perhaps aware of his son Philip's deficiencies, he divided his legacy in two. He gave Germany, Austria and eventually the title of Holy Roman Emperor to his brother, Ferdinand (1558–64). Spain, the Netherlands and the New World went to Philip. From now on, Spain's briefly dynamic role in Europe's history was diminished and gradually detached from the drama of central Europe. Its future was entombed in Philip's majestic citadel of stone.

The age of the princes was coming to an end. Charles's rival, Francis of France, predeceased him in 1547. Francis's successor, Henry II (1547–59), died in a jousting accident, and three young kings followed, requiring Henry's shrewd widow, Catherine de' Medici, to serve as regent. A similar state of affairs came to England after Henry VIII's death that same year. His fervently Protestant son, Edward VI (1547–53), died at the age of fifteen after just six years on the throne. His sister and successor, Mary (1553–8), briefly wife to Philip of Spain, plunged her country into an English Counter-Reformation that included the public burning of Protestants. To this brutality even her husband objected.

Mary died in 1558, only two months after her father-in-law, Charles V. Though her husband, Philip, claimed the throne and later offered his hand to her Protestant sister, Elizabeth, he was rejected. When Mary was succeeded by Elizabeth (1558–1603), the Reformation won a sympathetic, if inactive supporter, while England won a monarch of rare charisma and intelligence.

II

Wars of Religion
1560–1660

St Bartholomew's Day massacre

As the three princes departed the scene, they left Europe's conflicts unresolved. The Habsburgs remained at odds with the French House of Valois. Philip of Spain remained at odds with Elizabeth of England. Protestant north Europe was at odds with Catholic Rome. The crucial compromises reached at the 1555 Peace of Augsburg relied on the senior personalities of the Holy Roman Empire to respect them. That was a fragile reliance.

In 1559 first blood of a new era was spilled by Philip with an auto-da-fé in Valladolid. Thirty-one Protestants were burned alive in the main square. Philip, rebuffed as a suitor by England's Elizabeth, became ever more isolated. Unlike his father, who was constantly on the move, Philip ruled his vast empire chiefly from his Escorial apartment. He was obsessed with heresy. The Inquisition had all but eradicated Islam and Judaism from Spain, though not from the Spanish Netherlands. In the Americas Spanish rule now stretched south from Mexico to Peru and Chile and north to Florida. Its Roman Catholic Church had become, intermittently, a force for the humane treatment of the local population. It was a ban on the enslavement of native Americans throughout the Spanish empire that encouraged the importing into the Americas of African slaves.

In France, Catherine de' Medici as queen had long been forced to live in the shadow of her husband's mistress, Diane de Poitiers. On his death in 1559, she ruled France as regent of his young successors, effectively for thirty years. A true Medici, she upheld the Renaissance tradition of her father-in-law, Francis. She built the Tuileries palace in Paris, amassed a large art collection and is credited with devising and producing dances in the form of modern ballet. She was fascinated by the occult, under the influence of the fortune-teller Nostradamus.

Catherine's most intractable problem was Calvinism, which had spread to at least ten per cent of an otherwise solidly Catholic country, predominantly to the Huguenots. Her task was to mediate between the Huguenots, entrenched in sections of the aristocracy, and the Catholic House of Guise, pretenders to the French throne. In 1561–2 her attempts to grant the Huguenots freedom of worship led to Catholic riots in Paris, answered by Huguenot risings in Rouen, Lyon and Orléans. In 1563 Catherine achieved a compromise Edict of Amboise, which proved more a pause than a settlement.

Tension returned as Philip of Spain began the suppression of Protestantism in Flanders. The introduction of the Inquisition, requiring every Dutch citizen to adhere to the Council of Trent, was the last straw. The Netherlands, a crucial source of revenue to the Spanish crown, rose in revolt, and in 1567 Philip dispatched the Duke of Alva to enforce his Inquisition. Alva condemned to death several Dutch rebels, who died in Brussels' main square. The Dutch leader, William 'the Silent' of Orange (lived 1533–84), had been a favourite of Philip's father, Charles V, even holding his arm during his abdication speech. Alva's heavy hand turned William into a champion of rebellion, to wage what became an eighty-year war of independence of the Netherlands from Spain.

Philip's beleaguered realm was briefly diverted by its loyalty to Rome into a confrontation with a renewed Ottoman advance in the Mediterranean. Suleiman had died in 1566, having conquered most of the old Byzantine empire. The Ottomans' capture of Cyprus in 1570 led the pope to form a Holy Alliance to oppose them. Ships were contributed principally from Barcelona, Genoa and Venice, under the command of Philip's twenty-six-year-old half-brother, Don John of Austria.

In 1571 John confronted the Ottoman fleet at Lepanto, off Corinth, in what was the last set-piece battle between oared warships. Some five hundred vessels were crammed into confined waters, where they soon became gridlocked, their decks forming a continuous blood-stained battlefield. The Christian victory was overwhelming and much celebrated across Europe. Its strategic significance was limited, though it confined the Ottomans to the eastern Mediterranean.

Philip's campaign in the Netherlands now went from bad to worse. In France Catherine had sought a conciliatory marriage between her daughter, Elizabeth, and Philip's son, Don Carlos – supplying the plot to Verdi's eponymous opera – but politics dictated that in 1559 she instead marry Philip, widower of Mary of England. Catherine was now enmeshed in France's religious civil wars. As if to balance Elizabeth's marriage, she proposed another daughter, Margaret, to the Huguenot leader and claimant to the throne, Henry of Navarre. But in 1572, during the Paris wedding festivities, a prominent Huguenot, Admiral Coligny, was wounded in an assassination attempt. In the ensuing chaos, and fearing Huguenot reprisals, Catherine panicked and recklessly gave the Guise faction licence to assassinate Huguenot leaders.

The order was carried out on St Bartholomew's Day, 24 August 1572, and developed into a full-blown massacre. No one knows how many died, between 3,000 and 10,000 by various accounts. Protestant Europe was horrified, while Catholic Europe saluted a triumph. Philip declared it 'of such service, glory and honour to God and universal benefit to all Christendom' and 'the best and most cheerful news which at present could come to me'. The pope sent

Catherine a golden rose, and ordered a Te Deum to be sung. He also commissioned Vasari to paint a set of frescoes in celebration of the massacre, which he ranked in importance with the victory at Lepanto. Europe's religious divide deepened.

Many Huguenots fled to the safety of the northern Netherlands, now in open rebellion against Spain, and to England. Elizabeth offered asylum but refused military aid. Indeed, just before the massacre in 1572, Elizabeth had agreed the Treaty of Blois with Catherine against Spain. She unleashed her 'privateer' sea captains to prey on Spanish galleons, in what amounted to state-sponsored piracy, with Elizabeth taking a personal cut from their winnings.

In the Netherlands, the rebellion of William of Orange gained strength. In 1576 Philip sent his brother John to assess the rebellion, and he reported back that 'the Prince of Orange has bewitched the minds of all men. They love him and fear him and wish to have him as their lord.' Philip had no option but to capitulate. William was elected stadtholder, or de facto monarch, of a breakaway Dutch republic. Spain was left with just Catholic Flanders – part of modern Belgium – in the south. In 1581 the Protestant Dutch United Provinces declared formal independence.

The Spanish Armada

Mortified by the loss of his Dutch territory but uplifted by Catherine's scourge of the Huguenots, Philip raised his crusade against heresy to a new and spectacular level. As widower of Mary I, he still claimed England's throne. Elizabeth's Catholic cousin Mary, Queen of Scots, was also a claimant. French educated and daughter of a Guise mother, she had also been married to Francis II, briefly king of France (1559–60). Fleeing plots against her in Scotland, she in England became the focus of rumoured Catholic plots against

Elizabeth. Her execution at Fotheringay Castle in 1587 outraged Catholic Europe and gave Philip a casus belli for his long-planned assault on Elizabeth.

To Philip, such an expedition would honour his father's memory, win the blessing of the pope and deliver a blow against Protestantism. The plan involved a slow-moving Armada of 130 ships, laden with soldiers and priests to convert the English. It was to sail from Lisbon to Calais, where it would collect the Duke of Parma's Flanders army and cross to England. Parma would defeat Elizabeth, link up with a rising of English Catholics and put a Spanish infanta on the English throne. It was by no means an implausible venture. England's troops would have been no match for Parma's.

From the moment in 1588 that the Armada set sail it met disaster. It was assailed by English fireships when at anchor at Gravelines off the Flemish coast. Adverse winds then blew it up the North Sea and round the north coasts of Scotland and Ireland. Few ships were sunk by the English navy, but only half of the original fleet returned to Spain. Some 5,000 Spaniards perished.

The failure of the Armada greatly enhanced Elizabeth's reputation. Aided by the creation of an intelligence service under Sir Francis Walsingham, she contrived to balance personal and national security with a degree of religious tolerance. Above all, and despite pleas from at home and abroad, she struggled to limit her involvement in Europe's ongoing wars, though this did not prevent her indulging her favourites, the Earl of Leicester and the Earl of Essex, in a series of ill-fated expeditions to the Netherlands, France and Ireland. At the same time, England edged sideways into Europe's cultural Renaissance, honoured in the architecture of Robert Smythson and the music of William Byrd and Thomas Tallis. One Elizabethan Englishman did manage to cross every border and put a girdle round the continent. William Shakespeare's imaginative scope – from Greece to Rome, from Paris to Venice, from Scotland to Cyprus – embraced the commonality of the European experience in an emergent humanism.

The failure of the Armada humiliated Philip, further aggravated by the refusal of Pope Sixtus V to pay him the large subsidy promised for the conversion of the English. His advisers were single-minded. They attributed the fiasco to Philip's supposed leniency towards non-Catholics still in Spain. Yet the Spanish people seemed comfortable in their faith and loyal to their king. It was a remarkably peaceable country.

Paris worth a Mass

Spain's Catholic rival, France, experienced no such popular compliance. In 1589 its king, Henry III, was assassinated and his mother, Catherine de' Medici, died. A Jesuit-influenced Catholic League, led by the Guise party, ruled Paris but in an ongoing civil war with the Huguenots, who were led by the Bourbon successor to the throne, Henry of Navarre. This saw Henry's eventual victory at the Battle of Ivry in 1590. Though now formally king of France, he was refused entry into Paris unless he agreed to become a Catholic. After intense negotiation, Henry finally did so. On entering Paris he was said to have looked out from the hill of Montmartre and remarked, 'Paris is well worth a Mass,' one of history's many supposed quotations well-suited to the man but not known to be true.

Henry IV (1589–1610) was an unusual French monarch, wise, temperate and at times humorous. He said of Catherine's much-criticized reign, 'I am surprised that she never did worse.' He in 1598 negotiated France's version of Germany's Peace of Augsburg, the Edict of Nantes, ordaining religious freedom and tolerance for Protestants in public office and before the law. The edict was a compromise that did little to cross France's religious divide, and in 1610 it resulted in Henry's assassination by a Catholic fanatic. He had been a popular figure. In Paris he built the Pont Neuf, now adorned by his statue. As the first monarch of the House of Bourbon he was a French royalist hero after the Revolution, and is still regularly nominated in polls as France's favourite monarch.

As France struggled to secure peaceful coexistence between Catholics and Protestants, the Peace of Augsburg had brought the Holy Roman Empire half a century of relative calm. The king of Bohemia and Holy Roman Emperor, Rudolph II (1576–1612), made his capital of Prague, home of Jan Hus, the embodiment of Renaissance civility and taste. His collection of Mannerist art was celebrated, notably a portrait of himself as an arrangement of fruit and vegetables, painted by Arcimboldo. He was a reserved man who never married and was fascinated by science and the occult. Under pressure from his brother, Archduke Matthias, Rudolph in 1609 signed a Letter of Majesty conceding formal religious freedom to Bohemia's Protestants. Since Rudolph was a Catholic, this went beyond even the settlements of Augsburg.

The Thirty Years War

This emergent tolerance across northern Europe at the start of the seventeenth century was promising but insecure. In 1617 Augsburg abruptly fell apart. The Bohemian crown passed to a Jesuit-trained Habsburg, Ferdinand II (1617–37), who became Holy Roman Emperor in 1619. No succession could have been more disastrous for the peace of Europe. Ferdinand shared the missionary zeal of his cousin, Philip of Spain. But whereas Philip shared his faith with that of his own countrymen, Ferdinand's Bohemia was overwhelmingly Protestant, their freedom to remain so recently confirmed by Rudolph.

When news that Ferdinand meant to replace Bohemia's Protestant governors with Catholics reached Prague in 1618, it led to instant revolt. Ferdinand's emissaries were dragged to an upper window of Prague Castle and thrown into the ditch fifty feet below, the so-called Defenestration of Prague. Their remarkable survival was variously attributed to the wings of Catholic angels and the depth of dung in the ditch. The Bohemians promptly appointed Frederick V, the Elector Palatine of a small Rhineland state, in Ferdinand's stead. Frederick was a Calvinist married to Elizabeth Stuart, daughter of James I of England. Dubbed 'the jewel of Europe', she was to be a lasting object of Protestant veneration.

Ferdinand now summoned Catholic monarchs and mercenaries from across Europe to wage a war of faith on his Protestants. Spain, Poland and the papacy joined with him in a Catholic League, in effect an intra-European crusader force. Frederick on his side was backed by the Dutch Protestants, the Scandinavians, the French (deviously) and the English (half-heartedly). The ensuing Thirty Years War abrogated the Peace of Augsburg and all other edicts of toleration and non-intervention in the affairs of members of the Holy Roman Empire reached over previous centuries. It showed how far one man's faith could dictate the fate of nations.

The war's peculiar tragedy was to turn what had been Germany's strength – its detachment from Europe's dynastic wars – into a weakness. Most of Europe at least had a putative ruler to mediate between Catholics and Protestants. Germany had none. The Habsburgs had long guaranteed the autonomy of its disparate principalities. Now they were the enemy of autonomy. They set German against German. It meant catastrophe.

The first battle of the war, the Battle of White Mountain in 1620, took place outside Prague, and saw the Bohemians soundly defeated. Frederick fled, and he and Elizabeth became refugees in The Hague, known for the brevity of their one-year reign as the 'winter king and queen'. Rather than conciliate, Ferdinand reacted to his victory with brutality. Twenty-seven Bohemian leaders were executed in Prague's Old Town Square. All Bohemia's non-Catholic nobles had their lands confiscated and all Protestants were evicted, most fleeing west into Germany. Within ten years, the progeny of Hus's Reformation fell from three million to 800,000. So complete was this religious cleansing that Bohemia remains largely Catholic to this day, though a statue of Hus adorns Prague's Old Town Square.

Ferdinand soon found he could not pay the wages of his mostly Spanish mercenary army, which duly marauded beyond Bohemia into Germany. War became banditry, with soldiers living off the land in a state of medieval debauchery. Gradually all Europe was sucked into the conflict. The king of France, Louis XIII, and his adviser, Cardinal Richelieu, followed French policy in siding with any foe of a Habsburg, even a Protestant one. James I of England, an eager Protestant but with a Parliament averse to expense, sent a small detachment of soldiers.

More substantial allies of the Protestant cause were Denmark and Sweden, with Sweden's soldier-king, Gustavus Adolphus (1611–32), emerging in the lead. Gustavus had won fame as an innovative field commander. He would reposition his infantry, light artillery and cavalry constantly round the battlefield, keeping them well supplied. This was in contrast to the Spaniards' cumbersome guns and hard-to-manoeuvre *tercios*, blocks of pikemen twenty ranks deep. The Swedes won a victory at the Battle of Breitenfeld in 1631, but Gustavus was killed fighting a year later, a catastrophe that dashed hopes of an early end to the conflict.

In 1637, after nineteen years of war, Ferdinand died, but by then it had a momentum of its own. Concerned that Spain's Philip IV (1621–65) would use the war to reunite Charles V's Spanish and Austrian Habsburg empires, Louis and Richelieu officially declared France's war on Madrid. It was now not just Catholic against

Protestant, but Catholic Bourbon against Catholic Habsburg. At first the French fared ill and Spanish forces reached the outskirts of Paris. In return the French threatened Spanish Flanders and sent reinforcements to the Swedes in the north. The Ottomans were then involved, invited by the Protestants to attack Austria from the east. Europe was in turmoil.

Back in Germany the contest was no longer between dynasties and religions. It was a primitive struggle of people to survive. Undisciplined troops tore principalities apart and created conflicts where none existed before. One historian of the war, Veronica Wedgwood, wrote that there was little point to the fighting: 'Almost all [combatants] were actuated rather by fear than by lust of conquest or passion of faith. They wanted peace.' Eventually, in 1643, a charismatic French general, the twenty-three-year-old Duc d'Enghien, took the field against a Flemish army at Rocroi in the Ardennes, where he massacred the *tercios* and ended Spanish participation. Philip of Spain now realized that supporting Ferdinand might cost him Flanders and its revenues. Rocroi was the last pitched battle of the war.

For another five years, bands of soldiers wandered across central Europe, leaderless, hungry and desperate. German trade and manufacture collapsed. Sowing and harvesting ceased. A third to a half of twenty million German-speakers died. The Elbe city of Magdeburg had 20,000 inhabitants in 1620 and 450 in 1649. The medieval library of Heidelberg University was carried off to the Vatican. A Swedish general wrote home from Bohemia, 'I did not expect to find the kingdom so lean, wasted and spoiled, for between Prague and Vienna everything has been razed to the ground and hardly a living soul can be seen on the land.' The war is regarded as Europe's bloodiest before the twentieth century. To Wedgwood it was 'confused in its causes, devious in its course, futile in its result, the outstanding example in European history of meaningless conflict'.

The Peace of Westphalia

Diplomats representing the parties involved, eventually 109 in all, met in 1643 in the aftermath of Rocroi, camping separately in two adjacent towns in Westphalia, Osnabrück and Münster. Emissaries rode back and forth between the sides, reaching not one treaty but a series of local deals, designed to roll into a collective peace. Agreement took five years, being finally signed in 1648. It was in essence a reversion to Augsburg, to the principle of national self-determination in politics and faith, *cuius regio, eius religio*, to each country its faith.

As at Augsburg, Lutherans and Calvinists agreed to share parts of Europe with Catholics. There was to be a restitution of all, or most, confiscated property. The Catholic status of Austria and of now destitute Bohemia was recognized. Spain conceded formal independence to her lost provinces in northern Netherlands, and Jews were granted safe refuge there.

Westphalia restored the autonomy of German states and, once again, denied authority over them to the Holy Roman Empire. Though often awarded credit for fathering the concept of the nation state, it was more significant for its internationalism, for reasserting the autonomy of states and the legal sanctity of treaties. In this it was hardly a lasting success. None the less the participants celebrated their achievement in Gerard ter Borch's great portrait of them crowded into Münster town hall, the painting now owned by the National Gallery in London. England was one European country not involved.

The Peace accepted the reality of a Europe that had fought itself to exhaustion. France did well, gaining land deep into Germany in Alsace and the Rhine basin. This was the most unwise of the treaty's provisions, creating a lasting grievance among the region's German-speaking population. To the north, Sweden emerged as a regional power, winning a number of north-German territories. Germany was left ruined, a desert still of some fifty 'free cities', sixty ecclesiastical principalities and two hundred and fifty (some said a thousand) autonomous cities and statelets. It took a century for them to recover.

Protestant Prussia was the fastest to re-emerge, under the Hohenzollern family of the 'Great Elector' Friedrich Wilhelm (1640–88). His domain lay outside the Holy Roman Empire and was notionally a vassal of Poland. But during the war it had merged with Brandenburg, whose duke had long been a Holy Roman Empire elector. Since its capital of Berlin had lost half its population in the war, Friedrich Wilhelm opened its gates to refugees of all faiths, allowing the economic tonic of immigration (as it was to do again in 1945 and 2015).

Spain was left a shattered realm, decoupled for ever from the Holy Roman Empire. In the 1640s it had seen revolts in Catalonia and Portugal, protesting demands that they finance Philip's role in the war. Even Catholic Flanders was at risk, since Spain's antique navy was no match for growing Dutch sea power. No less shattered was the proxy instigator of the war, the papacy. Pope Innocent X was unrepresented at Westphalia, and denounced it as 'null, void, invalid, iniquitous, unjust, damnable, reprobate, inane and devoid of meaning'. Such papal edicts no longer carried force. Innocent took consolation in creating Rome's exquisite Piazza Navona, and in patronizing the genius of baroque architecture, Borromini. His stern portrait by Velázquez hangs in his family's Palazzo Doria Pamphilj in Rome.

Civil war in England

As the Thirty Years War drew to a close, a lesser encounter erupted in normally placid England. Though the issue was not freedom of worship as such, the antipathy of Catholic and Protestant was not far below the surface. The father of Elizabeth of Bohemia, James I

20. The Black Death plagues Europe – Tournai, France, 1349

21. The burning of Jan Hus by the Council of Constance, 1415

22. Burgundian plenty – October, from the *Très Riches Heures du Duc de Berry*

23. Constantinople falls to the Turks, 1453

24. Renaissance Rome – Ghirlandaio's *The Calling of SS. Peter and Andrew* in the Sistine Chapel, 1481

25. Johannes Gutenberg, first printer of the Bible in 1455

26. Isabella of Castile, Catholic monarch, scourge of heresy, *c.*1490

27. Girolamo Savonarola, instigator of the bonfire of the vanities, 1494–8

28. Martin Luther, master of the Reformation

29. (*below*) Europe spreads its wings south and west – the port of Lisbon, 1542

30. Charles V of Spain, Holy Roman
Emperor, 1519–56

31. Francis I of France, 1515–47

32. Henry VIII of England, 1509–47

33. Suleiman the Magnificent of Turkey,
1520–66

34. *The St Bartholomew's Day Massacre*, France, 1572

35. Catherine de' Medici, one of three women to rule France in the sixteenth century

36. Paris was 'worth a Mass' – Henry IV of France, 1589–1610

37. *The Defenestration of Prague*, 1618

38. *The Hanging* – horrors of the Thirty Years War, 1618–48

(1603–25), was a Protestant and proud commissioner of the King James Bible. All Catholics remained suspect – unsurprisingly, given the Gunpowder Plot of 1605 – but suspect too were extreme Puritans, such as the *Mayflower* voyagers who emigrated to America in 1620. Almost alone in Europe, England was devoted to the assiduous pursuit of a middle way.

James might have been Protestant, but he was an advocate of the divine right of kings and of 'God's mandate', which he interpreted as a mandate to overrule Parliament. Trouble began on James's death in 1625, with the marriage of James's successor Charles I (1625–49) to the devoutly Catholic Henrietta Maria of France. It confirmed widespread fears that the House of Stuart was unreliable in its commitment to Protestantism. In 1628 a Petition of Right to Charles reiterated parliamentary supremacy. It refused him revenue and also a standing army, both prerogatives of Parliament. Its author, Chief Justice Sir Edward Coke, declared, 'Magna Carta is such a fellow that he will have no sovereign.' Charles's reply was that 'kings are not bound to give account of their actions, but to God alone'. This was no basis for stable government.

In 1629 Charles dissolved Parliament and refused to summon another for eleven years, a period of the so-called 'tyranny'. To pay his expenses, he tried to impose an extra-parliamentary tax, 'ship money', but this proved uncollectable. Then, in 1637, Charles's conservative archbishop, William Laud, imposed what was widely seen as a Catholic prayer book on Calvinist Scotland. The Bishop of Brechin had to read it with two loaded pistols on his pulpit. Riots ensued. In Scotland thousands signed a 'covenant' asserting their reformed faith.

England now proceeded to compress into two decades a revolution that was to take two centuries in most of Europe. The Parliament elected in 1640 was overwhelmingly opposed to the king. It was unlike any yet seen, embracing landowners and civic leaders, merchants and professionals, in sum the new middle class that had been created and prospered under Henry's Reformation and Elizabeth's peace. They converted the Petition of Right into a Great Remonstrance, and demanded full parliamentary sovereignty over church and state. While the weak Charles might have assented to this, his Catholic wife was his implacable adviser.

In 1642 king and Parliament went to war. As in Germany the nation was deeply split. Royalist and parliamentarian stood proxy, if not for Catholic and Protestant at least for high church and Calvinist. Parliament's forces soon cohered under the austere Oliver Cromwell. Most armies at the time were rough assemblages of local levies, led by sons of aristocrats. Cromwell's New Model Army, largely drawn from Calvinist East Anglia, was recruited and paid as a professional force. The king suffered a series of reverses, culminating in Marston Moor in 1644 and Naseby a year later. The royalist army disintegrated and the king was later captured by the Scots and turned over to Parliament.

In 1647, as Westphalia reached its conclusion, Cromwell's soldiers met in a Putney church. For the first time European men in positions of power argued the fundamentals of politics in a manner still recognizable today. They debated universal suffrage, an end to conscription and the status of private property. The radical Colonel Thomas Rainsborough asserted that 'the poorest he that is in England hath a life to live, as the greatest . . . every man that is to live under a government ought first by his own consent to put himself under that government'.

Cromwell argued for retaining the monarchy, and even offered Charles emollient terms for ending the rebellion. But the king in captivity plotted a return to war, and as a result was tried for treason. In 1649 judgment was given for his execution, which took place outside the Banqueting House in Whitehall on a cold January afternoon. The king declared to the end that 'a subject and a sovereign are clean different things'. A groan went up from the crowd when the king's head was separated from his body. There was no revolutionary delight in victory or revelling in blood. A line had been crossed and it sat on the nation's conscience for years to come.

Under Cromwell, England never sought a stable basis for democratic rule. He attacked the Scots for switching sides to support the king, and treated Catholic Ireland with atrocious brutality, defying all claims to a tolerant Protestantism. For the first time he bound the nations of the British Isles under one central assembly, abolishing bishops and eventually dissolving Parliament itself. With the blind John Milton in support, Cromwell sought to rule his 'commonwealth' with prudence and justice. He invited Jews to return to England after three centuries of banishment, and he pursued a trade war with the Dutch on behalf of the City of London. For all the democratic pretensions of the English Revolution, its outcome was five years of dictatorship, a regime of 'grim godliness'. Before his death in 1658, Cromwell took refuge in kingly heredity, and appointed his son Richard as his successor.

Two years later, the army's General Monck consulted Parliament and invited the nation, in effect, to change its mind. Parliament did so, inviting the dead king's son, Charles II (1660–85), to return from exile on the clear understanding that he came at its will, not his. Monarchy was in its gift. The Church of England was re-established with its rights and property. Freedom of worship and parliamentary sovereignty were, supposedly, entrenched. A European nation had passed through the valley of revolution, tasting regicide, autocracy and commonwealth, and rejecting them all. England's 'constitutional monarchy' was a liberal state, at least in embryo.

Anne of Austria and the Fronde

Such a state was the last thing under discussion in France. Louis XIII and Richelieu were dead and Paris was ruled by Anne of

Austria, Louis's estranged wife and third in a line of cosmopolitan women to rule France in this period. She followed Catherine de' Medici and Marie de' Medici, mother of and regent for Louis XIII. Anne was for seventeen years regent for her son, Louis XIV. For much of the century from the 1560s, France was led by a woman.

Anne governed in collaboration and possible cohabitation with Richelieu's dashing protégé, Cardinal Mazarin. Both Richelieu and Mazarin were masters of the ruthless art of French politics. They were able, feared and pragmatic. With the end of the Thirty Years War, Anne faced a rebellion by an aristocratic faction known as the Fronde against taxes levied to pay for France's part in the war. The dispute threatened the House of Bourbon with a coup, but was eventually crushed in 1653. Though dubbed Paris's answer to England's civil war, the uprising left France with none of the political reforms won in both England and the Netherlands at the time.

In 1661 Mazarin died and the twenty-two-year-old Louis XIV took power from Anne. He was a shrewd young man, who had watched closely how his mother ruled, and learned what he regarded as a crucial lesson, that a monarch should never delegate power to others. Autocracy meant what it said. Later, Louis is alleged to have said, 'l'état, c'est moi'. The golden orb of Le Roi Soleil rose over the horizon. It was to dazzle all Europe.

12

The Climax of Autocracy
1660–1715

The Sun King rises

Louis XIV (1643–1715) dominated his age. He was dubbed 'le Dieu donné', given by God, and spent a lifetime trying to outdo his Maker. He faced a continent exhausted by the Thirty Years War and supposedly pacified by Westphalia. This had ended Catholicism's claimed sovereignty over the belief system of Europe. At the same time the energies of the Renaissance and Reformation had refreshed debate about the natural world and the human condition. Everywhere settled assumptions were challenged. The scientific revolution that had accompanied the Renaissance acquired new force. In 1642, the same year that Galileo died, condemned by the church, Isaac Newton was born. With him was born modern physics.

In France, Louis did not recognize any new Europe. Like a Roman emperor, he believed himself destined to 'the great, noble and delightful trade of monarchy'. A short man with a quick temper, he ruled by fear, splendour and guile. He brooked no opposition and delegated no authority. Secretaries of state could sign documents only in his name. They had to report to him personally each morning, and did so throughout his life. The Sun King glorified the twenty million people of Europe's most populous nation and left it a legacy of bankruptcy and revolution.

Louis's command centre was a new palace built outside Paris on the site of a royal hunting lodge at Versailles, into which he moved in 1682.

It was intended to be free of the influences and compromises of the capital. Unlike Philip II's grim Escorial, Versailles was a prison of gaiety and ostentation. In England, Elizabeth made her barons leave court, to guard and develop their provincial estates. Louis wanted no renewed Fronde, scheming behind his back. A thousand French nobles were incarcerated as if for life in the 350 apartments of Versailles. The Noailles family was so large it inhabited a whole corridor, known as the Rue de Noailles. Here courtiers fawned daily on the monarch, who responded with compulsory hospitality and entertainment. Like rats in a golden sack, they degenerated into petty feuding, ridicule and servility.

Louis loathed Protestantism, but he paid no deference to the Catholic pope. He was the totality of the state. Bishops were his servants. In foreign policy, he was obsessed with the dynastic and territorial disputes that had cursed France since the Middle Ages. He was a reversion to the pre-Westphalian age. Aggrandizement, he wrote, 'is the most worthy and agreeable of a sovereign's occupations'. He pursued it recklessly and with little success. Most of his income not spent on Versailles went on a standing army of 250,000 soldiers. No other European nation had anything like as many.

The king placed his finances under a controller-general, Jean-Baptiste Colbert, who had a feverish eye for detail and love of bureaucracy. A contemporary referred to him as having the accountant's 'chilly fixity of the northern star'. But even Colbert could not handle his monarch's extravagance. The result was a national economy that, behind a veil of splendour, was unsustainable. The only question was, would it outlast Louis?

The Franco-Dutch War

The king sought an early triumph against both the Spaniards and the Dutch in the Netherlands. To this end he sought a secret treaty with England's Charles II, signed at Dover in 1670. Charles was already finding Parliament as cheese-paring as had his father, and Louis mooted a large subsidy and the division of the Netherlands between France and England. In return, Charles promised sixty ships for an attack on Holland – and an English church brought back to Rome. These promises were absurd. Charles was so eager to ape Louis's extravagance he became his pawn, the secret deal being covered by a fake treaty pledging just friendship.

Louis declared war on the Netherlands in 1672, ostensibly over trade but in truth to seize land. Charles sent his promised ships, but this evoked such opposition in Parliament that, two years later, he had to renege on his treaty with Louis. The Dutch proved equally resistant. When the French invaded, the Dutch opened their dykes and flooded the country in the French path. The new stadtholder, the future William III of England, famously said his strategy was to fight 'until the last ditch'. The French invasion stalled and was eventually driven back. Under the Treaties of Nijmegen in 1678–9, Louis achieved only moderate territorial gains. But the war devastated the Dutch economy, at the time considered the richest in Europe. The golden age of Dutch painting, of Rembrandt, Hals, ter Borch and Vermeer, came to an end.

In 1683 Austria was distracted by yet another Ottoman incursion, this time reaching the gates of Vienna. In the culminating Battle of Vienna, a combined Austrian and Polish-Lithuanian force conclusively defeated the Turks. The battle included reputedly the largest cavalry charge in history, when 18,000 Polish horsemen charged into the Turkish force. Louis's France offered Austria no assistance in this resumed threat to the integrity of Catholic Europe. Yet again, Europe could not bring itself to co-operate.

Louis now turned homewards and directed his obsessive aggression against his Huguenot population, supposedly protected by Henry IV's Edict of Nantes. His view was that a single nation should have a single religion, that of its king. In 1685 he revoked the Edict of Nantes and ordered the Huguenots to convert to Catholicism or leave. The impact was traumatic. Estimates of the expulsion vary wildly, but between 250,000 and 900,000 Huguenots fled their homes for England, the Netherlands and Prussia. They thus blessed northern Europe with that boon to an emergent European capitalism, a network of skilled craftsmen, merchants and financiers.

The rise of William of Orange

The revocation of the Edict of Nantes cleansed England of any lingering traces of Francophilia, replacing it with a delight in all things Dutch. The French ambassador in London warned Louis that the only friend France had in England was the Stuart royal family. That too was not united. William of Orange was married to the then king James II's Protestant daughter and heir to his throne, Princess Mary. As hero of the Franco-Dutch War, William's eventual accession as Mary's husband became in England the eagerly anticipated guarantor of a Protestant crown. This hope evaporated when, in June 1688, James II's new wife, Mary of Modena, gave birth to a son, which made a presumed Catholic first in line to the throne. William and Mary were displaced and another Stuart crisis was at hand.

Parliament would not tolerate any return to royal Catholicism. The second thoughts of the 1660 Restoration had not turned out well. Third ones were required. The initiative was taken by William in the Netherlands. Within weeks of the new prince's birth he secured, via his agent in England, Hans Bentinck, a letter from seven peers requesting him to invade and usurp James's throne. British politics was dividing along lines going back to the Civil War, between supporters of parliamentary sovereignty and those of the

Stuart monarchy. They were dubbed, respectively, Whigs and Tories, abusive terms for Scottish drovers and Irish outlaws. The Whigs were strongly behind William's usurpation, while many Tories were Stuart sympathizers.

A Dutch invasion fleet of 463 ships and 40,000 men, three times the size of the Spanish Armada of a century before, set sail from the Netherlands in November 1688 and arrived off Dover, where a battery of guns boomed out a welcome. William did not land but cautiously headed west to Brixham in Devon. From there, the Dutch made their way across country to London, where the king's army, under its young commander, John Churchill, turned traitor and joined the invaders. James fled down the Thames, throwing the Great Seal of England into the water, where it is believed still to lie. He was allowed to escape to France and Louis's hospitality. William occupied London, and England was soon flooded with East India Company tea, 'china' porcelain, tulip-vases and red-brick gables.

William's invasion was as brazen as that of his Norman namesake, but this time few objected. He disregarded the terms of female succession and demanded the crown for himself on equal terms with his wife Mary (1689–94), so becoming William III (1689–1702). Parliament agreed, but insisted in return on the constitutional restrictions imposed, with limited success, on Stuart monarchs for the past century. These culminated in 1689 in a Toleration Act and a Bill of Rights. They permitted freedom of worship, though not (at least publicly) to Catholics or extreme Puritans such as Unitarians, who were excluded from public office. Parliament would retain control of state revenues, the army and foreign policy.

The bargain added that 'it has been found by experience that it is inconsistent with the safety and welfare of this Protestant kingdom to be governed by a popish prince'. An Act of Settlement in 1701 formally declared the succession to bypass fifty-five Catholic descendants of the House of Stuart, to rest on the Protestant House of Hanover in

Germany. Unless Mary or her sister Anne had a child, England's sovereignty would thus follow a French, Welsh, Scottish and Dutch dynasty with a German one. William's usurpation became sanitized as the 'Glorious Revolution', and set the seal on a turbulent half century since Cromwell's rebellion. A mildly representative Parliament had moved closer to the heart of a monarchical constitution.

The Nine Years War

A restless Louis was now at odds with virtually all the major nations of Europe. After the Franco-Dutch War, a defensive league was formed against him, with Spain in improbable coalition with the Netherlands, England and the Holy Roman Empire. This resulted in another war, the Nine Years War, which started in 1688 with Louis's armies pushing through the Netherlands into the Rhine basin, and into Savoy and Catalonia. They were also active in Canada, the West Indies and India, allowing historians to dub the conflict 'the first world war'. France's army was impressive, but without an overarching strategy, Louis was reduced to devastating towns and territory piecemeal and putting the university city of Heidelberg to the torch.

William was supposedly head of the alliance against Louis, but was opposed by Parliament in seeking English troops for service on the continent. It changed its mind only when in 1690 Louis dispatched an army to Ireland under the exiled James II, hoping Catholics would rally to the flag of rebellion. William defeated James at the Battle of the Boyne, north of Dublin, bringing 'King Billy' and the colour orange to grace, or curse, later Irish civil wars.

By 1697 European exhaustion at Louis's desultory adventures had set in on all sides, with the Treaty of Ryswick costing him most of his earlier gains. He was forced to withdraw from east of the

Rhine, lose Lorraine and return Luxembourg and Barcelona to the Spanish crown. He also had to acknowledge his enemy William as king of England. Pope Innocent XII sent a plea to the Protestant states to allow freedom of worship for Catholics. With memories of the Thirty Years War still raw in many minds, few were inclined to oblige.

The War of the Spanish Succession

For Louis, Ryswick was a setback, but a grander bone of contention loomed over the dynastic horizon. Years of intermarriage meant that French Bourbon and Austrian Habsburg blood flowed through most of the royal houses of Europe. The marital diplomacy pursued by Maximilian I, intended to bring familial concord to Europe's incessant conflicts, led to the opposite, a matrix of competing claims whenever a crown was vacant. Hardly a battle was fought that did not have first or second cousins on both sides. Louis said, 'If I must fight, I would rather fight my enemies than my grandchildren.' It was not easy to distinguish them.

Soon at issue was the succession to Spain's invalid king, Charles II, victim of generations of obsessive Habsburg inbreeding. Half of thirty-four Spanish Habsburg children died before they were ten. Charles was mentally disturbed, impotent and with an enlarged tongue that rendered his speech incoherent. Imprisoned in the Escorial, he lived under the control of a secretive cardinal. In 1697 as he approached death, his empire was disputed by three Habsburg minors. They were the twelve-year-old Charles, son of the current Holy Roman Emperor Leopold I; the fourteen-year-old grandson of Louis XIV, the Duke of Anjou; and a compromise candidate, the five-year-old Habsburg, Joseph Ferdinand of Bavaria.

The parties initially agreed on the Bavarian child, since Bavaria was an old ally of France and thus an Austrian–Spanish Habsburg empire was less likely to emerge and threaten Paris. The deal sustained what was a three-way balance of power in western Europe. But a year later the boy died and the deal was off. No new compromise candidate emerged and, despite frantic efforts on all sides, the parties resorted to force of arms.

The emperor Leopold was determined to win Spain for his son, and thus restore Charles V's united Habsburg empire. To what he saw as dangerous encirclement, Louis was adamantly opposed. In November 1700, Charles of Spain died and his will granted his throne to Louis's Duke of Anjou. An overjoyed Louis could thus envisage a French empire stretching from the Ardennes to the Straits of Gibraltar and the Americas. He recognized his grandson as Philip V of Spain and, for good measure, heir to his own French throne. He declared, 'Henceforth there are no Pyrenees.'

This was too much for the allies of Austria's Leopold. In March 1701 the Austrians, Dutch and English met in The Hague to form an alliance against Louis, despite Leopold's ambitions being hardly less grandiose than those of the French. In England, William III delegated negotiations to his commander and former ally, John Churchill, now Earl (later Duke) of Marlborough. Churchill was put in charge of the allied armies, and instructed that, 'in conjunction with the Emperor and the States General [the Netherlands], for the Preservation of the Liberties of Europe, the Property and Peace of England, and for reducing the Exorbitant Power of France', the allies would support the Holy Roman Emperor in his claim to the throne of Spain on behalf of his son.

The War of the Spanish Succession was a rerun of most previous wars. Louis returned to the familiar starting line of Flanders. Against him, the allies were hamstrung by disunity. Austria's constant and primary concern was with its eastern border with the Ottomans, while England's Marlborough lacked the support of anti-interventionist Tories in Parliament, some of whom still harboured Jacobite sympathies with James II's French patron.

Louis was in his sixties and isolated in Versailles. With Colbert dead, he lacked wise counsellors to challenge his supposedly divine decisions. War between France and Austria's allies was formally declared in 1702, and saw Louis's army advancing up the Rhine towards Austria. The French hoped to join their Bavarian allies on the upper Danube and make a joint Franco-Bavarian assault on Leopold's Vienna. It was a brazen aggression against the capital of Europe's greatest power.

The 1704 campaigning season opened with the arrival of Marlborough on the Rhine with a small army of some 20,000 British soldiers. He joined a larger allied army and staged what became a famous forced march of 250 miles in five weeks. He made a rendezvous with the other allied commander, Prince Eugene of Savoy, recent victor over the Ottomans in Hungary at the Battle of Zenta. With an army now grown to 52,000, Marlborough and Eugene met the French at the village of Blenheim in Bavaria, securing a crushing victory and forcing the French to retreat. Marlborough returned to an England ecstatic with war fever. Queen Anne made him a duke and awarded him the unique right to a 'palace', a term usually reserved for royals and bishops. It was designed in the baroque style by Vanbrugh on crown land at Woodstock. As Blenheim Palace, it stands to this day.

Louis did not admit defeat, and the war degenerated into a series of battles, mostly in the Low Countries during successive summers. Marlborough won a clear victory at Ramillies in 1706. Further French defeats followed at Oudenaarde and Lille in 1708. Louis was now driven from the Netherlands, and the Savoyards and Austrians forced him out of northern Italy. England, however, grew tired of the war and, in 1707, realized Queen Anne's passion, the formal union with Scotland in a new 'Great Britain'. Henceforth English mostly becomes 'British'.

The Treaty of Utrecht

The chief obstacle to peace was Louis's refusal to concede the Spanish throne, and hostilities took on the relentless character of the Hundred Years War. In 1709, a set-piece battle at Malplaquet on the Belgian border saw two armies with a combined strength of 190,000 fight each other to a bloody but indecisive finish. Though Marlborough drove the French to retreat and accounted it a victory, allied losses of 25,000 dead and wounded were double those of the French. A French general remarked to Louis, 'If it please God to give your majesty's enemies another such victory, they are ruined.' Louis could only wail, 'Has God forgotten what I have done for him?'

From 1710 Louis was eager for peace, and it was the allies who could not agree. The maritime states were content just to have France evicted from the Netherlands, which had now been achieved. Leopold wanted nothing short of the Spanish throne. In England an election saw the anti-war Tories win a majority, caused in part by revulsion at the bloodletting of Malplaquet. The argument staggered on until negotiations between the Tory Earl of Oxford and the French culminated in the 1713 Treaty of Utrecht.

The war ended with the armies of all parties depleted. Under the treaty, the new Holy Roman Emperor, Charles VI of Austria, lost his claim to the Spanish throne, which was a victory for Louis and his candidate, Philip V. On the other hand Louis had to concede the formal separation of the French throne from that of Spain, along with France's withdrawal yet again from the Rhine. Austria was compensated with Spain's former territories in Italy and the Spanish Netherlands (roughly western Belgium and Luxembourg).

Utrecht's principal achievement was thus to restate a balance of power between the old foes, Bourbon France and Habsburg Austria. Despite the roles of Marlborough and Oxford in the outcome, Britain had no continental territory at stake. Its interest lay overseas, where it won Gibraltar, Minorca and Newfoundland, as well as a thirty-year monopoly on trading African slaves with the Spanish colonies, a trade that had become hugely lucrative. With each redrawn boundary, each new shift in sovereignty or marital alliance, the kaleidoscope of Europe grew ever more complex. Like Westphalia, Utrecht was not so much a peace treaty as a storing up of trouble for another war.

Britain's Hanoverian dawn

Utrecht coincided with a seemingly trouble-free shift of power in the new Great Britain. In 1714, as the Stuart Queen Anne lay dying, a group of Tories staged a half-hearted bid to restore the Stuart succession through James II's son, known as the Old Pretender, in Paris. But the law was clear and Parliament upheld it. The succession to the British throne lay with the fifty-four-year-old German, George of Hanover. When he arrived for his coronation, he spoke little English. He had already incarcerated his wife in a castle as punishment for infidelity and brought with him two mistresses, fat and thin, known as the Elephant and the Maypole. He played cards with each on alternate nights. His major hobbies were military activity and hunting, and chief gift to his new nation was the composer Handel.

A more significant blessing emerged with time. George cared little for government or politics. He said he preferred Hanover, where his subjects did what they were told. He tried to chair cabinet meetings in French but soon gave up, and left them to the Whig Sir Robert Walpole, First Lord of the Treasury from 1715. This genial Norfolk landowner was the first Englishman to be titled 'prime minister'. British monarchical authority thus decayed, not through revolution but through lack of interest. Party government, the key to properly accountable democracy, was born of a power vacuum. There now began a long 'Whig supremacy', almost continuous, from 1714 to 1760, initially dominated by Walpole. The liberties for which Britons had fought in the seventeenth century were entrenched not by further petitions, rights and constitutional statutes but by custom and practice.

In 1715, a year after George was crowned, Louis XIV lay dying. Aged seventy-six and tormented by the misery he felt he had inflicted on his country, he advised his bemused great-grandson and heir, the five-year-old Louis XV, 'Above all, remain at peace with your neighbours. I loved war too much. Do not follow me in that, or in overspending.' Repentance was too late. At the king's funeral, the bishop pronounced the pointed banality, *Mes frères, Dieu seul est grand*, My brothers, God alone is great.

Charles of Sweden

Utrecht fixed west Europe's borders for half a century, but east Europe enjoyed no such stability. States had been marked out by the rough imposition of kingship over tribes, stretching from the Baltic and Estonia down through Poland to the Balkans, Hungary and Ukraine. To their east lay Russia, to the south, the Turks. To the north, Sweden had seen the eccentric, dazzling reign of Queen Christina (1632–54), daughter of the hero of the Thirty Years War, Gustavus Adolphus. A lesbian intellectual and supporter of the arts and sciences, she made Stockholm a Protestant Athens of the North. Then, in 1654, at the age of twenty-eight, she abruptly abdicated after an argument with her courtiers over her refusal to marry. Dressed as a man, she left for Rome, where she set up home as a Catholic with a lavish personal court. Her celebrity was much enhanced by a papal indictment calling her 'a queen without a realm, a Catholic without faith and a woman without shame'.

Christina's reign was followed by monarchs as meteoric as they were catastrophic. Charles X (1654–60) was tactless and lacking in judgement, but had a genius for battle. He overran Denmark, Poland and Estonia, securing the enmity of all his neighbouring powers. His ambitions were capped by his grandson, Charles XII (1697–1718). In 1700 he confronted a Russian army four times the size of his own at the Battle of Narva in Estonia, crushing it utterly. He killed 10,000 Russians for the loss of just 660 Swedes. Europe saw the emergence of a new power to its north.

Charles was determined to topple the tsar of Russia no less, hoping for the assistance of a revolt by the Cossacks, a militarized local gentry, that failed to materialize. He now came face to face with Peter the Great (1689–1725), one of those occasional Russian leaders with a charisma and ability to match the scale of their country. In 1707 Charles declined Peter's offer to grant him sovereignty over Poland, but by the winter of 1708 his army was suffering severe losses in the worst weather in living memory. The following summer the Swedish army, depleted to half its original size, reached the Russian fortress of Poltava in Ukraine, where Peter annihilated it. Charles fled for his life to Turkey. What might have been a Swedish empire was now divided between Russia and Prussia. Peter realized the strategic significance of the Baltic, announcing that the defeat of Sweden 'laid the final stone in the foundations of St Petersburg'.

Peter the Great

As Sweden subsided, Russia rose. Peter had inherited a country that was still in the Middle Ages. It was ruled by the tsar through regional barons or boyars, under whom Cossacks owned and farmed much of the land. Beneath them was a population of some twenty million serfs. Education was virtually non-existent and women lived in seclusion. The tsar ruled as an autocrat, with no parliament or civil rights. Men wore long beards and dressed traditionally in coats down to the ground.

Peter, like Vladimir in the tenth and eleventh centuries and Ivan in the sixteenth, was eager to bring his country into what he saw as the European mainstream. In 1697, before the Swedish war, he had set out on a year-long 'grand embassy', ostensibly incognito, to Amsterdam, Dresden, Vienna, London and Oxford. He studied everything from military strategy to city planning and art history. On his return, he imitated Constantine and planned a new capital at St Petersburg. It was designed by Swiss and French architects in the classical style, built on the labour, and reputedly the corpses, of Russian peasants and Swedish prisoners-of-war. It was formally founded in 1703 and its white palaces, gilded churches, squares and canals made it one of the handsomest cities in Europe. It remains so to this day.

Peter established a modern civil service, a reformed Orthodox church, a school system and a Russian navy. He abolished the boyars' council or duma, and replaced it with a twelve-man senate and a new aristocracy, based on service to the state. Peter removed eight letters from the Russian alphabet, and ordered males to shave and wear shorter western-style jackets. For all that, Peter remained Russian to the core. He was brash, high-living, persistently drunk and unable to brook opposition or contradiction, a Sun King of the steppe. He could adapt his country to western innovation, but he was immune to political reform. He opened Russia's door on Europe's emerging intellectual enlightenment, but never stepped through it.

In foreign policy was there a sort of symmetry between Peter's Russia and Walpole's Britain. Both sat on the continent's geographical extremities, and both viewed its conflicts with some detachment.

But there the similarity ended. Britain's outlook was maritime, global and commercial. It behaved as if it was supreme over every ship at sea. Russia's ambitions, on the other hand, were land-based, with half its gaze towards the vast territories of Asia and the riches of the Orient. Between these two pillars of what was to become a global imperialism lay a new Europe.

13

From Reason to Rebellion
1715–1789

Wars of the Polish and Austrian succession

Like most of Europe's grand treaties – often hopefully called 'peaces' – Utrecht initially ushered in a period of relative calm. Britain settled into Hanoverian lethargy and what became called 'Walpole's peace'. France under the child king, Louis XV, fell to the care of his counsellor, Cardinal Fleury (1726–43), a cerebral diplomat who shared an obsession with Walpole, that the duty of men of affairs was to steer clear of war. He acknowledged Walpole's adage, 'Let sleeping dogs lie.'

For two decades, Europe's dogs mostly slept. Borders opened and travel prospered. Rich northerners travelled south to France and Italy on the Grand Tour. They absorbed taste in the new European baroque and sent home ships filled with paintings and other treasures. In Britain, Lord Burlington's Italianate taste dominated Georgian fashion for a century. The pre-eminence especially of Italian and German culture suggested that European civilization had no need of the stimulus of a nation state, indeed might benefit from its absence. As Bach was completing his B-minor Mass in 1749, the prince-bishops of Würzburg were building their incomparable Residenz, with frescos by Italy's Giovanni Battista Tiepolo.

The Utrecht peace was broken in 1733 by another bout of 'succession-itis'. At issue was who should sit on the Polish throne, which saw France, Spain, Austria and Russia fight each other across much of Europe. It was a miniature rerun of the Spanish succession conflict, pitting Bourbons against Habsburgs, with this time a Habsburg winner. England's Walpole again held emphatically aloof. In 1734 he boasted to Queen Caroline, George II's wife, 'Madam, there are fifty thousand men slain this year in Europe, and not one an Englishman.'

No sooner was Poland's throne settled than a similar conflict followed over that of Austria. This was near intractable. Charles VI of Austria, Holy Roman Emperor and failed claimant to the Spanish crown, lacked a male heir and eagerly hoped that his daughter, Maria Theresa, would succeed him. As this was in defiance of German Salic law, Charles proposed a 'Pragmatic Sanction', setting aside the law. He won the agreement of his various electors and allies, until he died in 1740 and the sanction was activated. Austria, Hungary, Bohemia, Silesia, Croatia and much of northern Italy was now to be ruled by a frail twenty-three-year-old woman. Though they had never objected to an equally youthful Habsburg man, old fears and new opportunities surfaced.

Prussia had emerged from the Thirty Years War as a kingdom in three parts, distinct from Germany and lying to the east of the Elbe. These were East Prussia, based on the Teutonic knights' former colony in Poland, the German province of Pomerania or West Prussia, and the dukedom of Brandenburg with its capital in Berlin. East Prussia still retained serfdom under its Junker nobility and sported the Iron Cross of their founding fathers. To sophisticated Germans, Prussians were a tribe beyond the pale, with a history and fighting tradition alien to the gentle patchwork of autonomous Germany.

In 1713 the Hohenzollern Frederick William of Brandenburg (1713–40), grandson of the Great Elector of the Thirty Years War, had become elector and then king of Prussia. He was cut of classic Teutonic cloth, a stern Calvinist and a meticulous bureaucrat. His civil service manual ran to thirty-five chapters, and his army was the best drilled and best equipped in Europe. But his attitude towards his effete son, also Frederick, was terrifying. The boy was awoken each morning by a cannon, and was given a regiment of children on which to practise military command. To his father's horror, Frederick emerged a homosexual, which the king tried to correct, allegedly, by forcing him to watch the beheading of his best friend.

The boy survived such ordeals to emerge as Frederick II, later 'the Great' (1740–86). He built himself a palace at Potsdam outside Berlin in the manner of Versailles, calling it Sanssouci, Without Care. He founded a new Academy of Arts in Berlin and commanded that French be its language rather than 'barbarous German'. Frederick played music and wrote poetry, corresponding with the French philosopher Voltaire (1694–1778), whom he said had 'the lovableness and maliciousness of a monkey'. Voltaire admired and flattered him – until they fell out when Frederick inherited his father's addiction to war.

Frederick proved to be an authoritarian and a militarist. He viewed his people as 'a troop of stags in the great lord's park, with no other function than to stock and restock the enclosure'. He told Voltaire that 'three-quarters of mankind are made for slavery to the most absurd fanaticism'. He doubled the size of his army until it consumed over eighty per cent of the Prussian budget, built on the Junker tradition of an inherited officer class, with soldiers recruited on a cantonal basis. Frederick remarked that 'friends and relations who fight together do not lightly let each other down'. Soon the French had a saying: 'Prussia is not a nation that has an army, but an army that has a nation.'

As a result, when in 1740 Maria Theresa succeeded to the Habsburg empire bequeathed her by her father, Frederick decided to invade Austria's Silesia, without any pretext. He said, as had Louis XIV, that for every state big or small 'the principle of enlargement is the fundamental law of life' – a political Darwinism that lay at the root of much of Europe's history. The acquisition of Silesia increased the size of Prussia by at least a quarter and deprived Austria of a quarter of its tax revenue. The subsequent war pitted Austrian and Dutch troops and British subsidies against a Prussia allied with France as natural enemy of Austria. It was settled in 1748 by Maria Theresa keeping her Austrian empire, and Frederick holding on to Silesia.

Maria Theresa was to rule Austria for forty years, while her husband, Francis Stephen, became Holy Roman Emperor with her as his empress. They enjoyed a happy marriage with sixteen children, including the unfortunate Marie Antoinette of France. With her dazzling palace at Schönbrunn, Maria Theresa's Vienna was as much an eastern outlier of French taste as was Frederick's Berlin. One of the many tragedies of eighteenth-century Europe was that these two monarchs, of states that might have forged a new continent, should have found themselves in implacable conflict. Frederick found Maria Theresa 'impossible', while to her he was 'that evil man'.

The Enlightenment

By the time of his death in 1715, Louis XIV had seen Paris become the unchallenged cultural capital of Europe. From now until the outbreak of the French Revolution, it flowered not just as a centre of art and fashion but as home to the so-called Age of Enlightenment, roughly spanning the eighteenth century from Louis's death to the French Revolution. Its roots lay in the rationalism of the French philosopher René Descartes (1596–1650) and the father of British liberalism, John Locke (1632–1704), continuing the Renaissance movement away from religion as the dominant force in the realm of ideas. It took inspiration from the scientific revolution associated with the Royal Society in London and the work of

Robert Boyle in chemistry and Isaac Newton in physics. Its creed was a curiosity about the natural and philosophical world, drawing on the methodology supplied by the Scotsman David Hume (1711–76), that of empirical investigation and a sceptical mind.

The Enlightenment reached its climax in 1751 with the start of publication in Paris of the *Encyclopédie* edited by Denis Diderot and Jean le Rond d'Alembert. Diderot dedicated it simply to changing 'the way people think'. The encyclopaedists were not just confronting the Catholic church, as Luther and others had done. They were confronting all conventional knowledge, embracing philosophy, science, economics and politics. Contributors included Voltaire, Rousseau and Montesquieu. The encyclopaedia's initial twenty-eight volumes were Europe's most impressive intellectual enterprise since Plato's Academy. It was as if a wall long erected round the European mind, undermined by the Renaissance and the Reformation, had finally crumbled.

The Enlightenment posed a challenge that was also institutional. Voltaire wrote to Frederick of Prussia that the Catholic church in France was 'the most ridiculous, absurd and bloodthirsty that ever infected the world'. The Jesuits succeeded in having the *Encyclopédie* banned by Rome, and some of the contributors went to jail. But such was the mood in Paris that this proved counter-productive. A campaign began for the Jesuits' suppression, fuelled by a widespread resentment at their privileges and power. It was successful. In 1759 Jesuits were expelled from Portugal, then from France, Austria and even Spain. Eventually, in 1773, the Pope decided he had no option but to suppress the entire order. It had become unpopular even within the church. The cardinals in Rome descended on the Jesuits' headquarters, carted off its art collection and drank its cellars dry. The order's leaders were imprisoned in the Castel Sant'Angelo, for no crime worse than running out of friends. The order was restored in 1814.

One area in which French encyclopaedists deferred to Britain was in political thought. Diderot said that in Britain 'philosophers rise to public affairs and are buried with kings, whereas in France warrants are issued against them'. In 1726, when Voltaire was hounded out of France, he came to London for three years, to study Locke's views on consent, toleration, free speech and education. Britain, he said, had 'succeeded in controlling the power of kings by resisting them'. Voltaire was followed by Montesquieu, who admired Britain's separation of powers. 'England is the freest country in the world,' he said, 'because the sovereign . . . is unable to inflict any imaginable harm on anyone.' The humour and broadmindedness of Samuel Johnson and Edward Gibbon were lauded, as was the satire of Alexander Pope and Jonathan Swift. In Britain critics of power could be cruel without being revolutionary.

Were these liberties exportable? To many of the French *philosophes*, freedom of thought was detachable from political emancipation. So long as the mind was free, who needed the ballot? Voltaire might be mischievous and occasionally exiled for his opinions, but he was a favourite of Louis XV's mistress, Madame de Pompadour, as well as a correspondent of Prussia's Frederick. It was a cerebral and elite concept of political liberty but one that, in France, was soon to degenerate into chaos.

Another of Voltaire's correspondents was Russia's Catherine (1762–96), successor to Peter as 'the Great' and modernizer of a growing empire. Originally named Sophia, Catherine had arrived in Russia from Germany in 1743 as fourteen-year-old wife to the future tsar, Peter III. The prospect must have been terrifying, though a witness described her as having 'a cold, calculating and serious disposition'. She converted at once to Orthodoxy, 'to be Russian in order to be liked by Russians'. Then in 1762 she led a coup against her husband, assisted by a supposed lover, Grigory Potemkin. Her husband's mysterious death, said a contemporary, was evidence 'of God's divine intent in preparing the way for

Catherine to the throne'. Over four hundred people were rewarded for their presumed complicity.

Catherine determined to follow in the reforming steps of Peter the Great. She considered herself in the Enlightenment tradition, commissioning reports on the efficiency of her country and its government. She reformed the judiciary and education and continued to beautify St Petersburg. But like Peter, she understood the culture in which she was working. Catherine ordained that 'the sovereign is absolute . . . the purpose of autocracy being not to deprive people of their natural freedom but to guide their actions so as to attain the maximum good'. Serfs and peasants who disobeyed their masters 'shall be arrested and punished'. Unlawful petitions should be answered by the whip and penal servitude in Siberia.

Russia was ruled by Catherine through the agency of her consort and, when their ardour cooled, her friend and ally, Potemkin. Like Frederick, she dabbled in the Enlightenment, but as if it were an intellectual diversion, a French fashion. The admiration of Voltaire and Montesquieu for British political ideas was rooted in their practical outcome, in a genuine degree of popular liberty. They were ideas that changed society. To Frederick's Prussia and Catherine's Russia such ideas had no appeal.

The Seven Years War

By the 1750s Europe was bursting with too many egos for its own stability. In 1756, eight years after the War of the Austrian Succession, Frederick of Prussia made another unprovoked invasion, this time of the adjacent territory of Saxony, to add to Silesia. This antagonized his two most powerful neighbours, Austria and Russia. Like the biblical dog returning to its vomit, the continental powers again lined up for battle. With territory rather than succession an issue, France this time allied itself with Russia, Austria and Spain to confront the upstart Prussia. Britain's new leader, William Pitt (1756–61 and 1766–8) sided with Prussia, though only to the extent of paying subsidies to its army. His purpose, like Walpole's, was opportunistic, to use a European war to gain territory overseas. He was later to boast that his strategy was 'to win Canada on the banks of the Elbe'.

Frederick, though outgunned, outnumbered and often defeated, kept his army in the field, determined to hold on to Saxony. In 1757 he won a notable victory over Austria and France at the Battle of Rossbach, but despite such successes his resources were exhausted. Prussia's economy was devastated, reverting almost to Thirty Years War conditions. As much as a third of its population was estimated to have perished through starvation. Frederick had overreached himself, but he had marked his country as a player on the European stage.

Pitt sent troops to the continent, notably to protect Hanover, which led to a great victory at Minden in 1759, but his focus was on the conquest of France's colonies and the defeat of its fleet. In America in 1758 the French were driven from the Ohio valley, where they had threatened Britain's New England colonies from the rear. A year later, General Wolfe seized the French fortress of Quebec, a key defeat for the French (though not their language) in North America. Like Nelson at Trafalgar, Wolfe earned eternal glory by falling in the heat of battle. He died with Gray's *Elegy Written in a Country Churchyard* fresh on his lips.

In India, Robert Clive had similar success against the French through the agency of the private East India Company, and through tactical alliances with local rulers or 'princely states'. By 1759, the annus mirabilis of the burgeoning British empire, Bombay, Madras and Calcutta were all gathered into British hands. After the Americas, India was the most splendid of Europe's overseas conquests, for almost two centuries regarded as the jewel in the British crown.

These gains were recognized in the 1763 Treaty of Paris. In Europe the war was declared a draw. Saxony retained its independence but Austria did not regain Silesia. The treaty was more significant overseas. It distributed the new lands of the Americas between the European powers. Spain regained Cuba but gave Florida to Britain. France lost everything east of the Mississippi, but regained sugar-rich Martinique and Guadeloupe. British colonies and trading posts sprouted everywhere, served by its untrammelled navy. The imperialist Victorian historian John Robert Seeley remarked that Britain seemed 'to have conquered and peopled half the world in a fit of absence of mind'.

America's War of Independence

Pride came before a fall. An empire acquired almost incidentally would soon shrink through stupidity. In 1760 Britain's long-standing and little-loved George II, who survived his son, was succeeded by his grandson, the twenty-two-year-old George III (1760–1820). An intelligent and cultured young man, he was keen to assert his Englishness, yet he promptly behaved like a German princeling. He dismissed the experienced Pitt and appointed a cabinet that he would chair with his old tutor, the Earl of Bute, as prime minister. Together they sustained Tory support in Parliament through bribery and patronage. To their critics, George and Bute were almost a throwback to the Stuarts.

The young king's first need was to meet the costs of Pitt's overseas expansion, which had doubled the national debt and was consuming half the state's revenue in interest. In 1765 the government imposed a stamp tax on the American colonies, whose donation to the British exchequer was a derisory £1,400 a year. For this, the king pointed out, Britain defended them against both the French and the native Americans. When the colonists' representative in London, Benjamin Franklin, objected, George replaced the tax with one on tea. In 1773 a band of smugglers tossed tea into Boston harbour, and George raged at what he saw as a personal insult.

The king now achieved the near unthinkable. He sparked a successful uprising against Europe's most stable and admired proto-democracy. The thirteen British colonies in America already enjoyed virtual autonomy. They ignored treaties forged with the natives and played fast and loose with their debts. The economy of the southern colonies relied on slavery. Their one real complaint was over trade restrictions, yet these were intended to protect business in America as well as in the mother country.

From 1773 onwards, every move of George's government in London, now under the ineffectual Lord North, incited rebellion. While many colonists remained loyal, support for the dissidents was strong in Parliament, including from Pitt (now in opposition) and others such as Charles Fox and Edmund Burke. George's 'coercive acts' of 1774 suspended local assemblies in America and imposed trade sanctions. These led to a congress that year in Philadelphia, which drew up a 'declaration of rights' and a plea to end trade sanctions. What was a dispute essentially over taxes and trade could have been ended round a Whitehall table. As it was, decisions required weeks to pass the 4,000 miles across the Atlantic. By the time of their implementation, they were usually the wrong ones.

Fighting broke out in 1775. The cabinet told the governor of Massachusetts to deal harshly with any rebels. In July 1776, an exasperated American congress reassembled in Philadelphia and wrote a Declaration of Independence. This told the British king briskly that he was 'unfit to be ruler of a free people'. In the high-flown rhetoric of Locke and the Enlightenment, its author, Thomas Jefferson, wrote of 'self-evident truths' and 'inalienable rights'. These were partial, being inapplicable to women, 'Indians' or slaves. Nor were the motives of the rebels as noble as their later champions like to claim. Many rebels were speculators in western land seizures, land which the British, in 1763, had firmly allotted to native American tribes. Some were also alarmed at the growth of British anti-slavery pressure. They were more than happy to see their actions garlanded with Enlightenment texts on the equality of man and the pursuit of happiness.

Even then, the uprising might have been suppressed had it not been for domestic and foreign support for the rebels. There was little real determination in Britain to suppress the Americans. Burke savaged the king for using Hanoverian mercenaries, 'the hireling sword of German boors and vassals . . . against English flesh and blood'. France and Spain were still smarting from Britain's gains at the Treaty of Paris, and were happy to assist any embarrassment of Britain. The arrival of a large French force off the American coast in 1778 brought the rebels help, culminating in 1781 in their victory at Yorktown in Virginia. The American commander was a former British soldier, George Washington. He affirmed that 'we do not wish to be the only people who may taste the sweets of an equal and good government'. He hoped that the example of America would spread and that, soon, 'all Europe shall be freed from commotions, tumults and alarms'.

The defeat of Britain delighted much of Europe, and left George shattered. Largely by own actions, he had lost a much-prized British possession. Yet such was the support for the colonists that liberal opinion was not too sorry. Horace Walpole, Robert's son, predicted that 'the next Augustan age will dawn on the other side of the Atlantic'. In 1785, when America's first ambassador arrived in

London, even George greeted him amiably as offering 'the friend-ship of the United States as an independent power'.

After much dithering, the king in 1783 asked Pitt's son, William Pitt the Younger, to take over as prime minister. He was just twenty-four and the archetypal 'new man' of an outward-looking Britain. His bible was Adam Smith's *Wealth of Nations* (1776), a work that gave a theoretical framework to Britain's policies of free mar-kets and regulated trade. Pitt restored the government's composure and was to steer his country through the storms already gathering across the English Channel. England might have been wounded by defeat in America, but the nation that secured that defeat, France, was about to suffer grievously for doing so.

Louis XVI and France on the brink

The American War of Independence was a first example of the Enlightenment principles of equality and liberty in action. A major European power had been shown vulnerable to successful rebel-lion. Liberals and revolutionaries alike could look across the Atlantic and see a European people in a relationship to their state that was contractual, not subservient. It was the practical enact-ment of Rousseau's widely read *Social Contract* of 1762.

The American revolution could not be ignored. Some European rulers, such as Frederick and Catherine, reacted in the only way they knew, by the further suppression of dissent. France, however, saw itself as more progressive, the fountainhead of the new think-ing. It had aided the rebels and its general, Lafayette, had lent them his military leadership. Paris was thus seething with debate. On assuming the French throne, Louis XVI (1774–91) proved a weak monarch but with a strong-minded Austrian wife, Marie Antoi-nette. French political institutions were not fashioned to handle change. In 1780 Louis made partial reforms, liberalizing censorship and abolishing judicial torture and serfdom. But he also had to pay the bills for Lafayette's American adventure.

France in the 1780s was drifting towards bankruptcy. Louis's Swiss comptroller, Jacques Necker, demanded a universal land tax to balance the books. The country was suffering from harvest failure and famine, and the tax was met with immediate riots. As a result Louis backed down, with one region after another sliding towards anarchy. The nobility looked to the security of their châteaux. Officers doubted the loyalty of their soldiers. Visitors from Britain reported food shortages, extreme poverty and talk of impending insurrection.

14

The French Revolution
1789–1804

Rebellion erupts

France at the start of 1789 faced what the best-known student of its politics, Alexis de Tocqueville, called 'the most dangerous moment for a bad government . . . when it sets about reform'. Alarmed by incessant riots, Louis XVI summoned his three somnolent 'estates' or assemblies, of the nobility, the clergy and a Third Estate composed of 612 ordinary citizens, mostly merchants and professionals. He brought them to Versailles, but the Third Estate's rumoured radicalism unnerved him, and his soldiers refused it admission. Its members retired to an indoor tennis court near the palace, where they declared themselves a National Assembly. They swore an oath that they would stay in session until a new French constitution was written.

The Tennis Court Oath of 20 June 1789 precipitated change, but not revolution. It was recorded by the artist Jacques-Louis David, with the participants shouting and waving while a breeze of freedom billows through curtained windows. Under the leadership of Honoré Mirabeau, a disgraced nobleman later known to be in the king's pay, it set to work on a new constitution. Back in the streets of Paris the atmosphere was feverish. In July, a mob stormed the city's old Bastille fortress to obtain weapons, releasing not the expected hundreds of political prisoners but seven bemused convicts. Though of small tactical significance, the fall of the Bastille was symbolic. The monarchy could not defend even its castles against the mob.

Louis summoned an army 17,000-strong to Paris, but he was advised not to rely on its obedience or that of its officers. The advice spelled Louis's doom. One witness, Antoine Rivarol, wrote that 'the defection of the army is not one of the causes of the revolution, it is the revolution'. A Paris commune was now formed and, by the end of July, there were insurrections in cities across the country. Much of the French nobility gathered up its treasures and fled abroad, mostly to England. The old regime was collapsing.

In August the assembly published a Declaration of the Rights of Man and the Citizen, drawing its language from Rousseau's *Social Contract* and America's Declaration of Independence. It was drafted by the hero of American independence, Lafayette, working with Mirabeau and Thomas Jefferson, then American ambassador in Paris. The document repeated references to 'inalienable rights', including liberty, property, security and protection from oppression. It enshrined freedom of association, speech and religion, and the right to free and open trial. *Liberté, égalité, fraternité* were the watchwords of the hour. None was to be much in evidence in the ensuing months.

The declaration went on to describe the nature of a new state. 'The principle of any sovereignty resides essentially in the Nation. No body, no individual can exert authority which does not emanate expressly from it.' Government required the voting participation of 'active citizens', not what it regarded as passive ones – thus excluding women, servants and non-taxpayers. A series of decrees, some 11,000 in all, upheaved the French establishment. Nobility, titles, privileges and patronage were abolished. The church was made subordinate to the state, and the clergy became civil servants. Protestants were given equal rights to Catholics. The national debt was relieved by seizing and selling the property of the church, owner of ten per cent of productive land. State appointments were to be on merit.

The administrative districts of France's Ancien Régime were overturned, and the country divided into eighty-three roughly equal *départements*. The names of provinces were erased and replaced by natural features – mountains, rivers and compass points – such as Var, Alpes-Maritimes and Seine-et-Marne. It was a deliberate stripping of local identity, imitated in Orwell's *1984* and Britain's 1972 regional government reform. The tricolour became the national flag. New measurements were to be based on the metre, defined as one ten-millionth of the distance from the North Pole to the Equator. A National Gendarmerie and a National Guard were formed, the latter led by Lafayette. A 'humane' guillotine replaced messier forms of execution. Existing dates were abolished, with a fierce argument over when the new age of 'liberty' was to begin (eventually set at 1792).

The Revolution: Europe's reaction

News of these events mesmerized Europe. France was the continent's most populous nation and its most fashionable and significant. What happened in France mattered. Thus while conservatives were shocked, radicals were exhilarated, not least in Britain. The young Wordsworth wrote, 'Bliss was it in that dawn to be alive, / But to be young was very Heaven.' In a rare misjudgement, Pitt greeted the news from Paris as presaging fifteen years of peace. Only the judicious Edmund Burke sounded a note of caution. He remarked in his *Reflections on the Revolution in France*, published as early as 1790, that it had 'subverted monarchy but not recovered freedom'. Looking to the history of ancient Rome, he predicted that sooner or later 'some popular general will establish military dictatorship in place of anarchy'.

There were early imitative risings across Europe, in the Dutch republic, the Austrian Netherlands and Geneva. In Dublin an independence movement was formed by Wolfe Tone, who came to Paris to seek military support from the revolutionaries. In Poland-Lithuania, King Stanisław Augustus introduced a liberal constitution based on elections and described even by Burke as 'probably the most pure public good which ever has been conferred on mankind'. Back in Paris, Louis was forced to abandon his base at Versailles and move to the Tuileries in Paris, where he became a virtual prisoner. For the next few months, he appeased the Revolution. He signed its edicts and, in the summer of 1790, tactfully joined the anniversary celebration of 'Bastille Day'. He then unwisely sent a plea to Austria for rescue.

Relations between monarch and assembly swiftly deteriorated. In June 1791 Louis sensed the inevitable and tried to escape, disguised as a valet. He was recognized, captured and returned to Paris, his duties summarily suspended. He now had to sign a new constitution, ending a throne that dated back to Clovis and Pepin. Power would lie with a new Legislative Assembly of 745 deputies, which first met in October 1791. Under the control of the moderate Girondin party, many hoped that this marked the end of the Revolution, with Louis remaining as a constitutional head of state, British style.

France was handicapped by lacking any tradition of evolutionary reform or customary assembly in which political conflict could be channelled by the courtesies of debate. Over the course of 1792, the moderate Girondins were outvoted by radical Jacobins, led by a fastidious and fanatical Maximilien Robespierre. Seated in the upper tiers of the assembly, the Jacobins and their allies became known as the Montagnards, mountain-dwellers, the moderates below becoming La Plaine or Le Marais, the plain or the marsh. The loyalties of the army and Lafayette's National Guard wavered, and by the summer Paris was at the mercy of local gangs of sans-culottes, named for wearing trousers rather than aristocratic knee-breeches. They smashed their way into the Tuileries, harangued the king and made him drink their health wearing a red Phrygian cap of revolution.

Monarchy across Europe was now aroused. Prussia and Austria had in 1791 published the Declaration of Pillnitz, demanding 'the restoration of monarchical government in accordance with the rights of sovereigns'. They assembled a coalition to rescue Louis, composed of Austria, Prussia and the Dutch, supported as so often by British money. In September 1792 a Prussian army under the Duke of Brunswick came to Louis's aid, advancing across Champagne towards Paris with the express purpose of restoring the monarchy.

In 1793 the assembly reacted by raising three armies totalling 300,000 troops, Europe's first conscripted *levée en masse*. The northern army confronted Brunswick at the Battle of Valmy, where it was luckily reinforced by veterans of the royal artillery. One cannonade after another crashed into the Prussian ranks, putting them to flight and leading to a stunning victory for the Revolution. The supposedly best-trained soldiers in Europe had been vanquished. An exhilarated Paris assembly declared it would 'intervene in any country where people desire to recover their freedom'. Valmy unquestionably saved the Revolution, and terrified Europe's established regimes.

The cry of revolt was again taken up across the continent, in Basel, Frankfurt, Brussels and Savoy. Catherine of Russia was shocked by Stanisław Augustus's 'revolutionary' reforms in Poland-Lithuania, so admired by Burke. Despite his being among her former lovers, she invaded his country and suppressed its constitution. She then invited the rulers of adjacent Austria and Prussia to share the spoils of her action with a tripartite partition of Poland. Russia took Lithuania, Austria took Kraków and Prussia took Warsaw. By 1795 Poland was no more. Catherine's action ranked with Frederick the Great's seizure of Silesia as unprovoked aggrandizement. Not for the first time – or last – Poland paid the price for disobliging its more powerful and unscrupulous neighbours.

The Revolution: from terror to collapse

Over the course of 1792 the assembly found it could unite against an outside enemy but only divide against itself. It fragmented. The Paris commune formed a 'secret committee' under Georges Danton and Camille Desmoulins. Lafayette was disowned and a tribunal set up to try traitors. The assembly was replaced by a more radical 'National Convention', which declared the king dismissed and a republic established. It then debated Louis's execution, with Robespierre, Danton and the radical journalist Jean-Paul Marat in full cry for the motion. When Robespierre was reminded of his earlier decision to abolish the death penalty, he replied, 'Louis must die in order that France may live.' In January 1793 the king went to the guillotine, his last words to the crowd drowned out by a drum roll.

The Revolution began to splinter. The National Convention was supplemented by a 'committee of public safety'. The remaining Girondin moderates were arrested by a mob, and twenty-one of them marched to the guillotine. The committee, under Robespierre, now formally instigated 'the Terror', a specific policy, not a later description of anarchy. Robespierre said, 'The foundations of popular government in a revolution are virtue and terror; terror without virtue is disastrous; virtue without terror is powerless. The Government of the Revolution is the despotism of liberty over tyranny.' The phraseology became the thinking of dictators down the ages.

The Terror was aimed partly at curbing chaos in Paris and partly at a counter-revolution in the Vendée region. This was suppressed with savage brutality and up to 400,000 deaths. The general in charge boasted that he had 'crushed children under the hooves of horses, and massacred women so they breed no more brigands . . . We take no prisoners as it would be necessary to feed them with the bread of Liberty.' In Paris, meetings of the committee of public safety took place to a background chorus of the mob, either in the street outside or camped in the Hôtel de Ville, ready to lynch anyone to whom it took a dislike. At one point it 'liberated' a prison and a convent, only to slaughter or rape the inmates in an orgy of violence. In October 1793, nine months after her husband's execution, Marie Antoinette was tried and guillotined. Her infant son, briefly Louis XVII, was sent to die of disease with proletarian foster parents.

By the start of 1794, the Revolution was consuming its own. Danton and his associates were executed for 'an excess of moderation'. Marat had been murdered by Charlotte Corday, a Girondin sympathizer, while writing an article in his bath. David depicted the corpse, pen in hand, a painting that became an icon of the revolution. As for Robespierre, he was gradually losing his mind. He declared Notre-Dame a 'Temple of Reason' and initiated 'a cult of the Supreme Being', celebrated with a festival in the Tuileries garden glorifying the republic. Robespierre with torch aloft announced the death of Christianity and led a procession of thousands dancing with flowers. It was a forerunner of an Olympics opening ceremony.

Three weeks later, Paris was enveloped in anarchy. Mobs roamed the streets fighting each other. Meetings were unattended, their members fearing daily executions. Soldiers had no one to obey. Then Robespierre made a two-hour speech to the convention, which drove even his supporters to jeer at him. He was arrested, shot himself in the jaw and was guillotined screaming with pain. A hundred associates died with him.

A Paris awash in fear and blood collapsed from sheer exhaustion. In three years the convention had sent 2,600 victims to the guillotine. The prisons were full and the streets lawless. By the end of 1794 a craving for sane leadership was gaining the upper hand, and the National Guard asserted control. Sans-culotte leaders were arrested. Tribunals and committees of public safety were dissolved. The Girondins, such as survived, were reinstated in power and general amnesties proclaimed. A new constitution created a bicameral assembly modelled on the British Parliament and led by a five-member cabinet, the Directory.

Further uprisings during 1795, by both radicals and royalists, were suppressed. At one point, royalists took revenge on revolutionaries in what was called the White Terror. A royalist uprising in Paris in October that year was defeated by a small detachment of soldiers under the command of a diminutive twenty-five-year-old officer from Corsica, Napoleon Bonaparte. He fired cannon into the enemy's ranks, dispersing them he said 'with a whiff of grapeshot'. Thomas Carlyle concluded, 'A whiff of grapeshot . . . and the thing we specifically call French Revolution is blown into space.' The self-assurance of the officer so impressed the Directory that it appointed him head of the army of the interior.

Bonaparte rose swiftly to the challenge. He took control of the revolutionary forces, and married his aristocratic mistress, Joséphine de Beauharnais, six years his senior. Alongside Bonaparte, the Directory brought back from exile a former bishop, Charles-Maurice Talleyrand, a shrewd, energetic figure with remarkable powers of persuasion. Talleyrand had been present at the Tennis Court Oath and had helped draft the Declaration of the Rights of Man. He had avoided successive purges by living and serving abroad. Talleyrand, a towering figure in French history, was soon France's foreign minister.

The rise of Bonaparte

The new, moderate, Directory now had to establish its credibility. It had to restore order in Paris and across the country. It had to deal with the two powers with which it was still officially at war,

Austria and Britain. And it had to cope with the clearly burgeoning ambitions of its military commander, Napoleon Bonaparte. In 1796 he was removed from the scene 'to carry the flame of revolution' to Italy, then seething with rebellion against Austria. In a series of battles, Napoleon's mastery of fieldcraft defeated every army sent against him. He conquered northern Italy, replacing its dukedoms with new republics and occupying Venice in May 1797. Without bothering to consult Paris, he negotiated the Treaty of Campo Formio, giving Venice to Austria in return for France taking Lombardy and Flanders. Overnight, an employee of the French state had redrawn the map of Europe and made France the master of most of Italy, an achievement that had defied his predecessors.

The capture of Venice after a millennium of continuous independence was sensational. This city state, its merchants once supreme over the Mediterranean, had declined over the eighteenth century into what its biographer Jan Morris called 'a paradigm of degradation . . . besotted with hedonism'. Its aristocracy lived out a gilded existence in their canal-side palaces, evolving from the vitality depicted by Carpaccio in the sixteenth century into the sinister licentiousness depicted by the artist Pietro Longhi in the eighteenth. Casanova, icon of its jaded reputation, died in 1798. When Napoleon arrived the city was said to boast 136 casinos and 852 hairdressers.

Napoleon was merciless, declaring himself the 'Attila of Venice'. The constitution was overturned. The great barge was broken up. Thousands of art treasures were looted and sent to Paris's Louvre. These included the horses of St Mark's and Veronese's masterpiece, *The Wedding Feast at Cana*, which was cut in pieces and has never been returned. Napoleon ended the curfew in the Jewish ghetto, and converted one side of St Mark's Square into a vice-regal palace. The best that can be said of his 'sack of Venice' is that, by rendering the city insignificant, he probably saved it from rebuilding.

In the winter of 1797 Napoleon set himself up with his new wife in what amounted to a court at Monte Bello outside Milan. Any pretence that he was a servant of the Revolution was gone. He posed as neither a Jacobin nor a royalist, but as a pragmatic egocentric. In 1798 he sent to Paris the winnings of his Italian campaign: a parade of twenty-nine floats loaded with the loot of Italy's churches, museums and palaces. They included the Apollo Belvedere and works by Raphael and Correggio. There were also lions, bears and camels from various zoos.

Britain remained a thorn in the side of a regime that still retained some revolutionary ambitions. The Directory had at first set its sights on invasion, and various expeditions were sent to aid the rebels in Ireland. In 1798 French troops landed in County Mayo but were soon rounded up and Wolfe Tone was arrested. The effect on Pitt's government was sufficient for it, in 1801, to end Ireland's separate parliament and establish a formal union with Great Britain. An unsung result of the French Revolution was a new 'United Kingdom'.

Paris switched its focus to the Mediterranean. The classical world, including Egypt, had long been the Revolution's lodestar. Neoclassicism infused the art of David and the new architecture of Paris. To Napoleon, the Mediterranean was also gateway to Britain's power base in India. He told a sceptical Talleyrand that 'to destroy England it is necessary to seize Egypt'. He would strangle Britain's trade and destroy its empire. He would also open the wonders of the Nile to French scholarship.

In 1798 Napoleon set sail for Egypt, where he defeated an Ottoman army and captured Cairo. However, he lost his entire fleet to Britain's Horatio Nelson at the Battle of the Nile, and thus found himself and his army isolated far from home. He spent the following year campaigning through the Levant and Syria, with mixed success, though much to the benefit of his heroic reputation back in France.

From first consul to emperor

By 1799 the future of the new France was becoming ever less clear. The ruling Directory was unstable, with Jacobins and royalists in constant discord. In August that year Napoleon, stranded in Egypt without news from home, was sent by the British commander, Sidney Smith, a package of French newspapers recounting the political disarray in Paris. He sat up all night reading them, and the next day deserted his army and, with a group of followers, sailed for France.

By October Napoleon was in Paris, where he was treated as a victorious general returning in triumph. He chose as his ally a revolutionary ideologue, the Abbé Sieyès, with whose help he staged a coup d'état against the Directory. He was appointed 'first consul' (with Sieyès as second), and a swift second coup eliminated any implied check on his power. Sieyès's sentiment was, understandably, *J'ai vecu*, I have survived.

By the end of 1799 Napoleon, barely turned thirty, was fashioning a new France, and a more personal revolution. French armies had pushed east into the Netherlands as far as their old goal, the banks of the Rhine. Habsburg Europe was in retreat and Germany's autonomous states were at Napoleon's mercy. Germany, Prussia and Austria could not formulate a defensive coalition, despite numerous attempts to do so. This left Napoleon able to defeat Austria at the Battle of Marengo in Italy. He then in 1802 signed the Treaty of Amiens with Britain, leading to a sudden British tourist invasion of Paris, not least to inspect Napoleon's Italian hoard.

In 1804 Napoleon crowned himself in Paris as Charlemagne's heir. Though the pope was present, it was Napoleon who placed the laurel wreath on his own head. 'For the pope's purposes,' he said, 'I am Charlemagne. I expect him to accommodate his conduct to my requirements.' His first coins bore the ironic motto, 'République française – Napoleon empereur'. Beethoven had just dedicated his third symphony, the Eroica, to Napoleon, but on hearing news of his coronation he flew into a rage. 'Now he will tread under foot all the rights of Man, indulge only his ambition,' he cried. He tore off the first page of the score, requiring an assistant to copy the opening bars.

15

Napoleon's Europe
1804–1815

Master of Europe

The French Revolution lasted barely five years, but it shook Europe to the core. It witnessed in turn representative government, mob rule, terror, collapse and eventual dictatorship – as Burke had predicted. The evolution of any state so swiftly into chaos was sobering. As the oriental saying went, better a hundred years of tyranny than a week of anarchy. But its lesson was unclear. Regimes in Austria, Prussia and Russia saw events in Paris as a warning against democracy in any shape or form. Others, such as Britain's Whigs, took the opposite view, that the events proved the necessity of reform. On one irony all might agree, that the cradle of revolution had morphed into Europe's most potent autocracy.

By crowning himself Charlemagne's heir, Napoleon left no doubt as to his intentions, and they were not confined to the battlefield. Clothed in the raiment of imperial power, he was charismatic, decisive and with astonishing energy. In 1800 he had set up a commission, sometimes with himself in the chair, to draft France's new legal framework, the Code Napoléon. It was promulgated in 1804 as a legal template for government and society, not just in France but across its new empire. Borrowing from the 1789/90 revolutionary decrees, the code was mostly advanced and liberal. It reiterated equality before the law, religious tolerance, the right to private property and family security. Marriage and divorce were to be civil matters, not religious. France's public realm would henceforth be secular. 'I wish to throw granite blocks on the soil of France,' declared Napoleon.

The republican nation state had been developing since the late Middle Ages. Now formalized as a specific constitutional entity, it was to be Napoleon's most lasting legacy. In France it enshrined the Revolution's obsession with control and the suppression of provincial diversity. Local government, already reordered by the Revolution, was supplanted by departmental prefects, centrally accountable. A national university was established, together with a network of secondary *lycées*. Every teacher was told what to teach, a dirigisme that applies to this day, and that was first ridiculed and then imitated in Britain.

Trafalgar and Austerlitz

The government in London was unconcerned by the revival of French expansionism in Europe. Napoleon, on the other hand, regarded an independent Britain as a blot on his European escutcheon. In 1803 he revived his ambition to invade the islands with main force, convinced that, once he reached London, Britons would rise against the hated Hanoverians and welcome him. The activities of London's Francophobe press – such as his popular depiction as a midget dictator by the cartoonist James Gillray – in no way deterred him.

A French army of 200,000 soldiers was duly assembled at Boulogne, with an armada of 2,343 transports. But the French navy could not assure them a safe crossing. British ships were blockading France's northern fleet in Brest. Another squadron under Nelson was blockading Toulon in the south. None the less Pitt took the threat seriously. Across England's east and south coasts a chain of Martello towers was hurriedly built. Local militias were recruited against invasion, though it is hard to see what they, or their medieval-style towers, could have done against Napoleon's Grande Armée.

In the summer of 1805, the Toulon fleet under Admiral Villeneuve managed to escape Nelson's blockade and reach Gibraltar and the Atlantic. Its plan was to combine with French ships in the West Indies and sail to assist Napoleon in the Channel. Blighted by poor communications, Villeneuve eventually found himself in Cadiz, where he was blockaded by Nelson and attacked off Cape Trafalgar as he sailed forth. In the ensuing battle, Nelson deployed his twenty-seven ships in two lines directed at a right angle to the thirty-three French and Spanish ships deployed facing him. The French disposition was disastrous. Nelson destroyed twenty-two enemy vessels without losing one of his own. The victory was lent poignancy by Nelson's death to a sniper's bullet at the moment of triumph.

Napoleon had already abandoned his invasion plan by the time of Trafalgar, but Britain was now safe from further threats from France. The captured Villeneuve was allowed to attend Nelson's state funeral in London, which later acquired a new square and column in honour of the battle and its victor. England, said Pitt, 'has saved herself by her exertions, and will I trust save Europe by her example'. The implication was that Britain had done its bit against Napoleon.

For others in the anti-French coalition, Trafalgar was small comfort. Napoleon had already taken his army from Boulogne and, one day before Trafalgar, defeated an Austrian army at the Battle of Ulm in southern Germany. He proceeded to occupy Vienna, conquering the capital of the Holy Roman Empire that had never before fallen to an enemy force. In December 1805 he won an even greater victory over a Russian-Austrian combined force at Austerlitz, leaving a terrible carnage of 26,000 dead and the Russians fleeing home. Napoleon's fieldcraft at Ulm and Austerlitz was taught in (old-fashioned) military academies into the twentieth century.

Ulm, Austerlitz and the overrunning of Germany meant that the Holy Roman Empire was effectively dead. Napoleon told Talleyrand he 'no longer recognized the empire's existence'. It was 'an old whore who has been violated by everyone for a long time'. Napoleon ordered Germany to cohere into thirty-six states (not including Prussia), forming a loose Confederation of the Rhine under his authority. The states sent polite apologies to the Austrian (and Holy Roman) emperor, Francis II (1792–1806), pleading force majeure. They had no option. Napoleon's intention for the confederation, which embraced some fifteen million people, was chiefly to supply him with money and manpower for his ongoing wars.

The remaining Holy Roman Empire was now indeed a pathetic spectacle. It was shorn of Germany and northern Italy. It had shrunk to Austria, Bohemia, parts of Hungary and Venice. Francis was persuaded by his advisers urgently to 'disband' it, lest Napoleon seize the title for himself. Officials drew up papers, vassal states were relieved of feudal ties, accountants worried over pensions and property deeds. There was an argument over what should happen to the crown jewels. Then, on 6 August 1806, a herald in full regalia rode to Vienna's Jesuit church, climbed the tower and summoned the citizens with a silver trumpet. He declared that the Holy Roman Empire was no more. The crowd wept.

The empire had lasted a millennium and brought, at least to the people of Germany, eight centuries (mostly) of peace, prosperity and cultural glory. For all its lack of potency, it had outlasted every European association since Rome. As its biographer Peter Wilson writes, its weakness was its strength. To its members, 'the wider imperial structure guaranteed their local privileges and autonomy. Their sense of belonging was multi-layered, from household, parish, community, territory, region to empire.' It was a measure of its success to have produced some of Europe's greatest architects, artists and composers. The only European writer widely regarded as a

39. Louis XIV of France and his family dressed as classical deities, *c.*1670

40. (*below*) Versailles, palace and gilded prison of the Sun King

41. Battle of Blenheim, 1704

42. Frederick the Great of Prussia, 1740–86

43. Maria Theresa of Austria, 1740–80, with her family

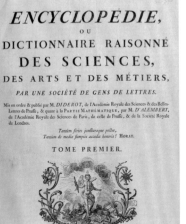

44. (*left*) Diderot and d'Alembert's *Encyclopédie*, title page

45. (*below left*) The Enlightenment personified – Voltaire in old age

46. (*below right*) Catherine the Great of Russia, 1762–96

47. The breeze of revolution by David – the Tennis Court Oath, 1789

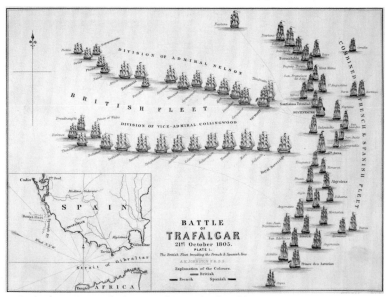

48. England saves Europe 'by her example' – Battle of Trafalgar, 1805

49. From consul to emperor – Napoleon, 1799–1815, by Ingres

50. Nemesis – the retreat from Moscow, 1812

51. The Congress of Vienna in session, 1815, with Castlereagh seated in the centre, and Talleyrand seated second from right

52. First year of revolutions – Delacroix's *Liberty Leading the People* in Paris, 1830

53. Second year of revolutions – barricades in Vienna, 1848

54. Britain's revolution – industrial Bradford, 1849

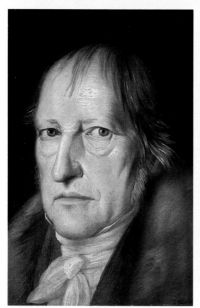

55. The state as 'God walking on Earth' –
Georg William Frederick Hegel

56. 'You have nothing to lose but your chains' –
Karl Marx

rival to Shakespeare, Goethe (1749–1832), was a humble court official in tiny Weimar. This coat of many colours now passed to Napoleon. His new confederacy laid the foundation of what would one day succeed not only the Holy Roman Empire but also his own France, a new German state.

Prussia and Russia

Where now for Napoleon? Talleyrand later said he could never detect any strategy, any objective, in his master's mind beyond an awareness of 'what had just happened, and what he thought of doing next'. In October 1806 it was Prussia's turn to feel the might of Napoleon's army. Its king, Frederick William III (1797–1840), had declined to support the alliance at Austerlitz, and had thereby contributed to its demise. To make amends he now sent his army, without allies, to confront Napoleon at the Battle of Jena, where it suffered a humiliating defeat. Napoleon's troops swept east and entered Berlin in triumph.

Ahead lay Russia. In February 1807 Napoleon marched east from Berlin and met and defeated a Russian army in two bloody battles at Eylau and Friedland. Tsar Alexander I (1801–25) was forced to sue for peace at the Treaty of Tilsit. During these negotiations, Napoleon is said to have toyed with the idea of France and Russia dividing Europe, east and west, between them. Together he imagined they could drive the Turks out of the Balkans, hand Constantinople to Moscow and march across Asia to British India. Despite this enticing invitation to emulate his ancient namesake, Alexander was unpersuaded. He knew that Napoleon was not good at keeping his word, let alone sharing.

Instead, Napoleon punished Prussia by reducing its land area and population of over eight million by more than half. He restored to Poland the lands lost in Catherine's 1795 partition. He also helped himself to a Polish mistress, Marie Walewska, induced to join him by Polish aristocrats desperate to cement their buffer status against Russia. Napoleon then reverted to his obsession with Britain by seeking to undermine its trade. In 1806 he had established a 'continental system' of European customs controls, aimed at excluding British goods from continental markets. In an intriguing premonition of the twentieth-century European Union, he announced, 'There is not enough sameness among the nations of Europe.' There should be a single dominant power 'with enough authority to force [the nations] to live in harmony with one another'. That power should, of course, be France.

Napoleon's blockade was a fiasco. British ships dominated the trade routes of northern Europe, including in the Baltic. Almost all Russia's exports, from furs and linen to tallow and iron, left in British ships that crowded the harbours of St Petersburg. There was no way Russia could or would cut off this business. In addition, in 1807 Britain's proactive foreign minister, George Canning, seized and destroyed most of the Danish fleet in Copenhagen harbour, denying Napoleon its use for a blockade. The same year, the British Parliament passed a law formally abolishing the country's Atlantic slave trade. That trade had in theory been abolished in the French Revolution, but was partly reinstated by Napoleon to appease local interests in France's Caribbean empire.

The Peninsular War

In response to Copenhagen, Napoleon decided to punish Britain's only firm continental ally, Portugal, and deny British ships the use of Lisbon. In 1807 he dispatched an army into Spain, ordering its monarch, Charles IV, to join an attack on Portugal. The result was calamitous for all concerned. Spain was a conservative country that had avoided Europe's revolutionary upheavals. There were no barricades in Madrid to assert the Rights of Man. The nation was ruled by a bizarre ménage of Charles, his queen, her lover Manuel de Godoy, and Godoy's wife and mistress. They were unreliable allies for France, or anyone, but they caused Napoleon no trouble. He could well have left them alone.

The French invasion divided Spanish loyalties. It precipitated Charles's abdication and replacement by his probably illegitimate and certainly incompetent son Ferdinand, ghoulishly depicted by Francisco Goya. Napoleon lost patience and in 1808, after a sequence of inspired feuds and coups, he sent the Spanish royal family into exile, replacing it with his brother, Joseph Bonaparte. The Portuguese royal family fled to Brazil.

Uncharacteristically, Britain overreacted. In 1808, after the failure of Sir John Moore's intervention at the head of one army, Britain sent to Portugal an army under the hero of the Indian wars, Arthur Wellesley. He led a joint Portuguese and British force against the French and Spanish. The resulting Peninsular War was to be the most gruelling of Napoleonic conflicts, five years of campaigning across the dusty plains of central Spain, with heavy losses on both sides. Its most innovative feature was the use of Spanish irregular units, known as *guerrilleros* (later guerrillas), informal skirmishes, on Wellington's side. The chief benefit was to sap Napoleon's resources at a time when he needed everything for his new venture to the east.

Moscow and endgame

Napoleon was wrestling with demons, not least his own. He had spent over a decade supposedly 'liberating' nations across Europe. For the German-speaking lands, freedom meant little but taxation, conscription and state intervention. Napoleon could win battles and crush regimes, but he could not rule, let alone instil loyalty. His empire had mutated from a revolution to a family business, a parody of Maximilian's 'conquest by marriage'. Bonapartes wore crowns in France, Spain, Holland, Westphalia, Italy, Tuscany and Naples. *La gloire* applied not to France but to its emperor.

Slowly the defeated governments of Europe regathered their strength. Austria found in the aristocratic diplomat Klemens von Metternich a foreign minister of brilliance and cunning. He came to power too late to stop Austria recklessly taking the field again against Napoleon, in 1809 at the Battle of Wagram, only to be mercilessly crushed. The best Metternich could do was send his emperor's nineteen-year-old daughter, Marie Louise, to be Napoleon's new wife, Josephine having been divorced for not bearing children. Though the girl was horrified at the prospect, she became devoted to Napoleon and bore him a son.

The emperor's megalomania was now all-consuming. In 1810 he moved his army into Prussia and gazed eastwards. Russia was openly breaching Napoleon's attempted blockade of British trade and now Alexander told him to leave Prussia in peace and cease his machinations in Poland. Diplomatic manoeuvres intensified, with Austria's Metternich offering Napoleon, if he withdrew, a Franco-Austrian alliance against any future Russian advance into Europe. Napoleon reputedly replied that he would 'wade through the blood of millions' to assert his dominance over Europe. Austria reverted to a policy of what Metternich called 'armed neutrality'.

In the spring of 1812 Napoleon assembled an army of some 650,000 men, fewer than half of them French and mostly conscripted from Germany. With little casus belli beyond forcing Russia to stop trading with Britain, he crossed the Russian border and embarked on one of the great marches of history. He avoided the capital, St Petersburg, as he sought the heart of Russia and Alexander's army, which was steadily retreating towards Moscow before him. In August he reached Smolensk, 230 miles from Moscow, where his generals pressed him to halt, mindful of the forthcoming Russian winter.

Napoleon was now showing signs of delusion, and he insisted on pursuing the Russians eastwards. With each mile covered, the long French supply train weakened, and soldiers had to live by foraging an increasingly denuded land. Eventually the Russian general, Kutuzov, halted seventy miles from Moscow at Borodino. Battle was joined. The result was dreadful slaughter, of some 45,000 Russians and 30,000 French, but it was indecisive. Napoleon described it as 'the most terrible of all my battles . . . the French worthy of victory, but the Russians of invincibility'.

Kutuzov now evacuated Moscow of virtually all its 250,000 citizens. 'Napoleon is a torrent we cannot stem,' he said, 'but Moscow is a sponge that will suck him dry.' When Napoleon entered the city he found it empty and much of it in flames, with eventually three-quarters of its buildings destroyed. There was no news of any Russian surrender, and a month later, at the end of October, the French in turn withdrew, taking with them a hollow triumph on the long, freezing road home.

Tolstoy's account of the Moscow campaign in *War and Peace* charts the pointlessness and arrogance of Europe's incessant wars. It describes the militaristic culture of elites to whom finding someone and somewhere to fight was a hangover of some drive deep in their cultural DNA, even if it meant the deaths of thousands. Napoleon's retreat from Moscow had no such romance. Its enemies were Russia's oldest friends, General Distance and General Winter. The Grande Armée starved and it froze. By the time it reached East Prussia in December, barely 40,000 of the original 650,000 soldiers were in a condition to fight. Some 60,000 were walking wounded and they had lost virtually all their horses. The outcome was not a Russian victory, except that to Russia survival always meant victory. Thus could Tchaikovsky celebrate 1812 with bells and cannons in his rousing overture.

As soon as Napoleon left Russian soil, he raced to Paris to stem rumours of insurrection and raise new troops, which he did with remarkable ease. By then it was clear that his Spanish strategy was in disarray. Wellesley, now the Marquess of Wellington, had liberated Madrid in 1812 and would soon defeat Napoleon's marshal, Jean-Baptiste Jourdan, at the Battle of Vitoria, driving the French back over the Pyrenees.

For Napoleon, both Russia and Spain were avoidable disasters resulting from imperial overreach. His most persistent critic, the Prussian strategist Carl von Clausewitz, fought against him at Jena and Borodino, and became a leading theorist of war. He sought to synthesize its 'primordial violence, hatred, and enmity' into its serious purpose, to act as 'a continuation of political intercourse, by other means'. Above all, he warned, war should never become an end in itself.

For Napoleon, war had become just that. It preceded policy rather than followed from it. As success turned to failure, the emperor had no strategy on which to fall back. He had refused Metternich's offer of an alliance against Russia, which might have saved his empire. Russian and Prussian armies were now pursuing his forces across Europe. Coalitions that had spent a decade forming and re-forming against him now found coherence. Over the spring and summer of 1813, Russia, Sweden, Prussia and Austria agreed to a 'sixth coalition', with Britain as usual offering money as well as manpower in considerable quantities.

The culmination was a 'battle of the nations' outside Leipzig on 16–19 October, involving over half a million soldiers under the Prussian General Blücher, and considered the biggest battle in Europe prior to the twentieth century. Most of the coalition's crowned heads attended in person, except England's now-ailing George III. Napoleon suffered the defection of many of his German allies, including Bavaria, and was at last outmanoeuvred in the field. He lost virtually his entire army. It was said to have taken a year for the local peasants to clear the field of corpses. France retreated to its homeland.

By April 1814 the Russian and Prussian armies were at the gates of Paris, whereupon Napoleon's marshals told him the war was over. Talleyrand, who had departed Napoleon's service, exasperated, in 1807, returned to the ascendant, advising the senate to demand the emperor's abdication. He should go into exile on the island of Elba, off the west coast of Italy. It agreed. The Bourbon Louis XVIII now took the French throne, with Talleyrand as his leading counsellor.

The indefatigable Talleyrand behaved as if he were suddenly arbiter of Europe rather than the supplicant of a defeated nation. He invited Alexander to lodge at his Paris house, and held talks with Britain's foreign minister, Castlereagh. He assured one and all that he represented not Napoleon but France and the French people. The French Revolution should be regarded as over. Napoleon's marshal Ney would later be executed for treason, and 60,000 Napoleonic officials were dismissed from their posts. In May 1814 the warring parties met and agreed the Treaty of Paris, which acknowledged the Bourbon restoration and put France back behind its pre-revolutionary borders. It also agreed to reconvene for a more comprehensive settlement in Vienna. It was to be the greatest assemblage of power in Europe's history.

16

Vienna and the Failure of Reform
1815–1840

Finale: Napoleon and Waterloo

The city of Vienna in September 1814 was on parade. The congregation of Europe's leaders had gathered to breathe a collective sigh of relief. Napoleon was gone and France defeated. Emperors, kings and princes came with retinues of military and political advisers. Present too, crowded into hotels and rented townhouses, were 200 German princelings and hangers-on, hoping to snatch crumbs from the deserted table of the Holy Roman Empire. To these were added representatives of cities, churches, banks, corporations, even publishers. Delegates were accompanied by courtiers, wives and marriageable daughters.

Vienna, humiliated by Napoleon, was overjoyed to be the centre of attention. One estimate had its population surge from 200,000 to 300,000, as its streets thronged with migrant servants, ostlers, cooks, tailors, 'courtesans and confectioners'. The winter was given over to entertainment, energized by the new waltz, with its exhilarating rhythms. Beethoven was summoned in November to stage a concert of his rousing Battle Symphony (now rarely performed), in honour of Wellington's triumph at Vitoria. The French, unabashed by their Leipzig defeat and led by Talleyrand, held a competition to decide Europe's finest cheese. Britain submitted Stilton and Switzerland Gruyère. Of sixty entries, France's brie de Meaux was declared *le roi des fromages*.

The formal proceedings were presided over by the practised statesmen Talleyrand, Metternich and Castlereagh. Against the wishes of the others, Castlereagh insisted on France's presence, lest it have grounds for disregarding any settlement. The earlier Paris treaty had already performed the customary ritual of readjusting the boundaries of old Lotharingia to form a buffer zone along France's eastern border. Vienna confirmed this, but also sought to rescue and restore Europe from Napoleon's blight. There were bilateral claims and counter-claims to be resolved. There were issues of restitution, compensation, trade and debt. There was France's colonial empire to be shrunk and reapportioned. Vienna was a United Nations assembly in embryo.

Proceedings were nearing an end in March 1815 when Vienna was shattered to hear that Napoleon had escaped from Elba and landed near Cannes in the south of France. He had then marched to Paris at the head of a new army. Louis XVIII had fled Paris and Napoleon resumed his old throne. The Vienna delegates declared him an outlaw and adjourned to assemble a seventh anti-French coalition, before struggling to complete their business.

The task of confronting Napoleon was assigned to Britain's now Duke of Wellington. He had replaced Castlereagh as head of the British delegation and, like Marlborough a century before, was regarded as a token of Britain's sincerity in seeking a new European order. He assembled a modest British army of 25,000, a third of them Irish, to add to an allied strength in Belgium of 118,000. Napoleon raced his 'army of the north' towards Brussels, to confront Wellington before he could be reinforced by the Prussians under Blücher.

Napoleon's advance found the allies ill-prepared and Wellington's prospects in doubt. After preliminary skirmishes on 16 June at Quatre Bras, battle was joined in earnest outside the village of Waterloo. Though the British infantry squares wavered before the force of the French cavalry, they ultimately held their ground. The outcome was thus inconclusive until the arrival late in the day of Blücher's Prussians on the French flank. Napoleon's imperial guard broke and fled, and the French were routed. The role of the Prussians was much debated afterwards, but exchanges between Wellington and von Clausewitz agreed that the Prussian arrival was critical. It was, as Wellington admitted, 'the nearest run thing you ever saw in your life'. When Napoleon's carriage was captured by the Prussians, it was found full of jewels, which were incorporated into the Prussian crown.

Waterloo was, on the day, decisive, although had Napoleon won, he would certainly have had to confront a larger coalition force, as at Leipzig. As it was, he was driven back to Paris with the British and Prussians in pursuit. This time his marshals told him emphatically it was over. In June 1815 he abdicated and fled Paris for the coast, writing to Britain's George III pleading for 'the protection of the laws . . . from the most powerful, most constant and most generous of my enemies'. It is said he dreamt of asylum as a British country gentleman. The letter was never delivered. Despite also contemplating escape to America, Napoleon was captured by the British, saving him from probable execution by the French or the Prussians. He was taken aboard HMS *Bellerophon* and transported by HMS *Northumberland* to the distant British colony of St Helena in the south Atlantic. 'I am the new Prometheus,' he told his secretary, 'chained to the rock to be gnawed by vultures . . . Before ten years have passed, all Europe will be Cossacks or republicans.' Six years later he was dead, stomach cancer the suspected killer.

Vienna: the settlement

The Congress of Vienna now completed its business, seeking to settle a Europe that had, in the past quarter century, seen carnage unprecedented since the Thirty Years War. An estimated five million people had died across the continent in the twenty-five years between the start of the French Revolution and Napoleon's departure, a greater proportion of the population than was killed in the First World War. France alone is thought to have lost one and a half million. All Europe's economies had atrophied and the emergent industrial revolution been put on hold, everywhere except in Britain.

The regimes present at Vienna craved the status quo antebellum. Instinct told them to return to the principles of Westphalia and Utrecht, to salvage Europe from its revolutionary trauma, in effect to pretend that Napoleon had never happened. Metternich's particular fixation was that a balance of power should obtain across Europe, Napoleon's empire being dismantled to this end. A new Netherlands incorporated Belgium to its south, the latter's fourth 'overlord' after Spain, Austria and France. Savoy was linked with Piedmont and Sardinia to form a buffer state on France's southeastern border. Poland and Saxony suffered for their brief flirtation with Napoleon by being dismembered, part going to Russia, part to Prussia, leaving mere fragments as independent.

Prussia wanted revenge for Napoleon's humiliations, and proved the chief beneficiary. It was awarded much of Saxony as well as much of north Germany as far as the Rhineland, including the mineral-rich Ruhr. The result was that what had been an 'east-Elbian' Prussia now stretched from Poland in the east to the French border in the west. Austria won Salzburg, the Tyrol and its old territories in north Italy. Venice, now under Austrian rule, regained its stolen bronze horses of St Mark's.

The delegates felt they had no option but to accept the demise of the Holy Roman Empire. Napoleon's thirty-six-state German confederation was refashioned as thirty-nine, with Vienna asked to chair its largely ceremonial gatherings in a Frankfurt Bundestag. The new entity was called a 'third Germany', alongside Prussia and

Austria. The identity of this third Germany was much discussed. The Holy Roman Empire had watched over it for a thousand years. There seemed little cause to disturb such a testament to local sovereignty, least of all with the hovering presence of an assertive, belligerent Prussia to the north.

Yet would a Bundestag talking shop be enough? German consciousness had been stirred to life by Napoleon's conquests. German universities, officers' clubs and the craft guilds of Hamburg, Frankfurt and Heidelberg wanted to be at Europe's top table. To be a people without a nation seemed antiquated, neither one thing nor another. As Simon Winder has noted, while this new Germany was being stitched together, Mary Shelley in Geneva was dreaming of Frankenstein's monster stirring 'with an uneasy, half vital motion' into signs of life.

Britain's Castlereagh was under strict cabinet instructions not to get embroiled in any continental horse-trading. Vienna confirmed Britain's wartime colonial gains, including Cape Town from the Dutch. As for Britain's future in Europe, as after Utrecht its job was done and its soldiers would stand down. The Whig Lord John Russell opposed further spending on an army, as it would risk turning 'a naval into a military nation . . . a mighty island . . . into a petty continental state'. The army was cut from 600,000 to 100,000, most of it for the colonies. Wellington was left to hold an annual banquet for his Waterloo generals in his house at Hyde Park Corner. A new London bridge was named after the battle, opened in 1817. The French later retaliated with the Gare d'Austerlitz, among others.

Vienna aftermath: the Concert of Europe

One outcome of Vienna was Castlereagh's concept of an ongoing congress, a 'concert of nations', to settle international disputes before they reached a battlefield. Britain, with Russia, Prussia, Austria and France, agreed to hold regular meetings to this end. The concert's intention was dubbed 'to keep Britain in, France down and Russia out'. The days of seemingly constant European wars should be over.

Less noted was Napoleon's principal innovation, his application of the apparatus of a modern state to the disciplines of war. It was an apparatus that once in place proved strangely resistant to dismantling itself. The question should have been how to curb such power, and make it accountable to its citizens, but Vienna did not ask it. Instead it discussed how to protect the continent's ruling autocracies against future rebellion. Monarchs in Prussia, Austria, Poland and France had tinkered with national assemblies, and mostly regretted the outcome. Castlereagh was here a radical, warning that popular sentiment could not be suppressed for ever. At home he might be a rigid conservative, but compared to Russia's Alexander or Austria's Metternich, he was a tearaway liberal.

One consequence of Vienna was the gradual but emphatic end to the most odious blot on Europe's overseas activities since the growth of empires in the seventeenth century, the Atlantic slave trade. Slavery had long ended, or at least elided into serfdom, in Europe itself. It had facilitated the opening up of plantations across the Americas in the eighteenth century, with the Spanish, Portuguese, Dutch, French and British all major traders. Cities such as Lisbon, Cadiz, Nantes, Bristol and Liverpool prospered greatly. Their ships conveyed manufactured goods to west Africa, picking up slaves from African traders, transporting them to the Americas, then bringing sugar, rum and cotton to Europe.

The horrific so-called 'middle passage' meant that most of the tens of millions of slaves did not set foot on European soil, though thousands still did. This made it more difficult for campaigners against the trade, formed by a group of British Quakers and William

Wilberforce in 1787, to publicize their case. Having ended its own trade in 1807, Britain entered a series of trade-banning treaties in 1818 with Spain, Portugal and the Netherlands, backed with British compensation to the former traders. The Royal Navy was deputed to enforce these, albeit spasmodically at first. This did not mean the end of slavery in Europe's colonies, let alone in North America, but ending the trade was a first step.

The genie in the bottle: the hesitant 1820s

Vienna might have dismantled the French Revolution, but it could not ignore that it had happened, or its arousal of hopes of a new order. As the years passed, young Germans, Italians, Belgians and Poles asked what had been gained from Leipzig, Waterloo and Vienna. Germany was still thirty-nine states, Italy was still nine and ruled by outsiders. Greece and much of the Balkans remained under Turkish rule. Vienna had nursed Europe back to health, but not cured the disease that preceded it. That disease, as Castlereagh said, was the lack in most of Europe of any mechanism for securing consent to power.

Though Louis XVIII restored the French monarchy and nobility, he did not wholly reverse the Revolution. France stayed secular. The Code Napoléon was entrenched, with an assembly, a National Guard and departmental prefects in place. Royalists constantly pushed for a return to the Ancien Régime, but against them were renascent radicals pushing for change. Louis attempted to walk a line between them. He tried to recapture the spirit of France's pre-revolutionary past, by combining aristocracy with the Revolution's bureaucratic statism. It was unlikely to be a stable marriage.

In 1820 Spanish radicals had seized power in Madrid through the Cortes (assembly) and reduced the absolute monarchy of Ferdinand VII to a mere figurehead. There followed the 'Liberal Triennial' of mildly revolutionary rule, until in 1823 France sent an army to restore Ferdinand to his full autocracy. They marched into Spain, flagrantly breaching the spirit of Vienna but returning Ferdinand to his throne. The attendant violence was horrific, to be chronicled by Goya in his grim Black Paintings series.

The turbulence in Spain had a seismic impact in South America. Spain's colonies took the opportunity of civil war back home to replicate North America's War of Independence. In this they were astonishingly successful. Driven by the charismatic leadership of Simón Bolívar, within a decade from 1821 they had swept aside Spain's colonial armies, creating Venezuela, Colombia, Peru and Bolivia. Other Latin American states, including Argentina, Uruguay, Chile and Mexico also achieved independence from Spain during the same period. In 1822 Brazil became independent of Portugal.

To the dismay of the Vienna Congress powers, Britain's Canning recognized each independent South American state in turn, under pressure from City interests eager for exclusive trade. Recognition also worried the American president, James Monroe (1817–25), who saw both the possibility of France backing Spanish reconquest and Canning's role as threatening. In 1823 he imagined the horror of Russia taking California and Peru, France taking Mexico and Britain taking Cuba. This would, he said, 'be dangerous to our peace and safety'. Thus was born the Monroe doctrine, that the Americas, north and south, should be no-go territory for their former European parents. They were now the United States' 'sphere of influence'.

1830 and the year of revolutionary failure

The French Revolution had led to aftershocks across the continent, but without serious damage to Europe's established order. As the nineteenth century progressed, the revolutionary urge began to resurface. First signs were in a surprising quarter, long-dormant Greece. In 1821 this orphan of old Byzantium staged a full-scale revolt against the Ottoman Turks. The struggle exhilarated Romantics across Europe, led by the heroic Lord Byron. The poet's death fighting for the Greeks in 1824 coincided with a craze for all things Hellenic. Classical architecture, stimulated by the French Revolution, was replicated in state buildings, country houses, churches and universities across the western world. America's Washington, under construction at the time, became the neoclassical city it remains today.

In 1824 France's Louis had died, and with him the slow meander to reform. His successor, Charles X (1824–30), was a reactionary spendthrift who, as a teenager, had been Marie Antoinette's dancing partner and darling of the Versailles court. He sought a return to the Ancien Régime, and was crowned in a truly spectacular ceremony in Reims, where medieval monarchs had been crowned. Greece was his opportunity for glory. In 1827 Charles joined Britain and Russia in sending ships to aid the rebels in Greece, where Russia was casting covetous eyes at the weakening Ottoman empire. An Anglo-Russian fleet engaged the Turks and Egyptians at Navarino off the Peloponnese, the same waters as had seen Lepanto in 1571. As Lepanto was the last major battle of oared ships, Navarino was the last exclusively under sail. The Turks were crushed by superior European gunnery and, by 1830, southern Greece was an independent if modest state. European nationalism had won a small but totemic victory.

That same year in Paris, Charles reacted to a series of assembly defeats with ordinances dissolving the assembly, ending press freedom and restricting the franchise. Mobs returned to their old haunt, the streets, but Charles was unmoved. He told the now ageing Talleyrand loftily, 'I would rather hew wood than reign like the king of England . . . I see no middle way between the throne and the scaffold.' Talleyrand soberly replied, 'Your majesty forgets the post-chaise.' Within days Charles took fright and fled to Britain, where he was allowed to settle only as a private citizen, the 'Count of Ponthieu'.

This miniature rerun of the French Revolution saw the throne pass to the king's cousin, the 'bourgeois' Louis Philippe of Orléans (1830–48). He greeted a delighted crowd from the balcony of the Hôtel de Ville, arm-in-arm with the elderly Lafayette. The amiable Louis Philippe proved a steadying influence. He steered a path between the hotheads of left and right, abolished France's hereditary upper assembly and brought France eighteen years of peace. Delacroix's revolutionary icon of Liberty, a topless maiden carrying a tricolour over a sea of corpses, referred to the 1830 coup and not, as is often supposed, to 1789.

Throughout 1830, Europe's capitals echoed to the cries of the Paris barricades. Riots broke out in Brussels among French-speaking Catholics, protesting the ill-matched Vienna union of the Netherlands, Flanders and Wallonia. They had been ordered to speak Dutch and accept equal status for Protestants. The Concert of Europe went into action. Britain's new foreign secretary, Lord Palmerston, collaborated with Talleyrand to separate Belgium from the Netherlands and guarantee its neutrality. In 1831 a separate Belgium was at last brought to life.

Italy next picked up the baton. Napoleon had given it a taste of unity and republicanism, but Vienna had returned it to Austrian overlordship. Moves for Italian unification proliferated, but they were largely confined to the Carbonari, secret revolutionaries' clubs with branches across Italy. They had little military clout and a rising against Austria in the northern provinces proved short lived.

Also in 1830, a group of Polish officers and landowners rebelled, yet again, against Russia. A new tsar, Nicholas I (1825–55), was a far cry from his predecessor, the pragmatic Alexander. To his biographer, he was 'autocracy personified: infinitely majestic, determined and powerful, hard as stone, and relentless as fate'. He reacted to the rebels by forcibly ending such autonomy as Poland was granted under Vienna and crowning himself king of Poland. Warsaw was devastated and saw a middle-class migration to Paris, to be entertained in its misery by Frédéric Chopin. 'I suffer and pour out my despair at the piano,' he groaned. Poland's ailment was what Palmerston called 'that sad inheritance of triumphant wrong'. With that, the revolutionary upsurge of 1830 was over. The architecture of Vienna remained intact.

A very British revolution: 1832

The greatest impact of the events of 1830, other than in Greece, was ironically in the nation least touched by revolution in France. Britain was experiencing the political backwash of economic success. The industrial revolution had changed its social geography to a degree as yet unknown on the continent. In 1801 the British population had been nine million. By 1841 it was sixteen million, plus eight million Irish. The countryside was depopulating and the cities were booming. Outside London, the biggest were no longer York, Bristol and Norwich but Manchester, Birmingham and Leeds. Social structures were changing and new leaders emerging. The defining British institutions were becoming less the country estate and the church and more the factory, the mill and the fledgling railway.

British politics did not reflect this change. Parliament might hold in check an unpopular Hanoverian monarch, but it was hardly accountable to the people. The hereditary and episcopal House of Lords held a veto on reform. Local government was patrician. The Church of England was moribund. Parliament represented a quarter of a million electors, mostly in rural counties and ancient boroughs, far fewer than in France and Spain. Most of the centres of industrial life were not enfranchised at all.

What had long guarded and developed the British constitution was the prevailing liberal ethos of its political establishment. It delivered the country leaders of remarkable ability, Walpole, the Pitts father and son, Lord Liverpool, Castlereagh and Canning. Each had tempered conservatism with tolerance of reform. The British people could pride themselves on free assembly and relatively free speech. A hearing was given to the radical philosophy of Jeremy Bentham, the prison reforms of Elizabeth Fry and the free trade of William Huskisson and Richard Cobden. Searing cartoonists such as Gillray and Cruikshank were tolerated, where they would have been guillotined in France.

In 1819 this outwardly serene state of affairs suffered a shock, when a peaceful rally for electoral reform at St Peter's Field in Manchester was dispersed by soldiers on the orders of a panicked local magistracy. Eleven died and some 500 were injured in what became dubbed by headline writers the 'Peterloo Massacre'. In most of Europe, the incident would have passed unnoticed – 'only in England would they call that a massacre', wrote one French commentator. But public and political opinion was appalled. To edgy conservatives, the event was a portent of British revolution. To liberals it was a summons to urgent reform.

In 1830 the long-decrepit George IV, so obese he scarcely ever appeared in public, died and the general election customary on the monarch's death was narrowly won by the Tory Duke of Wellington. He responded to calls for reform by saying that 'as long as I hold any station in the government . . . I shall always feel it my duty to resist such measures.' Reform, he said, was the beginning of revolution. The remark did something almost unprecedented in Britain. It drew mobs into the streets. Wellington was nicknamed the Iron Duke not for his military prowess but for his reactionary political intransigence.

Wellington felt obliged to resign and the Whigs under Lord Grey took power. In 1831 Grey introduced a 'great reform bill', abolishing nearly sixty 'rotten' (that is virtually empty) constituencies and unseating 168 MPs. It more than doubled the franchise to over 650,000 and brought to Westminster representatives of the new cities. The bill met opposition, first from Tories in the Commons and then, after a second election delivered a pro-reform majority, from the Lords. Politics was in turmoil. Pressure on the new king, William IV (1830–37), to create pro-reform peers finally brought him and Wellington to their senses. The Reform Bill was voted through in June 1832. Parliament had rescued itself.

Though hardly 'democratic', Britain in 1832 showed that political reform could be achieved within a constitutional framework and without civic upheaval. The central institutions of the state, the king, Parliament and its leaders, never lost control of the debate. Even Wellington took it in his stride. When asked to comment on the newly reformed Commons in 1833, he replied, 'I never saw so many shocking bad hats in my life.'

The new Whig Parliament confirmed the fears of conservatives everywhere. It banned child labour, and introduced a poor law, albeit in a form harshly satirized by Charles Dickens. Parish vestries were replaced by municipal corporations. Trade unions were legalized, and those unionists who had been deported to Australia for 'combination' – such as the Tolpuddle Martyrs – were brought home. In 1833 a bill abolishing the slave trade throughout the colonies was passed, Wilberforce dying just days after being told of its passage. In 1834, as if symbolic of a political spring cleaning, the Palace of Westminster burned down, to be replaced by a palatial new structure. This was in a gothic style that came to be associated with a new post-classical age, in church and state alike.

Three years later, a demure eighteen-year-old Princess Victoria took the British throne, shortly to marry an impeccable German husband, Prince Albert. The new Victorians might be smug, but they were not idle. No British troops sailed to support Spanish liberals, Polish rebels or Italian liberators. The Whig Parliaments of Grey, Melbourne and Palmerston held mostly to the non-interventionism of Walpole and the Pitts. Britons were more like Californians of a century and a half later. Their obsession was to explore new technologies and new horizons. While the rest of Europe was making revolutions, Britain was making ships, steam engines and cloth. In 1841, Brunel's new railway completed a run from London to Bristol. Abroad, the British empire grew to cover much of the world's land area and a quarter of its population under what was declared (by Britain) to be a worthy successor to the Roman peace, a new Pax Britannica.

17

The Old Order's Last Cry
1840–1850

The dawn of ideology

The failure of the reformist upheavals of 1830 may have disappointed revolutionaries, but it galvanized ideologues. Past wars had led to the reactionary settlements of Westphalia (1648), Utrecht (1713) and Vienna (1815). These waystations in Europe's history changed its map hardly at all. But the revolution in France had expanded the political conversation from elites to ordinary people. Europeans in all walks of life debated how societies should be ordered. They pondered personal liberty and national identity, the distribution of wealth and the role of class. Newspapers and railways widened visions and shrank distances. From now on, threats to established order no longer lay in palaces, churches and castles. They lurked around street corners, in barracks, universities and taverns.

The theorists of the American and French revolutions had taken their cue from Locke, at heart a practical empiricist. In Britain one of his most prominent interpreters was Bentham, who saw the purpose of government as essentially 'a felicific calculus', its purpose to secure 'the greatest happiness of the greatest number'. By the mid-nineteenth century other voices were being heard. Rousseau had seen government as a 'contract' between the chains of the state and the freedoms of equal citizens. He in turn influenced French philosophers of socialism and anarchism such as Saint-Simon, Comte and Proudhon.

Over these towered one man, G. W. F. Hegel. Hegel gave a

framework to the emergent German consciousness. He saw history as a 'dialectic' of contending forces, with their synthesis in the 'rational state'. Such a state was, to Hegel, 'God walking upon Earth'. The welfare of the state was what mattered: in contrast, individual freedom was of little account. This was an echo of the seventeenth-century English philosopher Thomas Hobbes (1588–1679), whose monarchical nation was the benign expression of society as against the condition of raw nature. The harbinger of Hegel's state was a new Prussia, leading an empire of global Protestantism. To young Germans, impatient with Vienna and yearning for identity, Hegel was a god. In 1829 he became rector of the University of Berlin, where a certain Karl Marx arrived as a student in 1836.

Few periods in Europe's history can have lent themselves so readily to Hegel's dialectic as the 1840s. Industrial expansion and capital accumulation were drawing people in their millions from the country into towns. Here they could not rely on the soil for sustenance, but had to rely on markets to find them work and food. But a city tenement was proving healthier than a peasant's shack. Bellies were full, life expectancy rose by fifty per cent in three generations and populations soared. Between 1800 and 1850, France's rose from twenty-seven to thirty-six million, Germany's from twenty-three to thirty-three million, Britain's from sixteen to twenty-seven million, and Russia's from forty to sixty-eight million. Capitalism appeared to be delivering on its promise.

This growth generated tensions. An urban proletariat was more visible, more vociferous and easier to organize than in the countryside. The early promise of industrialization was leaving a 'working class' angry and free to combine. In 1844, as he emerged from his studies and observed Europe evolving round him, Marx formed a partnership with a fellow German, Friedrich Engels, staying for a time in Manchester. Here he was shocked by the living conditions of workers in the booming mills. The market place might feed the poor, but it appeared unable to meet humanity's demand for empowerment and a decent life. To Marx and Engels, capitalism presaged social instability and eventual collapse.

In the mid-1840s, Europe's agricultural economy faltered, with potato blight and widespread crop failure. This choked supplies to the new cities and threatened urban famine. It was a textbook case for Marx's analysis. He took Hegel's ideas and applied them in practice. His creed, written on his tomb in London's Highgate cemetery, was that 'the philosophers have only interpreted the world in various ways; the point is to change it'. In 1848 he and Engels published a manifesto in London, though in German, opening with the announcement, 'A spectre is haunting Europe – the spectre of communism.' It ended with the stirring words (depending on translation), 'Workers of the world unite. You have nothing to lose but your chains.' The manifesto had minimal impact when published and for a quarter century afterwards. It would then tear Europe apart.

The year of revolutions: 1848

Two groups of Europeans had seen their sense of nationhood ignored by the Congress of Vienna, the Italians and the Germans. In Italy, long-standing opposition to Austrian rule, dating back to the Middle Ages, was still confined mostly to private clubs and occasional street uprisings. In 1834 a much-travelled Italian, Giuseppe Mazzini, formed a group in Berne called Young Europe, composed of radical Italians, Germans and Poles. A continent-wide political liberation, said Mazzini, would start in Italy 'and radiate from there across Europe . . . gradually and irresistibly guiding society to form itself into a vast and united mass'. It was a spirit of the age.

In January 1848, Milan rebelled against its Austrian governor and set up a provisional regime. The king of Piedmont and Sardinia,

Charles Albert, came out in support and declared war on Austria. In Rome a new pope, Pius IX (1846–78), greeted anti-Austrian crowds with the cry 'God bless Italy.' He liberated Rome's Jews from their ghetto. On cue, Sicily declared its independence of Bourbon Naples, and a rare Venetian revolutionary, Daniele Manin, declared that city's independence of the Austrians. Gradually, as in 1830, uprisings occurred across the continent. In February it was France's turn. The Paris government decided to suppress reform gatherings, or 'banquets', which led to riots so violent that the elderly Louis Philippe retreated to his palace and meekly mumbled, 'I abdicate.' He and his queen fled to London as Mr and Mrs Smith. A Second Republic was promptly declared and elections held.

There were also uprisings in Poland, Switzerland, Norway and Portugal. Austria faced more serious trouble than in Italy. In a flurry of oratory, a Hungarian leader, Lajos Kossuth, proclaimed his country's independence of Austria. With Vienna already in turmoil over government corruption, the ageing Metternich resigned and followed Louis Philippe into exile in England, where he lodged in Belgravia and was visited by Palmerston and Disraeli. For a few months, Austria was unable to contest Hungary's independence, and Kossuth enjoyed continent-wide celebrity.

The spirit of rebellion finally extended to Prussia. In Berlin, a panicking police force – ever the unwitting ally of revolution – killed 300 rioters. This so dismayed the king, Frederick William IV (1840–61), that he publicly begged forgiveness of his citizenry. To the horror of his generals, he pledged constitutional reform and freedom of speech, assembly and the press. More significantly, he pledged his support for radical calls for German unification. He announced a parliament, or Reichstag, for all German people, to meet at the old confederacy headquarters in Frankfurt.

Frederick William then backed German-speaking insurgents in their revolt against the Danish-ruled duchies of Schleswig and

Holstein. The issue, the rival claims of Denmark and Germany, was so obscure that Palmerston later said only three people ever understood it: Britain's Prince Albert, who by then was dead, a professor who had gone mad and he, Palmerston, who had forgotten. The 'Schleswig-Holstein question' stood proxy for Europe's border disputes down the ages – and for the readiness of Europe's leaders to race to arms in any such case.

Britain was, in contrast, once more a revolutionary disappointment. A rally in support of the Chartists, founded in 1837 to back equal constituencies, a universal franchise and a secret ballot, was summoned to a rain-soaked Kennington Common in April 1848. Only 25,000 turned up, to be met by 10,000 constables and troops drafted in to keep order. When the rally proposed to march on Westminster, a policeman suggested that, in view of the rain, it send a petition in two hackney cabs. It was sent, and ignored.

Anticlimax and counter-revolution

As in 1830, these minor insurgencies had no bite. They rose and they subsided. In Austria, Russian troops invaded separatist Hungary and handed it back to Vienna. Kossuth went into exile, from where in London in 1851 he addressed rapturous crowds in the Shakespearean English he had learned in prison. The Italian revolt was suppressed by an Austrian army, leading Piedmont and Sardinia's Charles Albert to despair and give his throne to his son, Victor Emmanuel II (1849–61). Pope Pius fled Rome in November 1848 and a republic was declared, welcoming Mazzini the following spring, assisted by the charismatic Giuseppe Garibaldi, veteran of the South American wars. Garibaldi was soon defeated by French troops and fled to Tangiers. The republic ended in a matter of months and the pope returned. Venice's republic was crushed by an Austrian army after eighteen months.

Indeed, it was only in France's toppling of Louis Philippe that the year 1848 changed a regime. It was not a change the revolutionaries might have hoped for. A royalist assembly was returned, albeit under a government dominated by radicals. Its leader, the poet Alphonse de Lamartine, ordered factories to be built to honour the 'right to work'. This drew thousands of peasants to Paris for jobs that did not exist. In the resulting chaos, some 13,000 rioters and troops were killed, wounded or deported to the colonies by Lamartine's militia, the Garde Mobile. The 'June Days' became a metaphor for bourgeois treachery against revolution. The composer Hector Berlioz noted that the statue of Liberty on the Bastille column had a stray bullet hole in her breast.

The spectacle of the French republic killing its own devastated the revolutionary cause. In December 1848 elections were held for a new president of France. One candidate was the exiled pretender to Napoleon's crown, his nephew Louis Bonaparte. Dismissed as a charlatan and even a cretin, he had been living incognito in London, where he served as a constable during the Chartists' rally. All Bonapartes were supposedly banned from France. However, Louis's appearance in Paris caused a sensation. The sheer celebrity of his name won him over five million votes and the presidency.

French radicals followed earlier royalists into exile in London, where Britain's liberal politics and open-door asylum were attracting refugees of all political stripes from across Europe. It prided itself as a citadel of free speech, even as other European governments deplored it as a nursemaid of revolutionary subversion.

New Germany stillborn

The denouement of the events of 1848 in Germany was Frederick William's concession of a parliament of all German-speaking lands. Some eighty-five per cent of German males were enfranchised.

The new 800-member Reichstag, composed overwhelmingly of lawyers, teachers and public officials, met in May in Frankfurt's Paulskirche. It was hailed as a 'parliament of professors'. Over its chamber towered a painting of a mythical Germania, holding an ominously large sword and a very small olive branch. It declared a new German 'empire', its constitution embracing the thirty-nine groupings of the post-Vienna confederacy. Looking across the Atlantic, the parliament committed itself to American-style freedoms. Of all the creations of 1848 it was the one most filled with hope.

Like many such proto-democratic institutions, Frankfurt lacked contact with the levers of power. It had no revenues, no armies and no government. It was also outside the terms of the Treaty of Vienna – under which Austria was 'chairman' of a German confederacy. In addition it offended the ancient autonomy still treasured by many German principalities. While the parliament formally included Prussia and Austria, it excluded Austria's imperial territories, as well as Bavaria. Left out of the equation was the status of the existing governments of Prussia and Austria.

At its first session, the parliament invited Prussia's Frederick William to become its constitutional monarch. He declined, worried both over the intrusion on the autonomy of the German states and over the likely reaction of Vienna and St Petersburg. By early 1849 scepticism towards the parliament was growing across Germany and members were failing to attend. By summer it was inquorate and collapsed. Engels dismissed it as 'a mere debating club, an accumulation of gullible wretches'.

Frederick William was right on one score. Russia's reactionary tsar, Nicholas, had no interest in the growth of a liberal-minded, let alone democratic, German state, any more than did Austria. In November 1850 the tsar forced on Frederick William the bizarrely entitled 'humiliation of Olmütz'. His German initiative was declared dead. What might have been a new and liberal German state was stillborn, and the old German confederacy was restored under Austrian chairmanship. Despite this fiasco, the spirit of Frankfurt did not die. A clear message had gone out, that any moves to German unity would most likely be under the sponsorship of Prussia.

Reaction triumphant

The uprisings of 1848 had each been intended by their instigators as a turning point in Europe's history, but Europe failed to turn. The autocracies of Russia and Austria had stood shoulder to shoulder against German liberalism and Italian nationalism alike. A new Bonaparte had thwarted any return to revolution in France. As Brendan Simms points out, for all Marxism's much-vaunted internationalism, 'it was counter-revolution that proved to be international . . . Liberals and workers had not united, but conservatives and reactionaries had.' The conservative Vienna compact had held again.

In 1851, France's Bonaparte was legally unable to run for a second term, so a coup was organized that year to make himself president, although he did not become Emperor Napoleon III until 1852. France had put its constitutional clock back fifty years. 'Plus ça change,' declared *Le Figaro*, 'plus c'est la même chose'.

Napoleon's rule was to last twenty-two years until 1870, more than twice as long as that of his uncle. His first act was to unleash a drastic rebuilding of Paris under Baron Haussmann, his city planner. Haussmann said he would 'rip open the belly of Paris, the neighbourhoods of revolt and barricades'. In their place he would create a city 'as strategically ordered as any battlefield'. Thousands of mostly poor citizens were driven into the suburbs, and in the next thirty years Paris's population more than doubled. Napoleon and Haussmann created the central Paris we see today.

Yet again, Britain was detached from this turmoil. When a French visitor flattered Palmerston by saying, 'If I were not a Frenchman, I should wish to be an Englishman,' the statesman coolly replied: 'If I were not an Englishman, I should wish to be an Englishman.' In 1851, while the tsar was humiliating Frederick William and while Napoleon III was staging his coup, Prince Albert was opening a display of Britain's scientific and commercial achievement in a Great Exhibition in Hyde Park. Its contents were drawn from every corner of the globe. The iron and glass vault, the largest in the world, was replicated in the terminus roofs of Britain's booming railways. Those who wished could ease their consciences by reading Charles Dickens's *Bleak House* (1852–3) and *Hard Times* (1854). Less easy reading was Henry Mayhew's *London Labour and the London Poor*, published in the same year as the exhibition. Britain might have avoided the upheaval of revolution, but it still displayed extremes of wealth and poverty.

The Crimean War

Russia's Tsar Nicholas, hotfoot from bullying Prussia and rescuing Austria, now moved to centre stage. The Russian empire had been fast expanding. It had won Azerbaijan and eastern Georgia from the Persians in 1813, and eastern Armenia in 1828. The Ottoman empire was looking vulnerable. Most of Greece was now independent and Serbia was granted self-government by Constantinople in 1830. The Danube principalities of Wallachia and Moldavia had also won a degree of autonomy. The Turkish hold on the Balkan Slavs was weakening.

Nicholas now unilaterally declared himself sovereign 'protector' of Turkey's Christians and guarantor of their access to the holy places of Jerusalem. In 1853, without any provocation, he invaded Wallachia and Moldavia and sank Turkey's Black Sea fleet. The resulting war was, even by Europe's standards, baffling. It was fought because a number of European powers saw Russia as too big, too ambitious and too autocratic to be allowed to spread southwards. They regarded the Ottoman empire as no longer a threat but as a useful buffer across the eastern Mediterranean.

When the Turks sought help to repel the Russians, France and Britain provided it. Napoleon III was happy to flex his muscles, and Britain was eager to keep Russia in check. The Russians immediately capitulated by agreeing to withdraw from the Danube principalities, which should have ended the war. However, Paris and London decided to punish Russia for its aggression, opening a new front to the east in Crimea.

The Crimean War (1853–6) degenerated into a series of disjointed battles and sieges. These included Balaclava and its Charge of the Light Brigade, inspiration for Tennyson's poetic celebration of military blundering. The result was a humiliating Russian defeat. In 1856, under yet another Treaty of Paris, Russia was forced to demilitarize the Black Sea. Wallachia and Moldavia were granted full independence and eventually became Romania. The long-standing dream of Russia's rulers, of an empire that would match Byzantium, died another death. Instead the treaty affirmed Turkey as 'crucial to the peace of Europe'.

Despite its outcome, the Crimean War became so unpopular in Britain that the prime minister, Lord Aberdeen, was forced to resign and concede a critical inquiry into its conduct. The war was the subject of the first on-the-spot war reporting, by William Howard Russell of *The Times*, and of publicity for battlefield conditions generated by Florence Nightingale and her field hospital at Scutari. Crimea was Britain's first military intervention in Europe for forty years, and its last for another sixty. It cost the lives of 250,000, most dying from disease. The government's excuse was that Russia had to be stopped from threatening Britain's Indian empire. As Russia had no such intention, this was specious.

Crimea may have been a senseless war, but it rearranged Europe's balance of power. Nicholas died in 1855, reputedly of shame over Crimea, to be succeeded by Alexander II (1855–81), a comparative liberal who conceded the final abolition of serfdom. This coincided with an outburst of Russian creativity, as if defeat had induced Russia to join Europe's cultural community. Tolstoy fought at Crimea and brought the vastness of Russia into the drawing rooms of Europe. Dostoevsky brought its moral complexities. Russian composers such as Tchaikovsky, Mussorgski and Borodin and, soon after, the dramatist Chekhov were among Europe's most inventive and popular artists. Alexander's Moscow did not become a second Rome, but St Petersburg (Russia's capital from 1712 to 1918) became a second Paris.

Prussia and Austria had both held aloof from Crimea. Both had reasons for not alienating Russia. Austria's now elderly Metternich, who had observed a Europe at comparative peace for half a century, returned from England to Vienna. Shortly before his death in 1859, he was visited for advice by a young aristocrat from Prussia named Otto von Bismarck.

18

Italy and Germany
1850–1900

Italy renascent

Since the end of the Lombard invasion of 568, Italy had resisted all attempts at reunification. The north was fought over by France, Austria and the powerful cities of Genoa, Milan and Venice. The papacy retained uneasy sovereignty over the centre, and Naples and Sicily changed hands between Byzantines, Saracens, Normans, the Holy Roman Empire and France. The Congress of Vienna had recognized the kingdom of Savoy, Piedmont and Sardinia and given it Genoa, as a buffer against France. One historian of the Mediterranean, Fernand Braudel, described Italy as nothing more than 'a historical entity within which events had similar repercussions and effects, and were indeed in a sense imprisoned'.

In 1852 it was little Piedmont that took the initiative. Since Vienna, it had flourished under the liberal monarchies of Charles Albert and his son, Victor Emmanuel. It now acquired the clever and ambitious Count Cavour as its prime minister. An aristocratic champion of Italian unity, he promoted the cause in his personal newspaper, *Il Risorgimento*, Revival. Piedmont sent 15,000 troops to the Crimean War, thus winning a seat at the Treaty of Paris and a useful alliance with France. Two years after the treaty, in 1858, Cavour visited Napoleon in secret and won a promise of military support in any future war with Austria.

A year later, in 1859, such a war was engineered. France duly joined Piedmont to defeat Austria at the battles of Magenta and Solferino. Devious negotiations followed, under which Austria was able to retain Venice but lost all of northern Italy to Piedmont. Cavour had to cede Savoy to France, but he had gained enough of Italy to establish an embryo Italian state, validated by local plebiscites. Piedmont's Victor Emmanuel became its king.

Events now moved with speed. In 1860 the charismatic Garibaldi, briefly defender of Rome in 1849, emerged from self-imposed exile to revive his Redshirt irregulars in the cause of Italian unity. He asked for Cavour's support in marching south to liberate Naples and Sicily from their Bourbon monarchs. Cavour's ambitions had never extended that far. North Italians still regarded the south as almost part of Africa – much as how some Germans regarded Prussians as part of Asia. But he and Victor Emmanuel could hardly deny Garibaldi their blessing. Britain's Palmerston offered crucial help from British naval units stationed in Palermo.

The Redshirts landed in Sicily and drove the Bourbons first from the island and then from the kingdom of Naples. The campaign was vividly reported by Ferdinand Eber, a blatant Garibaldi partisan and *Times* correspondent. It won Garibaldi international celebrity. He dreamed of turning southern Italy into a liberal republic, but in October 1860, at a 'meeting on the bridge' at Teano with Victor Emmanuel, he donated his conquest to Italy. Cavour forbade Garibaldi from marching on Rome. The pope was being protected by French troops, Cavour's trusted and vital allies, but within a year two-thirds of the Papal States had joined the new Italy.

Garibaldi retired in glory to dig his garden on the island of Caprera off Sardinia, emerging later as a mercenary to rebellions across Europe, though with little success. Full Italian unity had to await a time when Austria (in 1866) and France (in 1870) were distracted by bloodier struggles elsewhere. But an almost united Italy had at last come into being, and in just two years. It had been fortunate to find in Cavour and Victor Emmanuel leaders of caution and liberalism, and in Garibaldi a soldier to capture the imagination of a continent. Britain even named a Bermondsey biscuit after him. The new Italy also had its own bard, Giuseppe Verdi. His chorus of the Hebrew slaves in *Nabucco* became the anthem of Italian nationalism.

Otto von Bismarck

For centuries the territories comprising Germany had kept apart France, Austria and Russia like a repelling magnet. Napoleon and the Congress of Vienna had turned repulsion into attraction. Germany now became a problem, a 'question'. It was a culture and a people but not a nation, let alone a government. Nor did it have defined boundaries. Was it 'Germany proper', the old dukedoms and principalities, or was it Greater Germany, possibly embracing Prussia, Saxony and Bavaria? And what of Austria and its shrunken empire? These were all German-speaking peoples, descendants of the tribes of the Rhine, Elbe and upper Danube. But they were leaderless.

One witness to the collapse of Frederick William's 1848 Frankfurt parliament had no doubt as to the solution. Otto von Bismarck was the Lutheran son of a Junker landlord from Saxony, a brilliant student who rose rapidly in the conservative administration of the Prussian state. He was multilingual, energetic and high-living. He said no man should die without having consumed five thousand bottles of champagne and a hundred thousand cigars. He was never a soldier, though he affected military costume. In an age when the profession of warfare was giving way to that of diplomacy, he combined implacable Prussian nationalism with a pragmatism so amoral as to acquire its own name, realpolitik. He was to tower over the century's diplomatic personalities, already including Talleyrand, Metternich and Cavour.

By 1851 Bismarck was representing Prussia to the restored German confederation of states. He openly preached Prussian hegemony to young Germans craving the status of nationhood. In a memorandum to his king, he said a Prussia-led Germany should have no truck with the German radicals of 1848. 'The position of Prussia in Germany will not be determined by its liberalism but by its power.' It should base itself on 'strong, resolute and wise rulers who nourish the military and financial resources of the state'. A true Hegelian, Bismarck held that a citizen should enjoy 'only the degree of freedom consonant with the public welfare and the course Prussia must take in European politics'.

In 1862 Bismarck, still a professional diplomat, made a visit to London and elaborated his ambitions to Disraeli and other guests at dinner with the Russian ambassador. He astonished them, listing his objectives as being to force the Prussian assembly to pay for a new army, find a pretext for war with Austria, dissolve the old German confederacy and unite a new Germany under Prussian leadership. Disraeli warned the Austrian ambassador, 'Take care of that man; he means what he says.' Later that year Bismarck became 'minister president' of Prussia, dominant over a new Prussian king, Wilhelm I (1861–88). He told his assembly that Vienna had left Prussia with unsatisfactory boundaries, while 'the great questions of the time will not be resolved by speeches and majority decisions – the mistake of 1848 – but by iron and blood'. The message was clear: when Prussia said the Concert of Europe was over, it was over.

Bismarck and Austria

The first obstacle in Bismarck's way was Austria, ghost of the Holy Roman Empire and recently humiliated by Cavour and France in Italy. Bismarck knew the German states were suspicious of Prussia, and would prefer the light-touch 'presidency' of Austria to his iron grip. He also knew that Russia would be crucial to his designs. It had been Austria's ally at Olmütz, but that alliance had become estranged through Austria's neutrality during the Crimean War. Bismarck took advantage of another Polish revolt against Russia in 1863, in which most of Europe was on Poland's side, by offering St Petersburg his support. In return Russia would stay neutral if Prussia found itself at war with Austria.

Bismarck had his ducks in a row. France was distracted by a proxy war in Mexico. In London Disraeli had loftily declared that Britain was 'no longer a mere European power . . . She is the metropolis of a great maritime empire, more an Asiatic power than a European one.' Austria's restless Hungarians were still demanding independence from Austria, which Bismarck encouraged. In July 1866, on a trumped-up excuse, he sent the Prussian army by rail into the Austrian province of Bohemia, under a general who became the 'iron and blood' of Prussian aggression, Helmuth von Moltke.

Prussia took the field against the Austrians at the Battle of Sadová (or Königgrätz) and defeated them utterly. Bismarck then insisted that Austria cede Venice to Italy, and grant Hungary parallel status in a new Habsburg 'dual monarchy' of Austria-Hungary. Budapest was declared the equal of Vienna, with a magnificent parliament built on the Danube, a bizarre cross between the Palace of Westminster and St Peter's in Rome. Hungary was given its own assembly and government, and also its own army. Such honour was conspicuously not conferred on others in Austria's remaining empire: Bohemians, Czechs, Slovaks, Croats and Slovenes.

Within months, most of the twenty-two north German states had been encouraged to join a Prussia-led northern confederacy under a new 'German' constitution and Reichstag, elected on universal male suffrage. This parliament had no control over the Prussian government or its defence budget. When King Wilhelm was shocked at even this reform, Bismarck told him that 'universal suffrage would put you on a rock from which the waters cannot reach you'. To Bismarck, the suffrage was a sop to democracy. A proletarian franchise would prove a conservative brake not a radical force, a bulwark for autocracy against bourgeois liberalism. Bismarck was an early populist.

The south German states remained independent, but were made to sign military treaties with Berlin. They were offered choices that they could not refuse: Bismarck later admitted, 'Our linen was not always of the cleanest.' Yet he proceeded carefully. He did not press territorial demands on Austria, or seek its further humiliation. It was enough that the Habsburgs had lost all claim over the new Germany, which was to be a Prussian domain. Bismarck was applauded as 'Germany's George Washington'.

In just six years, between 1860 and 1866, the political map of Europe had been transformed. A new and powerful Germany had come into existence, as had a new, if not powerful, Italy. This had come to pass not through riots or revolutions, but through the talents of two conservatives, Cavour and Bismarck. At that same time, across the Atlantic, the United States of America was recovering from a bitter civil war (1861–5), of which the outcome was a new American federalism that would advance economically at breakneck speed. These two great federations, a union of German states and a union of American ones, were born of the same north European Protestant origins and bred in the same decade. They were to dominate the next half-century in Europe's story.

Bismarck and France

Unlike Napoleon's, Bismarck's ambitions were strategic and limited. He did not seek an empire, merely Prussia's pre-eminence in the new Europe. Though officially a servant of the Prussian state,

Bismarck was already acknowledged across Europe to have at his call an obedient monarch, a well-equipped army and a capacity for unprovoked aggression. He had made an ally of Russia, crushed Austria and united Germany. Next on his agenda was France.

Why Bismarck should regard France as in need of conquest was unclear. It might still hover on the European stage as the land of Louis XIV, and still with a Bonaparte on its throne, but it threatened no one. To Bismarck its chief transgression was to exist and, like Austria in 1866, not to have been defeated by him. He duly asserted that its defeat 'must take place before the construction of a united Germany'.

The Franco-Prussian War of 1870–71 was as pointless as that over Crimea. Neither side had a serious territorial or similar dispute with the other. Napoleon was sensitive of France's virility, still dreaming of his uncle's glories. But the only reason for war was that Bismarck so evidently wanted it, and the French high command was happy to fight one, as it could not imagine it would lose. The excuse was a parody of the War of the Spanish Succession, a dispute over the suitability of a German candidate for the Madrid throne. France declared itself 'offended' at the exception taken by the Prussian king to France's stance on the matter. In truth, the dispute was engineered by Bismarck as a provocation – and was treated as such in Paris. As was drearily familiar, two European elites went to war because they had trained all their lives to do so.

By summer 1870 politicians on both sides were seized by the fever. In Germany the southern states rallied, as intended, to Bismarck's cause and joined the north. Armies were mobilized, in France chaotically, in Germany efficiently. Prussian units, aided by carefully disposed railways, were at the French border in a matter of days, with King Wilhelm and Bismarck in attendance. The French army took weeks to assemble and performed disastrously in initial encounters. It was soon defeated by von Moltke at the Battle of

Sedan, and Napoleon was captured. The Germans marched on Paris unopposed.

The city was besieged for four months, from September 1870 to January 1871. Parisians starved, finally eating cats, dogs and zoo animals. The killing of the two elephants, Castor and Pollux, caused a minor sensation, their meat selling at a premium in the Boulevard Haussmann. It was described by the English journalist Henry Labouchere as 'tough, coarse and oily' and not recommended to English families. A popular hero, Léon Gambetta, contrived to escape in a balloon and raise an army, even inflicting a minor defeat on a Prussian force.

When Paris finally capitulated, Prussian troops marched through its streets and on to Versailles. French humiliation was complete when a new German empire was declared in Louis XIV's Hall of Mirrors. A subsequent French election chose Adolphe Thiers, a veteran of the 1830 and 1848 revolutions, to negotiate a final deal with Bismarck. This secured the departure of the Prussian army, but at the price of the transfer of most of Alsace and part of Lorraine to the German crown. France did not forget this loss, so cynically engineered by Bismarck. Europe was widely said to have 'lost a mistress and gained a master'.

Thiers' settlement was extremely unpopular in Paris and, in March 1871, an uprising led to the brief establishment of a Paris Commune. It was a throwback to 1792, its anthem 'La Marseillaise' rather than the communist 'Internationale'. The commune was suppressed by the forces of the new republican government after two months, with a brutality typical of France's treatment of its rebels. As many as 10,000 people died in a round of fighting and mass executions. The writer Émile Zola noted that he had 'never in civilized times seen such a terrible crime . . . The sound of firing squads, which one still hears in the mournful city, atrociously prolongs the nightmare.' A Third Republic was declared, but Paris saw a mass exodus of any who could afford it to London, including the artists Tissot, Pissarro and Monet, the last exquisitely to evoke the Palace of Westminster in a London smog.

What had been a Prussia of sixteen million people, in confederation with some forty traditionally non-aggressive German states, was now a Germany of forty-one million people, the biggest nation in Europe after Russia. In 1873 Bismarck set the seal on his new creation with a Dreikaiserbund, a Three Emperors League, of Russia, Austria and Germany. He formally declared a new balance of power in Europe, assuring one and all that Germany was a 'satiated power'.

Bismarck and the Congress of Berlin

If Bismarck was satiated, that was not true of the Russian government under Alexander II. In 1875, long-simmering Balkan resentment against Ottoman rule erupted into fighting in Serbia, Bosnia, Herzegovina and Bulgaria. Bulgaria's uprising in 1876 was suppressed by the Turks with extreme violence, some 12,000 civilians being massacred in reprisals. European opinion was shocked at what was regarded as genocide by Muslim Turks against Christian Slavs. Alexander needed no invitation to recover from the Crimean fiasco. He decided he would head a campaign of pan-Slavic liberation from the Turkish yoke. War broke out in 1877 and saw the Russians drive ill-equipped Turkish forces from virtually all the Balkans. Under the Treaty of San Stefano, a Russian protectorate was set up over a large new Bulgaria, extending across the entire north of the Balkans and with the tsar's nephew as its king. The Ottoman empire – widely dismissed as 'the sick man of Europe' – was humbled and Russia brought once more to the gates of Constantinople.

Despite public sympathy for the Bulgars, Europe remained as averse to Russian expansionism as it had been at the time of the Crimean

War. Turkey was still a useful buffer against Russia. Diplomatic pressure – Britain said it would even declare war if Constantinople were captured – induced Russia to agree to a new Congress of Europe. This was summoned by Bismarck to Berlin in the summer of 1878, with the intention of doing for eastern Europe what the Congress of Vienna had done for the west. It was to be his hour of triumph.

Bismarck did not personally care about the Balkans, regarding them as 'not worth the bones of a single Pomeranian grenadier'. He did care about Russia. The congress severely clipped Russia's wings. It halved the new Bulgaria, propped up Turkey and splintered the Balkans between its component peoples, with an independent Romania, Bulgaria, Serbia and Montenegro. Turkey kept Macedonia, but was detached from Bulgaria. Bosnia went to Austria-Hungary. Berlin was a classic European carve-up, with no nonsense about consultation or self-determination. But it emphatically indicated where the continent's centre of power lay, in the new Germany.

For Britain's prime minister, Disraeli (1868, 1874–80), Berlin was a reversion to Castlereagh, a careful British toe dipped into European diplomacy. His strategy was primarily directed at India. In 1875 he had enhanced imperial security by acquiring almost half the Suez Canal shares from France. A year later he delighted Queen Victoria with the title of Empress of India. He made a room at his house at Hughenden a museum of the Berlin congress (now open to the public). As for Turkey, Disraeli had been savaged by Gladstone during the Bulgarian atrocities for going soft on the Turks. Gladstone was vicious: 'There is not a cannibal in the South Sea islands whose indignation would not rise and over-boil' at Disraeli's policy. The latter replied that Gladstone was, 'of all Bulgarian horrors, perhaps the greatest'. There is nothing new in political invective.

Russia was deeply unhappy. The tsar described Berlin as 'a coalition of Europe against Russia, under the leadership of Prince Bismarck'. Since an alliance with Russia had been an anchor of Bismarck's earlier diplomacy, this was a troubling sign of the great man's loss of touch. As he grew older, Bismarck grew paranoid, seeing leftist conspiracies everywhere. He professed to trust only Britain, though he deplored any country, he said, which kept sacking its rulers 'on the whim of an electorate'. Only exhausted Austria was in Bismarck's good books. With the ink barely dry on the Berlin agreement, he in 1879 duly signed a secret treaty with Austria-Hungary, committing both parties to help each other 'with the whole war strength of their empires' in the event of an attack by Russia. Three years later this was extended to embrace Italy. The Triple Alliance echoed the Holy Roman Empire. It also alienated Russia. Yet it was Bismarck who had once remarked, 'What we learn from history is that nobody learns from history.'

Europe in the 1880s was seeing the same industrial growth and social transformation that Britain had experienced a century before. With the opening up of the grasslands of the Americas and Australasia, costs across Europe were falling. Cheap grain and refrigerated meat flooded food markets but caused an agricultural recession across Europe. The new rich were not landowners but manufacturers and distributors, bankers and traders. The change in newly united Germany was most dramatic. Coal output quintupled and seaborne trade rose seven-fold in thirty years. The Berlin government sponsored industrial cartels, notably in the new technologies of chemicals and electricity, protecting them with tariffs. It promoted industrial training, built universities and planned suburbs.

Bismarck was alert to socialism's appeal. He introduced Europe's first hint of a welfare state, a government insurance scheme against sickness, accidents at work and old age, though with no protection against unemployment. It was a barter, in return for penal laws against the propagation of socialism and other forms of dissent. The German proletariat was to be kept protected, comfortable and subservient. Prosperity was exchanged for obedience as the motif of the modern state.

The climax of the age of empire

The 1878 Congress of Berlin had led to an undignified 'scramble for Africa' by European governments, supposedly prevented from pursuing further adventures at home. Leaders sought pride in distant conquests. French governments might be unable to regain Alsace-Lorraine, but they could conquer Tunis and settle Vietnam. Belgians were setting foot in the mineral-rich Congo basin, the Portuguese were confirmed in Angola and Mozambique and the Italians in north and east Africa. In the lead was still Britain, though its reach was starting to exceed its grasp. In southern Africa it was challenged by both Zulus and Dutch Afrikaners. In Sudan General Gordon was killed by the Mahdi.

To this aggrandizement Bismarck was immune. As a virtually landlocked nation, his Germany had concerns that were the opposite of Britain's. 'I am no man for colonies,' he said. But he was now Europe's unofficial 'chairman'. He duly called another Berlin conference in 1885, supposedly to settle the map of Africa. It acknowledged Britain's overwhelming presence 'from Cairo to the Cape', but was determined to keep Britain out of the Congo basin. Bismarck proposed it as the private fiefdom of King Leopold of Belgium, which the latter ruled with peculiar extortion and brutality. Against Bismarck's better judgement, even Germany joined in and accepted what are now Namibia, Tanzania, Togo and Cameroon.

Elsewhere in the world, boundaries were being drawn by European governments, as if the globe were their plaything. In the Far East, Britain and Portugal strengthened their position on the Chinese coast. The Dutch were dominant in the East Indies. The French expanded into Indo-China. In the central Asian land mass, Russia's empire reached the far coast of Siberia, until barely a quarter of its land area was west of the Urals. Russian Alaska had been sold to America in 1867, while Russia's southern border touched Persia and Afghanistan. The new tsar, Nicholas II (1894–1917), even dreamt of adding Manchuria and Korea.

The death in 1888 of the nonagenarian Wilhelm I of Prussia, and shortly afterwards of his son, passed the crown to his twenty-nine-year-old grandson, Wilhelm II (1888–1918). The new king was physically disabled, vain and bad-tempered. He immediately declared, 'There is only one master in this country and I am he.' Wilhelm shocked Europe by promptly dismissing Bismarck, to a flurry of cartoons depicting the ship of Europe dropping its pilot. Of all the statesmen who had fashioned modern Europe, Bismarck was the most effective. Germany would have come into existence without him, but not when and how it did. Circumstance gave him the opportunity to create a new nation and he took it, but he took it by the projection of extreme force. As the strategist John Lewis Gaddis writes, he 'unified the country by provoking wars, but then secured peace by balancing resentments'.

The legacy of Bismarck's diplomacy was that these resentments were unstable, when he was not present to control them. His triple alliance with Austria and Italy reopened old insecurities. Three years later, in 1891, France and Russia felt obliged to form a dual alliance in response, and this induced in the paranoid Wilhelm a fear of encirclement. Central Europe's states were constant victims of their own geography. Yet again they were returning to type.

Fin de siècle

The statesmen who had kept Europe free of cataclysmic war over the century since Vienna had passed on. Talleyrand and Metternich were long gone. Gladstone stepped down as prime minister in 1894. An election in 1895 was won by a Tory aristocrat, Lord

Salisbury. His foreign policy was traditional, one of 'splendid isolation', doing as little as possible while Britain 'drifted lazily downstream, occasionally putting out a boat-hook to avoid collision'. As for intervening in the internal affairs of other European states, said Salisbury, 'there is no practice which the experience of nations more uniformly condemns, and none which governments more consistently pursue'. He would not.

Despite Bismarck's departure, as the century drew to a close there seemed nothing that need trouble Europe's equanimity. Britain's Queen Victoria, sovereign to twenty per cent of the world's population, was grandmother to Germany's Wilhelm, who paid her regular visits. The Prince of Wales holidayed in France, and spoke its language fluently. Tourism to the *riviera* of France and Italy boomed. The years of 1871–1914 were rightly called the belle époque.

In honour of such optimism, the tsar in 1899 summoned a peace conference to The Hague at which he invited Europe to agree, if not to abolish war, at least to promote disarmament and limit any new and terrible weapons coming onto the production line. It took forward the Geneva Convention of 1864 on the treatment of prisoners and non-combatants. It banned the destruction and looting of occupied towns. It forbade the dropping of bombs and gas from balloons, and attacks on civilian populations. A court of arbitration was set up to which conflicting states could take their case. The text stated, 'The battlefield as a place of settlement of disputes is gradually yielding to arbitral courts of justice.' Everyone appeared to agree.

Against this hopeful background, Europe's capitals sprouted with exhibitions, museums and other attractions, many of them reflecting the continent's global supremacy. Imperial competition demanded domestic expression. Britain's India Office in Whitehall was built round a Durbar Court and Queen Victoria was attended at her house at Osborne by turbaned Indian servants. In Belgium, Congolese 'native villages' were constructed, with real natives diving for coins. In 1900, Paris built a Grand Palais, where it staged a Universal Exposition with pavilions by forty countries. It was declared 'a symbol of harmony and peace for all humanity'. It had fifty million visitors.

As the twentieth century dawned, Europe held half the world's population under its sway and controlled eighty-five per cent of world trade. London's six and a half million people made it by far the biggest city on Earth. No other continent or group of peoples had ever claimed such mastery over the planet. This supremacy gave rise to a sense that Europeans were a superior race, with a right – and perhaps a duty – to conquer others, to rule them and convert them to Christianity. This power represented a Europe that had reached an evolutionary climax, and was tempted to define the word civilization in its own terms. It was the moment when it flew too close to the sun.

19

The War to End War
1900–1918

Trials of strength

Memoirs of the turn of the twentieth century are tinted with nostalgia. They dwell on Indian summers and imperial autumns. They list moments when a bold statesman, a wise decision or sheer luck might have averted the forthcoming tragedy. In retrospect, the period was one of self-satisfaction and overconfidence, but its starkest feature was a lack of leadership. Nineteenth-century Europe had been built on the deeds of bold and perceptive statesmen, if not always well-meaning ones. Few at the start of the twentieth century merit that description.

Bismarck's legacy of divergent alliances had left Germany and Austria sandwiched between France and Russia. Like it or not, Britain held a sort of balance. It was well disposed to both sides, traditionally with Germany and currently with France. In 1898 Britain clashed with the latter over a French settlement in Fashoda on the upper Nile and over fishing off Newfoundland. Negotiations led to an agreement in 1904, dubbed the Entente Cordiale. It was not a military alliance but a colonial barter. But since France was now an ally of Russia, any sign of good relations between France and Britain made Germany's Kaiser Wilhelm nervous. The Kaiser's paranoia was to dominate the next decade in Europe.

Russia too was nervous. Nicholas II ruled a country that was industrializing fast. Its growth rate, albeit from a low base, was outstripping Germany's and approaching America's. Yet the regime was insecure. Sailors mutinied in Vladivostok and students rioted in Moscow. Anti-Jewish pogroms throughout Russia and its satellites scandalized Europe, driving hundreds of thousands of Jews to western Europe, America and South Africa. A holding shed outside Hull station records the passage of an astonishing 75,000 refugees in 1906 alone, quarantined as they transited from the continent to Liverpool and on to America.

Nicholas's desire to expand his empire eastwards was brought to a halt by the Japanese at the Battle of Mukden in Manchuria in 1905. The same year he lost his fleet at the Battle of Tsushima. This was a significant warning, the first crushing of a European power by a modern Asian one. A bruised Nicholas tried to pacify his people with a 'manifesto' of half-hearted internal reforms, including freedom of speech, religion and assembly. But Russia was like France in the 1780s. Reform was arriving too late and imperialism was no salve.

The leaders of Europe were becoming belligerent. Jingoism was rising and politicians and press were goading weak statesmen towards military bravado. The German chief of staff, General Schlieffen, drew up a plan to respond to the alliance between France and Russia with a pre-emptive invasion of northern France. This would remove any French threat before Russia could mobilize and leave Germany fighting on two fronts at once.

The Kaiser became obsessed with a navy to equal Britain's, producing an instant arms race. Public opinion forced Britain's Liberal government to respond with a fleet of Dreadnought battleships. Churchill recorded that 'the Admiralty had demanded six ships; the economists offered four; and we finally compromised on eight'. As costs soared, the Chancellor of the Exchequer, David Lloyd George, increased income tax to 3.7 per cent basic rate and 7.5 per cent top rate, leading to a veto in the House of Lords and a 1909 constitutional crisis. In 1911 it led Britain finally to curb the power of its hereditary upper chamber.

The decay of peace

In May 1907 the American president, Theodore Roosevelt (1901–9), decided to reassemble Russia's Hague peace conference of 1899. This was a shift in America's foreign policy, which had long been rooted in isolation from the feuds of its European ancestors. Now the president announced that, should the European equilibrium fail, 'the United States would be obliged to step in, at least temporarily, in order to re-establish the balance of power'. America had 'become a great nation . . . and we must behave as beseems a people with such responsibilities'. This came oddly from an America which, though now the world's leading economy, had an army just half the size of Belgium's.

Roosevelt's conference was a fiasco. The Russian foreign minister dismissed disarmament as 'the idea of Jews, socialists and hysterical women'. The Austrians declared that it was 'against the idea of heroism – an idea essential to the monarchical order'. Peace had no political purchase. Britain took the fateful step of formally joining France's dual alliance with Russia, producing a Triple Entente. Though presented as a tidying of the imperial map, it was clearly aimed at Germany and broke a cardinal rule of British foreign policy. It positioned the country, not as Europe's honest broker, but on one side of the balance of power. It is hard to believe Palmerston, Disraeli or Salisbury would have countenanced it.

Bismarck had once predicted that if Europe ever again came to war it would be the result of 'some damned fool thing in the Balkans'. That region now clattered noisily onstage. Slav nationalists in Austrian-ruled Croatia, Dalmatia and Bosnia were pressing for independence. They were encouraged in this by Serbia, a nation independent of the Ottoman empire since 1878 and with many nationals living in Bosnia. In 1908, Vienna responded to a Bosnian independence plebiscite by removing Bosnia's autonomy and formally annexing it to Austria. This infuriated Serbia, which looked to Russia. That country, however, failed to support its Slav ally, since Austria had agreed to support a similar Russian venture into Bulgaria. The issue was almost trivial, but Russia was now sensitive to the charge of betraying the Slav cause.

At this point Ottoman Turkey, for so long a somnolent presence on Europe's eastern flank, experienced something unprecedented, a rebellion. In 1908 a group of students and young officers, dubbed the 'Young Turks', met in Salonika in Greece and marched to Constantinople, demanding the sultan introduce a liberal constitution. He offered one, but was immediately toppled. In 1912 former countries of the sultan's European empire came together to form a Balkan League, composed of Greece, Serbia, Bulgaria and Macedonia. A joint army defeated one Turkish force after another and, by 1913, had driven Turkey entirely from the soil of Europe, other than Istanbul. The Balkan peoples had, without external help, reversed five centuries of Ottoman occupation.

No sooner had they achieved this success than they fell out among themselves, a case of what Sigmund Freud called 'the narcissism of small differences'. They had freed themselves merely to pursue their petty squabbles. Bulgarians, Greeks, Serbs and Romanians turned against each other in conflicts of intense ferocity. All attempts at mediation failed. Serbia eventually crushed Bulgaria and emerged dominant. It then pitted itself against a more substantial foe, Austria-Hungary. In such a confrontation, Serbia had a powerful ally in Russia, and Austria in Germany.

War frenzy

Albert Camus wrote that 'plagues and wars take people equally by surprise'. Yet by 1914 all Europe was anticipating war, horrified and exhilarated in equal measure. Uniforms tramped the corridors of power. Germany thought of little else. The British ambassador in Berlin wrote home that the country was 'like a great camp ready to break up for a war at a week's notice, with a million men'. France too was swept by a mood of 'national awakening'. Its high command began plotting an early thrust into German Alsace-Lorraine.

The starting gun came as Bismarck had predicted, in the Balkans. In June 1914 Archduke Franz Ferdinand, a thoughtful, liberal-minded heir to the Austrian throne, was assassinated in the recently annexed Bosnian capital of Sarajevo. The killer was a Serb nationalist, Gavrilo Princip. Of the many tragedies preliminary to the Great War, among the greatest was the loss of Ferdinand, a moderate voice among the warmongers of Vienna. Austria declared war on Serbia.

The confrontation could, and under more courageous statesmanship would, have been resolved peacefully. The issue was a Balkan crime in a Balkan context. At worst it was an issue between Austria and Serbia, and at very worst between Austria/Germany and Serbia/Russia. Yet within three days of the Austrian declaration, the dominoes of European alliances began to fall. Russia mobilized, Germany demanded a volte-face, Russia refused. Germany declared war on Russia, which activated Russia's alliance with France.

The German strategy was ruthless. The Schlieffen Plan needed to pre-empt simultaneous French and Russian attacks on Germany's western and eastern fronts, and went immediately in to operation. A German army drove towards France through neutral Belgium, where German troops committed atrocities against the civilian population that were heavily publicized in Britain. London might have stayed its hand, but the invasion of Belgium, whose neutrality Britain had guaranteed, decided matters. The security of the Channel and the North Sea was also central to Britain's naval strategy. Britain declared war on Germany and dispatched the army to France. Britain's foreign secretary, Sir Edward Grey, remarked, 'The lamps are going out all over Europe; we shall not see them lit again in our lifetime.'

As so often in Europe's wars, there was no real casus belli between the principal participants other than the defence of international order. France, Austria, Germany and Britain had no pressing claim on each other's territory, no grievance in need of resolution. The historian A. J. P. Taylor wrote, 'Nowhere was there conscious determination to provoke a war. Statesmen miscalculated [and] became the prisoners of their own weapons. The great armies, accumulated to provide security and preserve the peace, carried the nations to war by their own weight.' Europe seemed psychologically and institutionally incapable of peace. War seemed the nobler option, as if nothing had changed since the Middle Ages. The causes of the Great War remain much debated among historians. They are summed up in the title of Christopher Clark's cast list of the period, *The Sleepwalkers*.

Europe's leaders, the mediocre Wilhelm, the debilitated Nicholas and a French government divided for and against a war, were slaves to nationalist emotion. Their populations had been indoctrinated, taxed and promised a quick and glorious victory. Even the British, whose prime minister, Herbert Asquith, was the embodiment of caution, were seized by war fever. Anti-German feeling was so strong that the royal family was eventually forced to change its surname from Saxe-Coburg-Gotha to Windsor. This yielded a rare joke from the Kaiser, that Shakespeare's play be changed to *The Merry Wives of Saxe-Coburg-Gotha*. Churchill wrote to his wife,

'Everything tends towards catastrophe and collapse. I am interested, geared up and happy. Is it not horrible to be built like that?'

War in the trenches

The opening weeks of hostilities saw a repeat of Bismarck's assault of 1870. The German army advanced swiftly into France, and was soon on the banks of the Marne and within a day's march of Paris. The French government, with trainloads of papers, fled south to Bordeaux. The German advance was halted by a concerted French and British counter-attack, pushing the over-confident Germans back some fifty miles. By September 1914 a front had stabilized the length of France's north-eastern border, from Lorraine to the coast. At the same time, the Germans had to divert troops to confront a Russian invasion from the east, culminating in the Battle of Tannenberg. Though this was a crushing defeat for the Russians, it led to the pinning down of a large German army on the eastern front for three years, precisely the outcome the Schlieffen Plan was meant to avoid.

As the war progressed, armies that had been trained to fight set-piece battles to a swift result became literally entrenched. They were unable to manoeuvre across fields of barbed wire and ditches that were reduced to deep mud by the broken dykes of the Flanders plain. Machine guns and artillery rendered defence easy and attack suicidal. Any progress involved horrendous losses. Trench warfare took on a rhythm of its own. It was hard to lose, and even harder to win.

The war was not confined to Europe. Half a century of imperialism offered a theatre for a global conflict. A quarter of a million British and Empire troops, at Churchill's initiative as head of the navy, were sent to the Middle East to fight Germany's ally, Turkey. A campaign at Gallipoli in Turkey in the spring of 1915 met with disaster at the hands of German-led Turks, with appalling losses among Australian and New

Zealand troops. There was fighting too in Mesopotamia, Palestine and the German colonies, particularly east Africa.

The war at sea was of limited strategic importance, since both sides were initially reluctant to risk expensive tonnage in fleet-sized engagements. However, in May 1916 the Kaiser's battle fleet did eventually leave port into the North Sea and confront the main British fleet off Jutland. Fought in thick fog, this became Europe's last great contest between ships in line. Though the British took the worse casualties, the German armada was forced back to port and the Allied blockade continued. Germany fared better in the submarine war. During 1915, German U-boats devastated convoys bringing food and others supplies to Britain, sinking a hundred ships a month. The Royal Navy refused to guard these convoys, as it meant removing ships from the German blockade.

The war on the western front reached its nadir in the summer of 1916 in the carnage of Verdun and the Somme. British, French and German governments all sacked their commanders. In December the British government fell, and a new Liberal leader, the energetic David Lloyd George (1916–22), took over as coalition prime minister. The dawn of 1917 was perhaps the bleakest Europe had seen since the Thirty Years War. The attrition of lives lost at the front seemed remorseless and unproductive. Yet the belligerence of public opinion at home was sustained. The mood of the time was later recaptured in the ironic title of a London musical, *Oh! What a Lovely War*.

Revolution in Russia

While breakthrough proved elusive on both western and eastern fronts, two million Russian deaths had by 1916 produced a surging demand for peace. Food riots in the capital, Petrograd – its name changed from Germanic St Petersburg – saw mutinies and military defections. Nicholas was unable to maintain order and, in March 1917, he abdicated, handing executive power to a provisional government. This continued to prosecute the war, but against the demands of its rivals, the revolutionary Bolsheviks.

Germany now played a master stroke, to prove of seismic significance for the future of Europe. It arranged safe passage for the exiled Bolshevik leader, the charismatic Lenin, by secret train from Switzerland to Petrograd. There he was expected to stir the embers of revolution to life and bring an end to the war in the east. After surviving an initial coup, the provisional government was toppled in November 1917 and evicted by Lenin from the Winter Palace. The slogan was 'Peace, Land, Bread and all power to the Soviets'.

First came peace. Lenin immediately sought a treaty with Germany, but the terms offered by the German military commanders were so humiliating that even their own diplomats were shocked. The Russians were told to hand over virtually the entire tsarist empire in the west. This even Lenin could not bring himself to do. It was therefore not until March 1918 that the two sides signed the Treaty of Brest-Litovsk. Germany took Estonia, Lithuania and most of Poland. Ukraine was granted what proved to be a brief independence. Russia lost Riga and Kiev, as well as a third of its population, half of its industries and almost all its coal mines.

Russia might have suffered, but the Kaiser's greed proved disastrous. The delay of four months in the Brest-Litovsk negotiations postponed his freedom to move his eastern army to the western front. That delay cost him the war.

The turning of the tide

German submarine attacks on neutral shipping at last converted American opinion to intervention. It had already been enraged by the German torpedoing of the liner RMS *Lusitania* in 1915, with the deaths of 128 Americans on board. In the spring of 1917, a once reluctant president, Woodrow Wilson (1913–21), declared war on Germany, leading Lloyd George to remark presciently that 'at one bound, America has become a world power'. The question was now a practical one, how soon could American troops reach the western front. The British commander, General Haig, jotted in his diary, 'Please God let there be victory before the Americans arrive.' God did not oblige.

A crucial change was the initiation of armed naval escorts for Atlantic supply convoys. This abruptly tilted losses at sea in the Allies' favour against the U-boats. By spring of 1918 the tempo quickened. In March, Brest-Litovsk at least enabled the German general Ludendorff to transfer troops from the eastern front. He threw an army some three million strong at mostly British lines in Flanders, which were pushed back before him. He could resume his march on Paris. Guns shelled the city's streets from sixty-five miles away. For a moment in the spring of 1918, it seemed as if Germany might win after all.

The poorly conducted German advance came too late, and was again halted by fierce fighting at the Marne, this time with the aid of arriving American troops. Back along the Flanders front, Allied armies were reinforced by 400 British tanks, and by a new Royal Air Force. The Germans collapsed before a concerted counter-attack at Amiens, and soon Allied troops were streaming across open country towards Germany.

Germany could no longer resist. A debilitated land was afflicted by food riots and mutinies, and the high command pleaded for an armistice before its enemies reached German soil. This came into force on 'the eleventh hour of the eleventh day of the eleventh month'. The Kaiser abdicated and fled to the Netherlands. His generals vanished, leaving a civilian administration to agree peace terms with the Allies. Ten million soldiers had by then died, and probably another seven million civilians.

Nor was that the totality of horror. In 1918 an event occurred as if to remind Europe that natural disasters could top even the most terrible manmade ones. The worst flu epidemic on record swept the globe, from Polynesia to the Arctic. Estimates of deaths have grown to between twenty and fifty million worldwide, with more than 2.5 million in Europe alone. Young soldiers who had survived the war were crammed into barracks and field camps and died in their thousands. The Kaiser, Lloyd George and Woodrow Wilson all fell ill. The disease was dubbed Spanish flu because wartime censorship forbade reporting of deaths elsewhere. News came only from the press in neutral Spain.

The Treaty of Versailles

In January 1919, the victorious powers gathered in Paris to formulate what became the Treaty of Versailles. A British delegate, Harold Nicolson, recalled that they were summoned to 'found a new order in Europe . . . preparing eternal peace. There was about us the halo of some divine mission.' Delegates met in the almost mystical belief that the Great War had, in H. G. Wells's variously quoted words, been the 'war that will end war'. That anything like it might occur again was unimaginable. Peace was inevitable – an assumption that was to dominate European diplomacy over the next two decades.

Delegates then proceeded to make that assumption ever less plausible. The Germans had hoped for agreement on the fourteen-point programme put forward by Wilson in January 1918. These entrenched a new relationship between European states as constituted under principles of democracy, self-determination and free trade. Borders would be determined by local plebiscite. There also should be a 'general association', or league of nations, to monitor the peace. The proposals were well meant and well crafted.

Germany's hopes – and Wilson's – were dashed by France. Under a belligerent former journalist, Georges Clemenceau, the French were determined 'that the legacy of Bismarck must be destroyed'. Germany should be humiliated. It was stripped of lands that had been annexed from Poland and all the lands lost by Russia under Brest-Litovsk. Germany's short-lived overseas colonies were distributed round the victorious powers.

The map of east Europe was radically redrawn. The Austro-Hungarian empire, which in 1914 had been larger than Germany, was dismantled into some of its component national groups, peoples that had been melded, however reluctantly, into one federation for centuries. They were granted uncertain independence as Hungary, Czechoslovakia and Yugoslavia, though with no guarantees as to their security.

The Ottoman empire was abolished and a new state of Turkey was created, to fall within four years under the secularizing sway of Kemal Atatürk. The Arab lands of the Levant and Mesopotamia had been promised their independence, perhaps recklessly, by T. E. Lawrence 'of Arabia' if they supported the Allies. This pledge was broken and most of the Arab lands were mandated to the Allied powers.

A diminished Russia now emerged in a new guise, as Europe's greatest ideological experiment since the French Revolution. Lenin in July 1918 had murdered the former tsar, his family and servants. In Germany he welcomed the forthcoming 'transfer of power to the German proletariat', coupled with the fall of European capitalism. A soviet was briefly formed in Bavaria. Anglo-American concern at this new Russia was intense. Britain's Churchill called for a rebuilt Germany, as 'a dyke of peaceful, lawful, patient strength and virtue, against the flood of red barbarism flowing from the east'.

Versailles was deaf to all this. In June 1919 a new treaty was signed in Louis's great palace, chosen to avenge Bismarck's humiliation of France in the same building in 1871. Germany was now to be disarmed and forbidden any tanks or aircraft. The Rhineland was to be occupied by Allied troops for ten years, to prevent any new encroachment towards France. A starving and destitute Germany was presented with a staggering reparations bill, estimated in present-day money as $430 billion. Wilhelm's battle fleet was interned at Scapa Flow in the Orkneys, where it was scuttled by its commander. Seventy-four mostly new ships were lost, many to become a treasure-trove for divers ever since.

Versailles was heir to Vienna, Utrecht and Westphalia, but it outstripped them all in its redrawing of the map of east Europe. While its borders were hard to the west, they were soft to the east, and clearly vulnerable to ongoing tension between Germany and communist Russia. Besides, the treaty's overseer was not some 'concert' of European nations. It was a new and untried institution, a League of Nations, whose inventor and guarantor, America, subsequently declined even to join it. The league thus lacked the remotest means of enforcing its decisions.

20

The Years in Between
1918–1939

The aftermath of Versailles

The Versailles treaty was a low point in European diplomacy. It left resentment throughout Germany and bitterness that others were not sharing their war guilt. Only exhaustion and starvation forced Berlin's eventual capitulation. France, on the other hand, felt that Germany was insufficiently punished. Italy was dismayed, as it had switched sides to the Allies during the war but gained less than it had hoped from doing so. This dismay led to the emergence in 1919 of a 'Blackshirt' breakaway from the socialists of a charismatic war veteran, Benito Mussolini. In Britain the 1918 'khaki' election was fiercely anti-German, with calls 'to squeeze Germany until the pips squeak'. It was the first vote in which women, albeit those over thirty, were allowed to participate. Other northern European countries were enfranchising women at the same time. France and the Latin countries did not follow suit until the thirties and forties.

Not everyone saw Versailles in the same light. Lloyd George was so worried at its severity that he wondered whether 'we shall have to fight another war all over again . . . at three times the cost'. The British economist John Maynard Keynes attended the Paris conference as an adviser and reacted in a diatribe, *The Economic Consequences of the Peace*. To him, crippling Germany would render it politically vulnerable. 'The campaign for securing out of Germany the general costs of the war,' he said, 'was one of the most serious acts of political unwisdom for which our statesmen have ever been responsible.' Debate has since questioned Keynes's economic analysis, but he was more than vindicated politically. Versailles should have sought a revival of the pre-Bismarck liberal Germany, yet it poisoned the soil from which that liberalism might have emerged. It fostered a sense of siege. It weakened recovery and put moderation at a discount. A challenge was thrown down to Prussian extremism, which was soon accepted.

The war had other indirect consequences. Conflict on such an unprecedented scale had demanded mass mobilization, the dedication of the entire economic and political community to a common cause. This meant the state controlling markets, allocating resources and directing labour. It extended a state bureaucracy as never imagined before. While peace might demobilize an army, it offered no incentive for the state to disappear. As states make war, so wars make states.

This was most manifest in Britain. For the first time, industry had seen something called 'planning'. Over a hundred railway companies were rationalized into four groupings. A programme of house-building – 'homes fit for heroes' – was undertaken. This sprawled over the suburban countryside while the rest of Europe was mostly building flats. An incipient welfare state emerged, with the extension of Lloyd George's pre-war national insurance. Estate duty, rising in some cases to forty per cent, meant landed families faced what they saw as penal levels of taxation. Some emigrated, others married American heiresses. After a century of struggle, Ireland was in 1921 at last given its independence. Only six mostly Protestant counties in the north-east were to remain within the United Kingdom.

The craving for peace

German governments, mostly of the left, came and went amid mounting anarchy. Strikes were persistent. Berlin's initial inclination to reject Versailles was countered by the army saying it could not resume fighting. A new threat was emerging to the east. Soviet Russia, excluded from the League of Nations, in 1920 sent the Red Army into supposedly independent Poland, anticipating a communist uprising. The prospect of Bolsheviks advancing to the German border shocked the Allies and the outcome was a rare victory for Poland over Russia, the Red Army being defeated at the Battle of Warsaw. This little-publicized battle was historically crucial, halting a communist advance into central Europe when the latter was at its most vulnerable. The 1921 Treaty of Riga freed Poland and the Baltic states from the Soviet threat, for the time being, leaving Russia now dominant over Ukraine and the Caucasus.

Germany made its first reparations payment in August 1921. It then purchased foreign currency for its next payment and, as the value of the mark fell, it printed more marks. By 1922 the mark was in free fall, with the presses turning out ever more notes. Hyperinflation became rampant. Forty-eight marks to the dollar became 320 and upwards. In the second half of the year, the German cost of living rose fifteen times and the country lurched from post-war malnutrition into extreme poverty. By the following year the mark had crashed to four trillion to the dollar and Berlin saw spenders crowding shops, bars and the new jazz clubs, ridding themselves of increasingly useless currency.

At the beginning of 1923, with Germany unable to purchase foreign exchange and reparations payments having ceased, France sent 100,000 troops into the Ruhr to seize factories and coal mines as penalties. The move rendered Germany less rather than more able to pay, and certainly less inclined to do so. The French action was opposed in London, Washington and elsewhere, and united Germans in misery and resentment. The Ruhr workers went on general strike. France's economic aggression was conspicuously counter-productive.

By the following summer a degree of stability had returned to

Germany under a new chancellor, Gustav Stresemann. In 1923 he created a new Rentenmark, fixed to the price of gold bonds, and the printing presses fell silent. But the government in Weimar, to where it had moved in 1919, could not establish authority. There were uprisings by communists on the left and nationalists on the right, often fighting openly in the streets. Among the nationalists was a war veteran and jobbing artist in Munich, Adolf Hitler. On 8 November 1923, at a rowdy meeting in a Munich beer cellar, he leaped on a chair and, in a stirring speech, called for a 'national socialist' revolution. He had been inspired by Mussolini's march on Rome the previous year, which led to the fall of the Italian government and the Duce's assumption of power.

Hitler called for a similar march on the Bavarian government, but he and his followers barely got down the street before the army stopped them. Sixteen of Hitler's comrades were killed, including an associate shot dead at his side. The so-called Beer Hall putsch failed and Hitler was imprisoned for five years, though a complicit judge let him out after nine months. In prison he dictated his manifesto, *Mein Kampf*, to a fellow prisoner, Rudolf Hess. By the start of 1924 German inflation had peaked, but the nation was virtually ungovernable.

The spirit of Locarno

Allied governments were growing increasingly worried that Keynes's predictions were coming true. France's policy of revenge was inflammatory, stirring dangerous forces, left and right, within Germany. The French shipped coal from German mines to French power stations and sent Senegalese troops to 'guard' the campus of Frankfurt University. Communists did well in German and Austrian elections, with Russian agents supposedly active in both. To most of Europe, Hitler in a Munich beer cellar was trivial compared with Lenin on a pan-European crusade.

This did not last. In January 1924 Lenin died after a series of strokes. His brain was sliced minutely to be studied for signs of genius, and his embalmed body went on display in Red Square. Joseph Stalin moved swiftly to assume power. His series of five-year plans was to start in 1928, the first attempt to reorder what amounted to an imperial economy on communist lines.

In Britain an altogether milder socialist revolution occurred at the same time, when in 1924 a first (minority) Labour government briefly took office under Ramsay MacDonald. Its members had no five-year plans but rather worried over whether they should wear top hats to the Palace or create hereditary peers. The government lasted just ten months, to be replaced by the Conservatives under Stanley Baldwin. His slogan, promoted by the new medium of radio, was a reprise of Tory policy down the ages, 'freedom from adventures and commitments at home and abroad'. The Tories' most enlightened creation was another product of Great War upheavals, the conversion in 1926 of the older dominions of the British empire into a 'commonwealth'. As yet, it was a white commonwealth.

The Versailles treaty was now being recognized as unsustainable and a redrawing was suggested by an American politician, Charles Dawes. This proposed a withdrawal of French troops from the Ruhr, a reduction and staging of reparations and the offer of loans for rebuilding. The result was the Locarno treaty of 1925, involving Germany, Britain, France, Italy and Belgium. It was a mutual non-aggression pact, recognizing the Versailles borders and admitting Germany to the League of Nations. France acquiesced. Stalin's Russia remained excluded.

Locarno was the high point of diplomacy between the wars, a desperate attempt to reassert the inevitability of peace. The British Foreign Office named its chief reception room after it, and those involved secured Nobel Peace Prizes. The French foreign minister, Aristide Briand, recalled, *A Locarno, nous avons parlé européen. C'est une langue nouvelle'*, we have spoken European, a new language. Three years later, in 1928, the Kellogg–Briand pact went further and 'outlawed war as an instrument of national policy', with the crucial exclusion of 'national defence'. It was an eerie repeat of the Hague conference of 1899, and was signed by fifty states. In 1930 Briand even proposed a 'European Federal Union', to begin with economic co-operation. They were heady days.

Kellogg–Briand was a sincere attempt to extend the rule of law above and beyond the purlieu of individual states to govern dealings between them. From Westphalia, through Vienna to Versailles, this concept of replacing inter-state violence with a judicial and diplomatic process had eluded Europe's concert of nations. Now the so-called 'spirit of Locarno' was enhanced by a belief in the pacifying power of economic growth. Cars were filling Europe's roads, their number doubling each year. Cities sprouted factories for consumer goods, cosmetics, medicines and vehicles. Suburban housing estates, central heating and electric trains were freeing families from the pollution and overcrowding of cities. British home ownership rose from one household in ten in 1910 to one in three by the 1930s. Farm mechanization, notably the combine harvester, boosted agricultural productivity. Contraceptive devices arrived and divorce soared, as did jazz music, night clubs and luxury liners. A fashion revolution saw the Parisian couturier Coco Chanel replace extravagant Edwardian flounces with clean, slender lines.

Crash, recession and doubt

This optimism was dented by the financial crash of 1929. Its cause was the bursting of a speculative bubble on the New York stock exchange which spread swiftly to its counterparts in London and on the continent. This was exacerbated by what the economic historian Robert Skidelsky has analysed as 'a delayed reaction to the war': new European nations 'each with their own tariffs and misaligned currencies, and a Britain no longer serving as Europe's lender of last resort'. Faced with this crisis, finance ministries defied Keynes's advice. They tied their currencies to gold, restricted the supply of money and cut spending. Banks failed across the continent. In 1931 Germany proposed a customs union, covering the new states of east Europe and Austria, in effect a greater German economic space. When France objected, the Rothschilds' Vienna bank, Credit-Anstalt, collapsed and German unemployment rose from three to five million.

The Allies met in Geneva in 1932 and faced a German chancellor, Heinrich Brüning, pleading for relief. Again the French objected, and Brüning was forced to resign. It was a fateful moment. That November, the German electorate split left and right, with communists and Nazis both feasting on national humiliation. Nazi strength tended to be concentrated in the old Prussian provinces, while the left tended to be stronger in the west and Catholic south. Hitler emerged at the end of 1932 as leader of the largest party in the Reichstag, and secured the chancellorship from the ageing president, Hindenburg. A month later, a fire burned down the Reichstag building, possibly instigated by the Nazis but blamed by them on the communists. Hitler demanded and got from Hindenburg an 'enabling act', with dictatorial powers to suppress freedom of assembly and speech. His colleague Hermann Goering declared that 'every communist should be shot'.

The Versailles chickens were now coming home to roost. France had largely dictated the terms enforced on Germany after the war, and then undermined each moderate German leader. But the Allies all shared responsibility for the rise of German fascism. They were now so immersed in the Depression as to be indifferent to Germany's shifting power structure. If France's attitude to Germany was blinded by revenge, that of her fellow Allies was blinded by guilt. Either way, Hitler was left a free hand to build up his strength.

From 1933 the new German chancellor moved with speed. His programme was to eliminate communists, suppress 'international Jewry', end reparations and rebuild his country's military and industrial power. Manufacturing was put on a war footing. In 1934, the Brownshirt SA was suppressed – more than 150 of Hitler's former colleagues being murdered in a 'night of the long knives' – and replaced by a paramilitary SS, operating outside the law. It mimicked Junker militarism, including its black uniforms. The Boy Scouts became the Hitler Youth. 'Racial science' was taught in schools. To Germany, Versailles was dead, its signatories denounced as 'the criminals of 1918'.

Hitler in these early months was careful to court respectability. He slowed his campaign against the Jews during the 1936 Berlin Olympics, which he made a display of blatant chauvinism – which the games have retained in part ever since. Visitors to Germany at the time were often impressed by the vigour of the Nazis, as they were by Mussolini's Fascists. The Foreign Office's Robert Vansittart recorded that 'these tense, intense people are going to make us look like a C nation'. Young people across Europe, tired of talk of past wars, were eager for change. They warmed to upbeat confident leaders who could metaphorically 'make the trains run on time'. This spirit even infected corners of British society, from the *Daily Mail* to the Prince of Wales. In concluding his history of Europe in 1935, H. A. L. Fisher could see the ingénue Hitler as 'the wild hero of a Wagnerian opera'.

Slowly, Allied governments began to view events in Germany with alarm. Hitler, like the Kaiser before him, was obsessed with encirclement. He dallied with the idea of a united Europe, but his expansionism was essentially nationalist, seeking *Lebensraum* (living space) for a pure German *Volk*. Such space lay most obviously to the east, where, since Versailles, millions of Germans lived under an alien sovereignty, notably in Poland and Czechoslovakia. They were an open invitation to restore the integrity of what Hitler saw as the German-speaking Aryan race. As with Bismarck, at this point he sought a critical geography for a German nation.

Within a decade, Europe had lost the glad confident morning of Locarno, but Hitler could still call on enough guilt over Versailles to stave off pressure to curb him. At the 1935 British election, none of the parties proposed rearmament, Baldwin remarking that such a promise would have been electoral suicide. Britain's strategy, as so often in the past, was to stand apart from Europe, behind a moat of air and sea, defended by an air force and a navy. Nazi propaganda concocted a mythical headline, 'Fog in Channel – Continent Cut Off' to illustrate Britain's lack of concern for Europe.

In 1935, Locarno was finally shattered when Mussolini invaded Ethiopia, seeking to link it with Italy's colonies in Somaliland and Eritrea. The aggression was supported by Hitler, and the blatant breach of League of Nations rules went unpunished. Yet public opinion still assumed diplomacy would avert trouble. In Britain, the largest ever privately organized referendum in history, the Peace Ballot in the summer of 1935, attracted a turnout of eleven and a half million voters, thirty-eight per cent of the adult population. They were variously and overwhelmingly in favour of peace, the League of Nations and an end to arms manufacture. The ballot did, however, endorse by a majority that 'if a nation insists on attacking another, the other nations should combine to compel it to stop . . . if necessary by military measures'.

Appeasement and the descent to Munich

In March 1936 Hitler took his first overt act of aggression and sent troops to reoccupy the Rhineland. Neither France nor Britain responded. Had they done so, it is now known that Hitler had given the army an order to pull back. He would have concentrated on his eastern border. At the same time, Germany formed an 'axis' with Italy. Hitler next sent bombers to support the fascist General Franco in his rebellion against the left-wing government in Madrid. The Spanish civil war was to run for three years, with mounting atrocity. In April 1937 bombers attacked the Basque town of Guernica, the pilots incinerating or machine-gunning civilians on the ground. The attack was vividly recorded in a Cubist painting by Pablo Picasso. Hitler also negotiated a friendly understanding with Japan in the Far East, aimed at containing the Soviet Union.

That union was now experiencing its own horrors. Stalin's early plans were delivering improved industrial output. But the manner of their implementation, in particular the collapse of food production, drove people to starvation and him to obsessive paranoia. He particularly feared revolt in Ukraine, visiting on that country in 1932–3 a 'Holodomor', or killing by starvation. Deaths have been estimated at between four and seven million people, starved or killed, mostly as supposed enemies of collectivization. There were similar death rates in Kazakhstan. Unlike the Holocaust, these famines remained unreported for decades, and were therefore unacknowledged until 2008, when the Ukrainian Holodomor was recognized by the European Parliament as a crime against humanity.

By 1936–7 the Great Purge had brutalized the Soviet regime. In that period it is estimated that about a million people in the Soviet Union were executed or sent to death camps by their government. Not since the French Revolution had a regime murdered so many of its own, including officials, businessmen, intellectuals, farmers and even Stalin's colleagues. Stalin's rival, Leon Trotsky, had been expelled from office and exiled to Mexico, where Stalin had him killed in 1940.

Sabres were now rattling on all sides. In 1938 Hitler demanded that

Germany merge with Austria. When the Austrian government refused, Hitler invaded, telling delighted Viennese crowds that 'the German people will never again be rent apart'. He then cited the Versailles creed of self-determination and demanded Czechoslovakia's German-speaking Sudetenland. Again the former allies were in an agony of indecision. No government would seriously go to war for the Sudetenland, described in the British press as 'Germany's backyard'.

In September 1938 the British prime minister, Neville Chamberlain, and his French counterpart went to Munich to seek an accommodation with the Czechs and Hitler. He was in effect tearing up Versailles. He conceded the Sudetenland in exchange for a promise from Hitler of no more such aggressions, returning to London to declare he had won 'peace for our time'. Britons were hysterical with relief. Chamberlain unquestionably represented majority opinion in his country at the time. He had forestalled a European war that Britain would have lost, a conflict he described in a broadcast as over 'a faraway country, between people of whom we know nothing'.

Across the Atlantic, America had reverted to isolationism following Versailles. It had already helped end one war on Europe's behalf, and it was disinclined to do so again. The president, Franklin Roosevelt (1933–45), was aware of the risk from Hitler to the Wilsonian settlement of Europe, but he was constrained by Congress. When he heard news of Munich, Roosevelt cabled Chamberlain: 'Good man'. Hitler responded to Europe's timidity with *Kristallnacht*, a destruction of Jewish properties across Germany and Austria.

Over the winter of 1938–9, Hitler's reaction to these successive acts of appeasement led Britain to realize the need for rearmament. A public opinion wildly for peace now had to contemplate war. Chamberlain, despite having supported rearmament on taking office in 1937, went from hero to villain overnight. Hitler derided him as 'that silly old man . . . with his umbrella'. The French punned his name as 'Monsieur J'aime Berlin'. To the maverick Churchill,

'We have passed an awful milestone in our history, when the whole equilibrium of Europe has been deranged.' Britain and France even put out feelers to an alliance with Moscow, Hitler's putative foe.

Hitler next approached Poland for a pact allowing his armies to cross its territory in the event of conflict with Moscow. Poland refused, hoping to rely on western aid in the event of trouble. Hitler did not wait. At the same time in August 1939 when Allied negotiators were discussing an alliance with Stalin, Hitler's emissary, Ribbentrop, was signing a non-aggression pact with Russia's foreign minister, Molotov. It included a secret protocol agreeing to divide Poland and the Baltic states between them, an echo of the aggression of Catherine and Frederick the Great. When asked how he could treat with a fascist dictator, Molotov told journalists that 'fascism is a matter of taste'. It was pure opportunism on both sides.

On 1 September 1939, without ultimatum or negotiation, Hitler drove an army of one and a half million troops into west Poland, while Moscow did the same into east Poland. Stalin confided to his colleagues his intention to liquidate the Polish state. Some 70,000 Polish troops died on their eastern and western fronts. Ten times that number were taken prisoner. Thousands of officers were later shot and hundreds of thousands of civilians were slaughtered in cold blood. Poland was to suffer appallingly over the next six years.

These aggressions were such glaring breaches of Versailles, and so hostile to the peace of Europe, that Britain and France had no option. As Chamberlain said to the nation on the morning of 3 September, 'the situation in which no word given by Germany's ruler could be trusted, and no people or country could feel itself safe, has become intolerable'. Britain and France were therefore in a state of war with Germany. Since Hitler had as yet shown no aggression towards either country, both hoped such a conflict might be confined to Germany's eastern frontier, where it might also contain Soviet expansionism.

21

The Second World War
1939–1945

Germany's opening moves

The start of the Second World War was like an opening in a game of chess – predictable. As with the first war, Germany sought to escape its geography. It looked eastwards, towards the open lands beyond the Oder and Danube, and westwards across the Rhine into the ever-contested territory of old Lotharingia. Hitler was a keen student of history. Bismarck in the 1860s had carefully covered his back with an alliance with Russia, to give him room for manoeuvre against Austria and France. He had done so with conspicuous success. In 1914 Kaiser Wilhelm had failed to do likewise, and paid a terrible price by fighting on two fronts. By 1939 Hitler had neutralized Austria, Czechoslovakia and Poland, and had held the Soviet Union in check with the Molotov–Ribbentrop pact. He knew that he would one day have to reckon with the Soviet Union, but for the moment France had to be removed from the equation. The strategic clarity was Bismarckian.

Hitler had been a private soldier in the trenches, and was unencumbered by the received wisdom of generals fighting the proverbial 'last war but one'. He had learned the critical value of mobile armour. An army should move at the speed of its fastest tank, while everyone else should catch up. German industry rallied to the cause, turning out tanks, ships and aircraft by the hundreds in a matter of months.

Over the winter of 1939–40, Hitler took stock. He already had his *Lebensraum*, and there were rumours of peace feelers put out to Britain and France, to which Britain's foreign secretary, Lord Halifax, is known to have been sympathetic. But an Allied threat to block Swedish iron exports to Germany in Norwegian waters led him in April 1940 to invade Denmark and Norway. An Allied expeditionary force was forced to withdraw, and a Commons debate in London led to Chamberlain's resignation and his succession by a coalition headed by Churchill. On one matter all – or almost all – agreed, there could now be no deal with Hitler or any further British aloofness from a looming European war. Still it was hoped that war might prove 'phoney'.

In May, Hitler sent his tanks through the Ardennes forest in southern Belgium, bypassing France's supposedly impenetrable Maginot Line of fortresses. He swept aside a British force sent to northern France to stop him, driving it back to Dunkirk. Reluctant at this stage for open war with Britain, and wanting to rest his tanks, Hitler let its soldiers return home with minimal harassment. The Dunkirk evacuation was even portrayed in Britain as a sort of triumph. France's defences were hopeless. German troops swiftly reached Paris and Hitler was filmed driving down the Champs-Élysées and posing before the Eiffel Tower.

All northern France was soon in German hands, while the south came under the pro-German Vichy regime of Marshal Pétain. In contrast to the First World War, France's involvement in the Second was minimal. Less successful was Hitler's reliance on his axis with Italy to master southern Europe. Mussolini's attempt to expand Italy's 'empire' into the Balkans and Africa met with failure. German troops had to invade the Balkans themselves, and move on to Greece. In Spain, Hitler's negotiations with Franco foundered on the latter's unacceptable demands for French territory in Africa, though Franco affirmed Spain's promise of neutrality.

As for Britain, Hitler relied on its traditional detachment in the hope it would avoid a continental conflict. None the less, he allowed his staff to prepare Operation Sealion for an invasion of Britain's south coast, should the need arise. Since Germany lacked sea power comparable to Britain's navy, Hitler was adamant that Sealion should not proceed without the neutralization of Britain's navy and air force. An attempt to wipe out the RAF was baulked when it won the 'Battle of Britain' in the summer of 1940, a success brilliantly exploited by Churchill to restore morale after Dunkirk. Hitler was undoubtedly wise to doubt the feasibility of a German invasion of Britain. The British navy was as yet undefeated, and its air force had shown itself effective against the Luftwaffe. Hitler cancelled Sealion in September 1940.

The Anglo-German war now became a tit-for-tat of bombing, at great cost but dubious strategic value. Both sides' air commanders insisted that bombs would weaken war production and break popular spirit, such that governments would have to capitulate. It was a strategy that applied to the enemy but not to one's own side, which was supposedly strengthened by the 'blitz spirit'. This mutated into an argument over whether bombs should be aimed at military/industrial targets, or at civilian areas for maximum terror impact, even though attacking civilians breached the Hague conventions. Since military targets required precision and were heavily defended, air forces preferred easier objectives. The leading advocate of terror bombing, Britain's Arthur 'Bomber' Harris, sought 'a state of devastation in which surrender is inevitable'. The thesis was to be tested to massive destruction, and survives in the 'shock and awe' tactics of air forces to this day.

The Axis ascendant

In September 1940 Hitler signed an alliance with Italy and Japan, agreeing that Germany would support Japan in the event of war with

America. This risked repeating the Kaiser's error in 1915, when he also goaded America into opposing him. It jeopardized the isolationism that was overwhelmingly popular in America, so much so that Roosevelt fought for re-election in November 1940 with the pledge, 'I say it again and again and again. Your boys are not going to be sent into any foreign wars.' After he won the election, and under intense pressure from Churchill, he said the precise opposite, warning of a 'second world war' when America 'must be the great arsenal of democracy'. Roosevelt launched Lend-Lease in 1941 as a massive aid package to the British and, later, Soviet war efforts. American ships now became targets for German U-boats, even close to America's eastern seaboard. The U-boats were the one thing that 'truly frightened' Churchill.

By the end of 1940, Hitler had all but conquered continental Europe. No German army had suffered a defeat and German military casualties were small. Germany's neighbours now found themselves beholden to German military commanders. Their soldiers and war machines were requisitioned, their Jews, gypsies and communists rounded up and enslaved or killed. As under Napoleon, a single mind and a single obsession were again dictating the actions of rulers across Europe. Only Stalin and Churchill still had some freedom of manoeuvre.

Talleyrand had observed that a megalomaniac leader's next move is usually governed only by the opportunities opened up by the last. Hitler now adjusted his ambitions to circumstance. While ostensibly eager to avoid war with America, Hitler had to guard against the possibility of one. In February 1941 he dispatched General Rommel's Afrika Korps to Libya, to prevent a British army from occupying the Italian colony. He also needed to command the Atlantic littoral, to impede an attack from America and prevent supplies reaching Britain. Rommel would then move through Egypt to the oilfields of the Middle East.

At the same time Hitler decided it was the moment to commence his fateful gamble, a main-force assault on the Soviet Union. The objective was to colonize western Russia, replace or enslave its Slav population, kill its Jews and seize the Caucasus oilfields. In June 1941, Hitler abandoned the Molotov–Ribbentrop pact and ordered his high command to activate Operation Barbarossa. This involved four invading armies surging forward along a 300-mile front, with infantry units preceded by mobile Panzer divisions. Five thousand tanks were committed. These forces swiftly took Kiev in Ukraine and Minsk in Belarus and, in September 1941, laid siege to Leningrad. The siege was to last more than two years and see a million people die.

By the start of winter 1941, the Germans were just forty miles from Moscow. Their behaviour was abominable. All rules of war were disregarded. Passive civilians were slaughtered in their hundreds of thousands. Large areas were subjected to a 'hunger plan', whereby existing populations would be starved to death and later replaced by Germans. In a rage of preventative paranoia, Stalin killed or sent to Siberian gulags over half a million Russians and other minorities, lest for some reason they might collaborate with the Germans.

While this battle was taking place in the east, Roosevelt and Churchill were meeting aboard a warship off Newfoundland and formulating an Atlantic Charter. It reiterated Woodrow Wilson's fourteen points for world peace of 1918, including national self-determination and freedom, following the 'final destruction of Nazi tyranny'. America was not yet party to the war, and the unspoken bargain was Churchill's agreeing to dismantle the British empire in return for America's return to another European combat. By January 1942 the charter had been signed by twenty-six Allied nations as a 'declaration of united nations' against Hitler. But there was no guarantee of a Nazi defeat. Only the Soviets were seriously fighting.

The charter talks were followed by an act of unprovoked aggression. In December 1941, 353 Japanese planes struck America's Pacific fleet in Hawaii's Pearl Harbor. They sank four battleships and destroyed or damaged fifteen other ships, with the loss of 2,400 American sailors. At the same time, Japan was attacking and occupying American, British and Dutch colonies throughout south-east Asia and the western Pacific. They invaded Hong Kong, the Philippines, Malaya, Singapore and the Dutch East Indies with a clear intention to move on to Ceylon and India. British forces were helpless against them. Europe's Asian empires faced oblivion. The war had gone truly global. But it also reached a turning point. Within three days of Pearl Harbor, the United States was at war with both Japan and Germany.

The turning of the tide

In January 1942 senior Nazi and SS officials met in conference at Wannsee outside Berlin. The topic was the 'final solution' to Europe's ten million Jews, a switch from using them as slave labour to their complete extermination. The officials were concerned at public reaction to such a plan in Germany itself, especially in the less-Nazified Catholic provinces. Extermination camps were therefore located principally in lands to the east, notably Poland. Though Europe had seen exterminations before – not least against Jews – for a modern state systematically to plan the eradication of millions of its own citizens was unprecedented. A European power was not just perpetrating a pogrom but doing so on an industrial and pseudo-scientific basis – justly to be termed a Holocaust.

That winter of 1941–2, the coldest of the century, saw German soldiers within sight of Moscow. The grease on German shells froze and the tanks needed hours to warm up before moving. Army clothing was inadequate and frostbite ubiquitous. Russia's old ally, General Winter, played his hand, as he had against Sweden's Charles XII and France's Napoleon. A mass Soviet mobilization ensued, with a million Russians pressed into an army that already topped nine million. These numbers proved successful. The Soviet commander, General Zhukov, pushed the Germans back from Moscow; for the first time, Hitler experienced defeat.

The following summer, Hitler retaliated with a massive assault on Stalin's southern flank towards Stalingrad. The resulting battle, involving two and a half million troops, lasted from July 1942 until the following February. In terms of numbers committed, it was probably the greatest battle in Europe's history. The Germans reached the centre of Stalingrad. Months of street fighting ensued, with the Germans at an increasing disadvantage. In the winter, a Soviet counter-attack encircled the Germans, and resupply became impossible. Rats were eating the insulation wires on the Panzer tanks, immobilizing half of them. In February 1943, defying Hitler's express orders, German commanders in Stalingrad surrendered.

Japan's ascendancy in the Far East proved brief. The American navy defeated the advancing Japanese fleet in the Battle of Midway in June 1942, sinking or incapacitating seven of the Imperial Fleet's capital ships, including four aircraft carriers. By December, British and Indian troops began a long, grim fight to regain Burma, achieved in 1944. The closer the Allies got to Japan, the slower was progress, until the war in the east proved longer than the war in Europe.

Rommel's advance across north Africa had also been halted. A British army at the Battle of El Alamein in October–November 1942 fended off the German threat to Egypt and the oilfields of Arabia. German and Italian forces were pushed back through Libya and Tunisia. In November, American troops under General Eisenhower arrived, to attack Rommel from the west. By May 1943 German activity in Africa had ceased. One hundred and fifty thousand Germans and Italians were taken prisoner and all their equipment was seized. Churchill described El Alamein as 'the end of the beginning.'

The tenor of the war now changed. From the summer of 1943

Hitler was turned from aggressor to defender. He was retreating from the Soviet Union and from Africa, and knew that, sooner or later, Allied forces would land on the continent. There followed an intense debate among the Allies as to whether to invade Europe from the north, along the French coast, or from the south, through southern France or Italy. The invasion route was decided at a meeting between Roosevelt and Churchill in Casablanca in January 1943.

The British war effort was now confined largely to maritime convoy operations and the nocturnal bombing of German cities. Germany's Blitz of Britain had almost ceased, the Luftwaffe being needed on the eastern front. The RAF's 'demoralization' campaign had switched to demolishing symbols of German culture, beginning with the destruction of the historic ports of Lübeck and Rostock in spring 1942. An enraged Hitler retaliated with the 'Baedeker' raids on Britain's cathedral cities, including Exeter, Bath, Norwich and Coventry. After Britain destroyed much of ancient Cologne, Germany desisted from this barbarism. Britain did not.

In July 1943 Hitler ordered a last desperate assault on the Soviet heartland at Kursk, south of Moscow, in a tank battle that dwarfed those in north Africa. Against him the Soviet Union was able to field vast resources, and an army of two and a half million soldiers and 3,800 tanks overwhelmed 780,000 German troops and 3,000 Panzers. Germany's attempted conquest of Russia was at an end. Near an end too was the war in the Atlantic. Anglo-American collaboration in anti-submarine warfare and the breaking of German Enigma machine codes were rendering U-boat operations near suicidal. Convoy losses dwindled over 1943 and supplies began to pour into Europe.

Hitler's defeat now seemed only a matter of time, but the time seemed long in coming. In July 1943 American and British troops landed in Sicily and swiftly captured Palermo. Within two days Mussolini, after making a minimal contribution to Hitler's war, was dismissed by Italy's grand council and imprisoned. He was rescued

57. Britain at peace – Queen Victoria at the Great Exhibition, 1851

58. (*below*) Britain at war – Charge of the Light Brigade at Balaclava, 1854

59. Revolutionary hero – Garibaldi in Sicily, 1860

60. Otto von Bismarck, 1890

61. Paris Commune – the toppling of Napoleon I's statue, 1871

62. Spark of war – Archduke Ferdinand en route to his assassination, Sarajevo, 1914

63. *The Taking of Vimy Ridge*, 1917

64. Steps to emancipation – women workers in a German munitions factory, 1915

65. (*below*) 'The peace to end all wars' – Treaty of Versailles, 1919

66. (*above*) The Nuremberg Rally, 1937

67. (*right*) The fall of Paris, 1940 – Hitler and Speer go sightseeing

68. (*below left*) Reshaping Europe – Churchill, Roosevelt, Stalin at Yalta, February 1945

69. (*below right*) Nadir of war – the destruction of Dresden, February 1945

70. Cold War begins: the Berlin airlift, 1948

71. Soviets triumphant – the Prague Spring, 1968, ultimately crushed

72. (*top*) Communism collapses – the fall of the Berlin Wall, 1989

73. (*above*) Last rites for the Cold War – Gorbachev and Thatcher, 1990

74. (*right*) Angela Merkel posing for a selfie at a migrant shelter – Berlin, 2015

75. A tsar in the making – Putin's reinauguration, 2018

76. Allies at odds – the G7 summit, 2018

by the Germans, but was later captured by partisans, shot and strung up on a building site. Although the Italian government officially capitulated, Italy was the theatre for a determined rearguard resistance by German units. It was not until June 1944 that the Allies captured Rome, for once respecting its historic buildings.

Back on the eastern front, German divisions round Leningrad were finally forced to retreat in January 1944, looting the Romanov palaces of their treasures as they went. The city was freed, and Stalin ordered starving craftsmen immediately to work on restoring the ruined palaces. In London, Eisenhower took over command of the prospective northern assault on France, his tact proving crucial in resolving three-way conflicts with Churchill and the exiled French leader, General de Gaulle. On 6 June 1944 came D-Day, history's greatest ever amphibious invasion along fifty miles of the Normandy coast.

The Allied conquest of Nazi Europe proved unexpectedly laborious. Not until the end of August 1944 did Paris fall to the Allies, its German commander defying Hitler's order to destroy the historic centre with explosives. In December, retreating German troops staged the Battle of the Bulge in the Belgian Ardennes, further delaying the Allied advance. But by February 1945 both Soviet and western armies were moving onto German territory.

British and American bombers were pulverizing German cities at will. Immensely destructive of property, the lack of impact on the war of this bombing was illustrated by German tank and plane production hitting an all-time high in the early spring of 1945. Post-war assessment was that barely seven per cent of German industrial plants were put out of action. The Wehrmacht was even able to deploy the V-1 flying bomb and V-2 ballistic missile against London. In February 1945 British and American planes visited a massive firestorm on the city of Dresden, crowded with unknown numbers of refugees from the Soviet advance. Estimates of deaths vary from 25,000 to over 100,000.

The fall of Berlin came on 2 May, two days after Hitler shot himself in his bunker, his wife Eva Braun taking cyanide beside him. Germany's generals surrendered to Britain's Montgomery in a bleak cabin on Lüneburg Heath in North Saxony. Others surrendered to the Soviets on the eastern front. Allied troops spread across a devastated land, trying to restore a modicum of order. Misery turned to horror as Hitler's concentration camps were liberated. About six million Jews, two-thirds of Europe's total, are estimated to have perished in the camps, along with as many again of Soviets, Poles, Slavs and Roma gypsies.

The germ of a settlement

By now diplomats in Allied capitals had been revising the Atlantic Charter. Roosevelt, already a sick man, was eager to act as elder statesman, leading a Europe that had again immersed the world in bloody conflict. The Allied powers were fighting as 'united nations', and Roosevelt put this concept at the heart of his post-war settlement. Already in the spring of 1945 at Yalta in Crimea, Roosevelt, Stalin and Churchill had taken the first steps on that much-travelled route, redrawing the map of Europe. Now it had to be made real.

The overriding question was once more what to do with Germany. The mistakes of Versailles had to be avoided. Germany had to be made secure for democracy, but few agreed on how. Churchill felt the need, as he had in 1918, for a strong Germany as a bulwark against Soviet communism. He had foreseen 'a United States of Europe . . . with an international police force, charged with keeping Prussia disarmed'. He did not say if Britain should be a member.

The Soviet Union had borne the brunt of the war and felt it should be duly rewarded. It got what Stalin wanted, a 'sphere of influence' over Germany's east European conquests. France regained

Alsace-Lorraine. For the time being, Germany was administered by the four Allied powers, America, Britain, France and the Soviets. Partitioned too was Austria and the German capital, Berlin, uncomfortably isolated within the Soviet sector.

Yalta preceded the German surrender. At the post-surrender Potsdam conference in July, the west found itself facing a more confident Stalin. Roosevelt had died and been replaced by his vice-president, Harry Truman (1945–53). Churchill was ousted by Labour's Clement Attlee in an election held in the middle of the conference. With the west lacking in leadership experience, Stalin was cock of the walk. He ignored western demands for a larger Poland, and emphatically rejected democracy or self-determination in eastern Europe. 'A freely elected government in every one of these countries,' he said baldly, 'would be anti-Soviet and we cannot permit that.' The words echoed across the continent. A new Europe would clearly be two Europes.

In August 1945, the war against Japan finally ended when the Americans dropped atomic bombs on Hiroshima and Nagasaki. Shock was mingled with relief as the Japanese emperor surrendered, vindication to many that such bombs could sometimes be used to secure victory. The war ended in an act of humanitarian obscenity. But it was over.

22

Cold War Continent
1945–1989

Post-war recovery and rebuilding

Europe in 1945 confronted a bald fact. A continent that fifty years earlier had confidently ruled a third of the world's population had torn itself to pieces. It had killed forty million of its own people, mutilated its historic towns and submerged half its population in famine and destitution. The economies of the combatant countries reverted to where they were in 1900, wiping out half a century of progress. Nothing so damaging to Europe's prosperity and culture had been seen since the religious wars of the seventeenth century. Hubris had led to nemesis. As the continent began to pick itself up, as in 1918 one thought was uppermost in every mind – never again.

The outlook of Europe's post-war leaders was very different from 1918. Then the redrawn boundaries echoed previous treaties, rewarding winners and punishing losers, creating new strains along old divisions. In 1945 Hitler's empire had vanished and Germany was traumatized. Its surviving leaders were tried as war criminals and most were executed. The country was partitioned four ways, its public realm depoliticized and central and local government given to Allied administrators. Germany was to resume its pre-Bismarck fragmentation. There was even talk of the country being deindustrialized and forced to return to agriculture.

In Germany's stead, a new balance of power had emerged, more blatant than any Europe had seen before. On the one hand was the triumphant Soviet Union, allowed at Potsdam to expand its sphere of control roughly to the Elbe and lower Danube. On the other was a replica of the Versailles alliance, a partnership of west Europe and America. These two 'blocs' swiftly diverged as Europe seemed unable to bridge its old fault line. This line, as the historian Tony Judt remarked, 'was one of the defining obsessions of the inhabitants of the continent'. As we shall see later, its shadow remains to the present day.

An immediate crisis was caused by massive refugee displacement. An estimated twelve million people were evicted from their homes by the collapse of Germany, mostly German speakers expelled by Stalin from Poland and elsewhere in eastern Europe, and others relocated by Russia to replace them. Millions fled from fear of ethnic retribution or of communism. It was the cruelties of peace, not war, which created the greatest forced migration in Europe's history.

The cry on all sides was for food, houses and work. A sophisticated market economy had been reduced to a struggle for survival. Economists with the Allied Control Council predicted social collapse and starvation, and frantic calls went to America for relief. Yet, while there was short-term famine, the years immediately following the war proved to be ones of astonishing recovery. Europe's economies, both communist east and capitalist west, were estimated to have returned to their pre-war output by 1950.

Two factors had been underestimated by the experts. One was the acceptance of continued wartime discipline. Governments and armies were still in place, and resources could be allocated at will. More significant, an entire continent was on the move, with millions desperate for work – and finding it in farm or factory. A British official, Ivan Hirst, sent to the Volkswagen tank factory, supposedly bombed to pieces, was ordered to dismantle and sell what was left. Ford of America declared it 'not worth a dime'. Within weeks Hirst was making cars and by 1946 was producing 1,000 a month. Crucial was the swift introduction of a new currency, the Deutschmark, by the economics minister, Ludwig Erhard. He disobeyed Allied orders to impose food rationing and price control, and abolished both, adamant that markets be left as free as possible so a cash economy could replace a barter one. He was proved right.

Aid from America was slow in coming. In 1947 America's secretary of state, George Marshall, pleaded that 'the patient is sinking while the doctors deliberate'. He declared the need for 'the revival of a working economy . . . to permit the emergence of political and social conditions in which free institutions can exist'. Eventually colossal sums in Marshall Aid were pouring into west Europe – Stalin refusing to accept any into the Soviet bloc. Britain's Labour foreign secretary Ernest Bevin described 'the generosity of it as beyond belief'. Historians have since questioned its impact, since by the time of its arrival recovery was already surging. More crucial was America's writing off of Germany's sovereign debt.

Even while Europe was struggling to feed itself, its rulers were determined on a path to a better society. Already in 1942, three years before the war's end, Britain had published a report by the economist William Beveridge, advocating universal insurance, unemployment assistance and free health care. It laid the groundwork for Europe's first comprehensive welfare state, introduced after 1945 by Attlee's Labour government.

This government also nationalized a wide range of public industries and utilities. Everywhere in Europe saw the mass rehousing of those evicted by bombing. Amid widespread social disintegration, governments deployed the disciplines of war to those of reconstruction – in Britain under the slogan 'winning the peace'. Elected politicians voted through programmes of social reform as yet unthinkable elsewhere in the world, even in America. Europe was no longer a smug, superior continent, rather a bruised, humbled and, many hoped, more socially responsible one. It saw the apotheosis of the state.

A continent divides

The supranational institutions proposed by the Atlantic Charter gradually moved into gear. A United Nations, replacing the defunct League of Nations, first met in San Francisco in April 1945, with fifty nations represented. This UN set up an international court and a peacekeeping force. It was described by the South African prime minister Jan Smuts as 'peace with teeth', intended to ensure that no would-be aggression should ever get started. As talisman of America's commitment, the UN would be based in New York. At the same time a World Bank and an International Monetary Fund were established in Washington. There was no doubt that, by the middle of the twentieth century, Europe had sacrificed any claim to be home to a new world order. That era was at an end.

On one matter America was adamant. It had not sent soldiers round the world for a second time to die for European imperialism. John Foster Dulles, later American secretary of state, said America was 'the first colony . . . to have won independence' and expected others to follow. Chief among these was India, where an independence movement was flourishing under the inspiration of Mahatma Gandhi. Britain's Labour government swiftly announced Britain's withdrawal from the subcontinent, leading to its bloodstained and controversial partition in 1947. Other nations such as France and Portugal were more reluctant, as was Britain with its other colonies. 'It is in union with its overseas territories,' said France's de Gaulle, 'that France is a great power.'

As for the Soviet Union, it had only just regained its empire, while the Potsdam agreement had removed any hope that it might join democratic Europe. Stalin had asserted not just his 'sphere of influence' but his right to dictate its ideology. Hesitantly democratic regimes that briefly emerged after the war in Poland,

Czechoslovakia and Hungary were, within five years, suppressed and drawn into the Soviet embrace. The wartime ally became a peacetime dictatorship.

It was in this spirit that the out-of-office Churchill told a gathering in Missouri in 1946 that an 'iron curtain has descended across the continent', an image borrowed from Goebbels. Behind it, he said, lay 'all the capitals of the ancient states of central and eastern Europe, Warsaw, Berlin, Prague, Vienna, Budapest, Belgrade, Bucharest and Sofia'. At the same time an American official in Moscow, George Kennan, sent home a secret assessment of Soviet policy, in a celebrated 'long telegram' of 8,000 words. This accepted that the Soviet destiny was 'to overthrow the political forces beyond its border', but since that destiny also saw capitalism in inevitable decay, Kennan felt the west's best policy was 'a long-term, patient but firm and vigilant containment of Russian expansive tendencies'. Containment by deterrence, became America's Soviet policy. America, he wrote 'should keep out of the Russian sphere of influence and Russia out of ours'. It kept the peace for fifty years.

The new Germany

Germany's three western zones did not long remain distinct. Since America had indicated a desire to withdraw from Europe within two years, there was an increased urgency to return it to some form of self-government. A decentralized federal constitution was fashioned to prevent the emergence of a renewed 'strong Germany'. Its capital would be in modest Bonn – like the pre-war seat in Weimar – and regular elections would keep government in check.

The new West German chancellor was Konrad Adenauer, stern but impeccably non-Nazi mayor of Cologne. Adenauer was deeply hostile to the Prussian/Saxon East Germany, and was eager to see

West Germany merge into a 'European' future. When travelling east, he is said to have closed the blinds when his train crossed the Elbe and remarked, 'Here we go: Asia again.' He and many like him were relaxed to see the east-Elbian provinces safe behind an Iron Curtain. He even pressed America to abandon Berlin to Stalin.

Stalin was furious at so early an end to the four-part division of Germany. In April 1948 he began to impede western access across the east zone to the still-multinational Berlin, which soon became a full-scale land blockade. The resulting crisis led the Allies to ponder enforcing a corridor, but as this would have risked a resumption of war, an airlift was needed to supply West Berlin with food. Sweets were even dropped from planes for children. Stalin ended the blockade in May 1949 and instead reacted to the German Federal Republic with one of his own, a 'German Democratic Republic' (GDR).

The Berlin crisis marked the commencement of a 'cold war'. The west's response was the formation in 1949 of a North Atlantic Treaty Organization (NATO), whose parties agreed that 'an armed attack on one or more of them in Europe or North America shall be considered an attack against them all'. Crucial was a guarantee that America would give NATO the cover of its atomic arsenal. Also drawn up was a European Convention on Human Rights, including 'rights' of migration and self-determination. In the summer of 1949 Stalin tested a Soviet atomic bomb.

By 1950, Europe's age-old 'German question' had been answered, not by union but by partition. Germany's post-war recovery was proving as dramatic as had been its interwar one. It was aided, not just by American debt relief but also by a running 'subsidy' from the communist east, a steady flow of able-bodied refugees eager for work. As each factory was rebuilt, productivity soared. West Germany's output soon exceeded Britain's.

Europe's industrial diplomats were also alert to the opportunities of a new west European economy. In 1951 West Germany, France and the Low Countries formed a European coal and steel cartel or 'community' (ECSC), initiated by the French foreign minister Robert Schuman, in part as a way to 'make war not only unthinkable but materially impossible'. It set up a common market in coal and steel and an assembly of national parliamentarians. It was a European union for beginners. Britain, eager to keep trade open with the Commonwealth, declined to join. The ghosts of Walpole and Pitt lived on.

Hungary and Suez

The death of Stalin in 1953 led to a gradual easing of east–west tension, aided by the coming to power in Moscow of Nikita Khrushchev. His programme of modernization and 'de-Stalinization' stimulated reformist governments in Poland and Hungary. There was even talk of 'peaceful coexistence', and toleration for each other's 'systems'. This proved short lived. When Hungary clearly began to plough an independent furrow, Khrushchev felt he had to restore hardline rule. In 1956 Soviet tanks appeared on the streets of Budapest, and Hungary's leader, Imre Nagy, was tried for treason and executed. He went to his death remarking, 'May God spare me the punishment of being rehabilitated by my murderers.' He suffered that fate, but not until 1989.

With America still eager to remain aloof, west Europe had no way of reacting to the Hungarian crisis, militarily or otherwise. Britain's foreign secretary, Anthony Eden, had often talked of Europe's 'progressive integration', and had in 1954 proposed a Western European Union (WEU) as a loose defensive alliance. But any move towards collective security foundered on the twin rocks of national sovereignty and the value of America's NATO shield. This paradox of the continent's dependence on and independence of its transatlantic offspring has never been resolved to this day.

Indeed, the paradox was highlighted by the inability of France and Britain to shed their imperial habits of mind. France had lost Vietnam in 1954, after America refused it military aid – a costly refusal, as America recklessly discovered a decade later. France was also under pressure in Africa, in its colonies of Morocco, Tunisia and Algeria. Its concern was with the forces not of communism but of Islam.

In 1956, at the same time as Moscow was crushing Hungary, Britain, France and Israel colluded secretly in an invasion of Egypt to regain control of the Suez Canal. This had been nationalized by Egypt, which was seen as threatening the imperial route 'east of Suez'. In Washington President Eisenhower (1953–61) was furious. He imposed financial sanctions on Britain and forced a humiliating withdrawal. The message was clear. If a neo-imperial war could take precedence over an anti-communist one, America would be wholly opposed.

Western Europe from alliance to union

A more constructive development came with the evolution of the six-member ECSC into a fully fledged customs union. It began with a conference in Italy's Messina in 1955, inspired by Jean Monnet, father of the post-war political reconstruction of Europe. The resulting European Economic Community (EEC) was formed in March 1957 under the Treaty of Rome. Both Monnet and the ECSC's Schuman saw this development not as a one-off but as 'the first concrete step towards a European federation, imperative for the preservation of peace'. Thus was born the defining ambition of post-war European politics, progress toward 'ever closer union'.

The EEC developed a permanent commission and a Council of Ministers composed of presidents or prime ministers of the member states, to be based in the old Lotharingian city of Brussels. The latter was to be the supreme policy-making body, guarding national sovereignty with the right of individual governments to veto decisions. There would be a consultative assembly and a European Court of Justice. Europe had seen nothing so coherent in all previous attempts at collective empire, co-operation or union.

Some aspects of forging a new European identity could be quaintly Ruritanian. The formation of the EEC stirred into life the custom of town twinning. The European Cup football competition began in 1955, won for the first five years in succession by Real Madrid. The following year saw the staging of a Eurovision Song Contest, with seven nations competing and Switzerland the winner. Gentle feuding took place over what might be a common European language, with France pushing French and lobbyists for the global tongue of Esperanto putting in a bid. The commission opted instead for a translators' Tower of Babel.

The United Kingdom could not bring itself to join in the new political institutions of Europe. It displayed the same aversion to continental adventures as had Britain's rulers down the ages. Britain saw itself as of Europe but not in it. London reacted to the EEC by in 1960 joining the Scandinavians and others in a seven-member European Free Trade Association (EFTA), with a more limited free-trading remit. But a year later the prime minister, Harold Macmillan, made a sudden switch in policy and decided after all to join the EEC. According to a cabinet paper, he feared that outside the EEC 'we shall run the risk of losing political influence and of ceasing to be able to exercise any claim to be a world power'. This was reflected in a much-publicized jibe from America's secretary of state, Dean Acheson, that 'Great Britain has lost an empire and has not yet found a role'.

To Britain's astonishment, France's ageing and Anglophobic president, de Gaulle, vetoed Macmillan's application. Britain, he said, was a Trojan Horse for America in Europe: 'Europe would eventually be absorbed into a colossal Atlantic community . . . under American control. This France could not permit.' In 1962 the increasingly maverick de Gaulle walked out of meetings of the EEC, leaving a conspicuously empty chair. He also withdrew from NATO deliberations and developed his own nuclear weapon, a gesture devoid of strategic force but complicating any collective European security. At this crucial stage in Europe's gestation, France stood in the way of a wider community.

The Sixties, from crisis to détente

In 1961 Khrushchev had been told by the East German leader, Walter Ulbricht, that the continued flight of his young people to the west meant that eventual 'collapse is inevitable'. Though the East German border was closed except to goods, East Germans could secure a passage to the west by moving across sectors within Berlin. Moscow duly agreed to the building of a wall across the entire city. As it was going up, migration rose to 2,000 a day. Khrushchev now became belligerent. He demanded an end to the west's presence in Berlin as a cuckoo in the East German nest. He also moved long-range missiles onto the island of Cuba in the Caribbean, insisting that NATO missiles be removed from Turkey.

As tension mounted in October 1962, the American president, John F. Kennedy (1961–3) promised to defend the status of Berlin, and demanded that the missiles be removed from Cuba. There was an intense stand-off with both sides – it was later confirmed – contemplating the ultimate horror of a nuclear exchange. Khrushchev swiftly backed down and America withdrew its missiles from Turkey. The following year Kennedy went to Berlin and declared, 'Ich bin ein Berliner.' It had been the first true crisis of the nuclear age. Deterrence had worked, just.

The sixties saw the wartime 'population bulge' come of age. The UK doubled the number of its universities in that decade alone. A distinctive European music began to free itself from American rock-and-roll imports. The first single by the Beatles was released in 1962 and by the Rolling Stones in 1963. A new generation arose with no memory of the war. Young Germans started asking their parents what happened in the thirties and forties – previously a taboo question. The idea of a specifically youth politics, distinct from traditional parties, took hold.

By the late sixties, street demonstrations across Europe were violently opposing America's mounting war in Vietnam. In 1968, riots in Paris were a self-conscious echo of past centuries, albeit motivated largely by a desire to reform French higher education. In 1970 the Baader-Meinhof Gang in Germany and the Red Brigades in Italy were formed, but degenerated into murdering corporate executives. Only in Czechoslovakia was there a coherent rebellion and brief 'Prague spring', under the moderate leader, Alexander Dubček. That too led nowhere. As in Hungary a decade earlier, Soviet tanks turned spring to winter. As it had in 1848, Europe in the sixties offered infertile soil for urban revolution.

The aftermath of the Cuban trauma produced an undoubted thaw in the cold war. A symbol of the new Europe was the election in 1969 of the first social democratic West German chancellor, Willy Brandt, with his policy of Ostpolitik, or engagement with communist states to the east. He formally recognized the GDR and promoted an easing of east–west travel and trade. A year later, long stuttering conversations over nuclear disarmament came to life with the first strategic arms limitation talks (SALT-I). An anti-ballistic missile treaty was signed in 1972, designed to reduce the risk of a pre-emptive 'first strike'.

By the seventies the mood within the EEC had changed sufficiently for the UK under Edward Heath finally to gain admission in

1973, a decision confirmed two years later in a British referendum. A remarkable two-thirds of voters were in favour, opposition being chiefly concentrated on the left. *The Times* demanded that schools in future 'teach a European history . . . rather than a narrowly British one'. At the same time, Europe saw the demise of its surviving wartime dictatorships in Spain and Portugal and the Greek military junta. They opted for democracy, joining the EEC not long after Britain. European union was at last coming of age.

The 'second cold war'

The period of détente had coincided with the dominance of Henry Kissinger over American foreign policy, from 1969 to 1977. A Jewish refugee who fled Germany in 1938 and never lost his thick German accent, Kissinger was a student of Bismarckian realpolitik. Though bogged down by the task of extricating America from Vietnam, he was less concerned with the cold war than with seeking to stabilize a global balance of power. To this end he was eager to triangulate America, the Soviet Union and a resurgent China. Europe was absent from this triangle.

Détente suited Kissinger's purpose, but it did not long survive his departure. When the Soviet Union invaded Afghanistan in 1979, the west seemed to lose collective patience. Containment, engagement and détente had delivered no gains. After Afghanistan, economic sanctions were imposed on Russia and sixty-six nations boycotted the 1980 Moscow Olympics. Newly elected conservative leaders in Britain and America, Margaret Thatcher (1979–90) and Ronald Reagan (1981–9), vied with each other in anti-communist rhetoric. Détente, said Reagan, had been 'a satanic device to blunt America's sword'. He pointed out that 'regimes planted by totalitarianism have had more than thirty years to establish their legitimacy'. The Soviet

Union was 'an evil empire'. To Thatcher, socialism was an ideology that had been 'tested to destruction and failed'.

Even as Reagan allowed disarmament talks to continue, he initiated a new east–west arms race, in the form of 'star wars' in space. The prospect was of missiles fighting an unimaginable conflict far beyond the Earth's atmosphere. Moscow was shocked at the cost of competing with star wars. Its paranoia was further inflamed by the formation of Lech Wałęsa's overwhelmingly popular Solidarity movement in 1980s Poland, and reports of similar movements across the Warsaw Pact of east European countries. Moscow ordered Solidarity's suppression, and Wałęsa became a hero in the west. He spent the decade in and out of prison.

Tension reached a crisis in 1983, with Moscow ruled by a dour, sick apparatchik, Yuri Andropov, convinced that America was planning at any moment to attack his country. In September 1983 the shooting down of a Korean airliner that had strayed into Russian air space precipitated a repeat of the Cuban missile crisis. Moscow claimed the plane was spying. A few weeks later NATO, in the midst of a major exercise, Able Archer, alarmed Moscow intelligence by changing its codes. Washington had stationed Pershing missiles in West Germany, ten minutes from Moscow. The dying Andropov had an aide stationed beside his bed, with his nuclear button at the ready. No one knew if anyone was serious – and the crisis passed. But once again Europe had diced with deterrence.

Nothing on the cold war front seemed to impede the evolution of the EEC. In 1986 it passed the Single European Act rendering relations between member states subject to majority votes, thus embodying a key transfer of sovereignty. This foresaw union in areas well beyond trade. Special funds would grant-aid 'social cohesion'. Rich regions would cross-subsidize poor ones. Thatcher was explicit in supporting the reform. On the Act's implementation two years later, she boasted to business leaders that 'Britain has given the lead in creating a single market without barriers – visible or invisible – giving you direct and unhindered access to the purchasing power of over 300 million of the world's wealthiest people.' They should make a success of it.

The signing of the Act was a high point in the UK's commitment to Europe, as Thatcher acknowledged when she later professed to regret it. The year 1986 was when London might have decided that enough European union was enough, and returned to the arms of EFTA. It could have chosen a lighter, looser form of European trading regime. Instead it opted for an 'in' phase of the in–out game that it had played for so long with continental Europe.

The end of the Iron Curtain

No sooner had the second cold war reached the brink in 1983 than, as after Cuba in 1962, the two sides stepped back. In 1985, Mikhail Gorbachev was appointed general secretary of the Soviet Communist Party and initiated what proved the terminal upheaval of Stalin's empire. Gorbachev was an unusual product of the Soviet system, intelligent, calm and outward-looking. With his stylish wife, Raisa, he copied Russian rulers down the centuries in seeking to modernize his country. Like them, he hoped to do so without losing control from the centre.

Revolutions rarely oblige the ambitions of their progenitors. They have minds of their own. Gorbachev announced two policies – or approaches to policy – perestroika (reconstruction) and glasnost (openness). They were intended to liberate Soviet politics within a framework of Party accountability. Corruption was countered, dissidents released, the Russian Orthodox church revived. Gorbachev returned to the concept of détente, of a 'common European home', and was duly idolized with 'Gorbymania' in

West Germany. He even developed a rapport with Thatcher in Britain and Reagan in America.

At home in Moscow, all was tense. The Soviet Union faced de Tocqueville's moment of maximum danger, when autocracy embarks on change. Nationalism was resurfacing across the Warsaw Pact, with no apparent objection from Moscow. New political groupings formed. People spoke freely, and were reported upon freely. Poland's Wałęsa and Czechoslovakia's Václav Havel were lionized in the west. Poland's communist leadership was clearly unstable, and Gorbachev sensed a single Soviet-style communism across eastern Europe was becoming untenable.

When Gorbachev and Reagan attended arms reduction talks in Reykjavik in 1986, they pledged deep cuts in nuclear arsenals. Reagan angered his own right wing by removing short- and medium-range nuclear missiles from Europe, while Gorbachev slashed troop numbers and missile bases across the Warsaw Pact. He then told the pact's party leaders that they should seek their own paths to internal reform. In June 1989 Poland held elections, at which Wałęsa's Solidarity won all the free seats and prepared to form a government. The lights on reforming European communism changed from red to green.

That summer of 1989, the bicentennial of the French Revolution, Moscow lost its grip on the handle of Soviet power. In August, history descended into irony when a member of the European Parliament, Otto von Habsburg, pretender to the Austro-Hungarian throne, co-sponsored a 'pan-European picnic' on the Austria–Hungary border. Hundreds of East Germans trekked to it and, in a gesture of friendship, officials temporarily opened the border gates. Six hundred 'picnickers' stampeded across before they closed – and did not return. Pandemonium ensued as thousands rushed to the spot. On 11 September the Hungarian government announced that they could no longer control the border. It opened, and some 30,000 East Germans crossed to the west.

The Iron Curtain was breached, and the East German leader, Erich Honecker, resigned. In October the Hungarian government declared a new republic and free elections. A month later, on 9 November 1989, East Germany announced that east–west movement through the Berlin Wall would be eased. As crowds rushed the gates, soldiers abandoned all attempts to stop them. Ecstatic masses climbed the wall and lined its fortifications. Pictures of this photogenic symbol of ideological collapse flashed round the globe.

The forty-year-old Iron Curtain fell because tens of thousands of people, long denied democracy, simply voted with their feet. They were able to do so because Gorbachev had abandoned the centralized discipline on which the Soviet empire relied. Other regimes lacked the political will to enforce the incarceration of an entire generation of Europeans. Later that month, I visited a small border village in Upper Saxony to witness local people cutting their stretch of the fence. They rushed through the gap to embrace their erstwhile neighbours, elderly relatives whom they had thought they would never see again. It was a tear-stained vignette of Europe's most uplifting moment since the end of the Second World War. A divide had been crossed, but had a division been ended?

23

Strains Past and Present
1989–

The end of history?

The world watched mesmerized as the once mighty Soviet empire gave a sigh, tottered and collapsed. It vanished in just over a year. No one had predicted it and the surprise was total. Europeans had, for half a century, taken for granted a divided Germany and a divided Europe. The gulf seemed a permanent shadow across the map of the continent. In terms both sides were careful not to use, the west had 'won' the cold war – Gorbachev shrewdly called it 'our common victory' – without a shot fired in anger, other than briefly in Romania.

The end did not come from any shift in the balance of power or any military supremacy, much though this was cited by defence lobbyists. The historian Robert Service attributed 1989 directly to 'Gorbachev's personal realization that communism was unsustainable'. It had to find new forms of consent. Moscow would have to relinquish control over its satellite regimes in eastern Europe, but it would also have to open up internal channels of accountability. Service stressed the value to Gorbachev of 'high-level political engagement by the United States', in particular Reagan's personal liking for him. Something synchronized between leaders in both east and west, a synchronicity so long absent from Europe's inter-state dealings.

For two years after the fall of the Berlin Wall, Gorbachev struggled to maintain control. He sought free elections to party soviets and thus the democratization of political life. It was not easy. In losing its autocratic character, the Communist Party lost its brain and its spine. It disintegrated, and with it the fount of institutional discipline within the Leninist-Stalinist empire. Into the resulting vacuum flowed empire's most insistent opponents, nationalism and anarchy.

In Moscow, the result was power shifting from Gorbachev's Kremlin to the headquarters of the formerly somnolent Russian republic in its 'White House' on the Moscow River. Here a new Russian president, Boris Yeltsin, was a boisterous, bibulous throwback to past Moscow rulers. He resisted a coup attempt in August 1991 by KGB hardliners, when Gorbachev was briefly absent by the Black Sea. By December, the Warsaw Pact regimes were going their own way and so was Russia itself. A weakened Gorbachev was finally forced to sign the formal dismantling of the USSR. It meant his own downfall and Yeltsin (1991–9) moving into the Kremlin. On New Year's Day 1992, the hammer-and-sickle that had graced the fortress battlements for sixty-eight years was hauled down, and the tsarist tricolour rose in its place.

Gorbachev remained a hero in the west, but there were no eulogies for the Soviet Union. In the history of absolutism, it was an empire without redemption. Stalin's rule in the thirties and forties brought more death and misery to the people of one European country than any government in history. In Norman Davies's words, the union finally fell because 'the grotesque organs of its internal structure were incapable of providing the essentials of life'. While those organs had, in the years since Stalin's death, maintained internal peace, it was a peace that denied its subjects the unprecedented prosperity and freedom enjoyed since 1945 by peoples across western Europe.

Communism's saddest epitaph became evident only under Yeltsin. Russia's most able and enterprising citizens did not stay to help reconstruct their blighted economy. In their thousands, they fled to the west, taking with them as much of its resources as they could grasp or steal. The curiously named 'oligarch' became the symbol of that flight. In the bitterest blow of all, Russia had to watch its old ally China adjust itself to entrepreneurial capitalism, without bothering to dismantle the framework of a communist state.

To the west the new order after 1989 was a moment of exhilaration. The American political scientist Francis Fukuyama declared it 'the end of history'. He said that the world had reached 'the end point of mankind's ideological evolution, and the universalization of western liberal democracy as the final form of human government'. In retrospect this was naïve, but it reflected a widespread optimism that swept across Europe in the 1990s, a repeat of the fin-de-siècle exhilaration of the 1890s. It was as if Europe's evolution had reached a sort of apotheosis, or at least become uninteresting.

West Europe's practical response to the fall of the Soviet empire did its best to defy Fukuyama's optimism. There was no lowering of tariffs or other barriers to trade with the east, and therefore little stimulus to growth in the post-communist economies. Brussels lobbyists opposed any inrush of low-cost produce, especially food, into the EEC's protected markets. Despite initial pleas from Gorbachev, there was no new Marshall Aid, nor substantial inward investment, at least until former communist states joined the EU. Instead London opened its markets to Russia's stolen roubles. At the same time there was a torrent of low-cost labour migrating westwards, bleeding the east of talent and further aiding the west's economies.

More dangerous was an instant NATO welcome to Russia's former Warsaw Pact allies. Those republics closest to Russia, such as Belarus, Ukraine and the central Asian 'stans', formed a Commonwealth of Independent States under Moscow's aegis. But the Baltic states together with Poland, Czechoslovakia and Hungary turned their backs on the east and began negotiations with NATO as guarantor of their future security. There was no doubt this is what these countries wanted, but the alacrity with which NATO seemed ready to advance its frontier eastwards rubbed salt into the gaping wound of Russia's national pride.

Yeltsin pleaded with the west to hold back, describing NATO's expansionism as 'a major political mistake'. He warned that 'the flames of war could burst out across the whole of Europe'. He was ignored. In this respect, there was an ominous sense of the cold war's demise replicating the casual triumphalism of Versailles.

A new Germany, a new Europe

West Germany's Helmut Kohl was on a visit to Poland in November 1989 when told of the fall of the Berlin Wall. It is said he wept tears of joy. He called for the immediate reunification of his country. Both France and Britain were less sure. Thatcher seemed to regret the passing of the old order, and warned that a reunited 'Germany would once again dominate the whole of Europe'. To Kohl it was a matter of practicality. In just two months from the opening of the wall, 200,000 East Germans migrated to the west. East Germany's economy faced collapse.

There was not even a plebiscite on reunification. Elections were held and by July 1990 new members from the East German provinces took their seats in the Reichstag. A vote was then taken on moving Germany's capital back to Berlin, decided on a tide of emotion driven by the East Germans. The new provinces became a sorely depressed part of Europe's richest state and were to emerge as its most conservative region politically. The former east contributed just five per cent to German output, but was to double the national debt.

At the very moment the eastern bloc disintegrated, the EEC mooted a major step in the opposite direction. The commission's head, Jacques Delors, proposed in 1990 that the EEC become an executive agent of the European Parliament, with the currently sovereign Council of Ministers as merely its senate. This would drastically increase the unelected commission's authority and diminish national sovereignty. It was constitutionally – not to mention politically – explosive. The EU was becoming a state without a nation.

Britain's Thatcher reacted in the House of Commons, 'No, no, no!' She later added, 'We have not successfully rolled back the frontiers of the state in Britain only to see them reimposed at a European level, with a European superstate exercising a new dominance from Brussels.' The Delors initiative won little support and was scrapped, but Thatcher's days were numbered. In November 1990 she was felled by a party coup and replaced by the Chancellor of the Exchequer, John Major. Apart from her dominant hold on British politics in the eighties, Thatcher's 'iron lady' stance in the cold war won her heroic status in east Europe. I watched her idolized at a Warsaw banquet in 1991, when some Poles pleaded with her to stand as their, presumably honorary, president.

The EEC went into conclave in Maastricht in 1991 to decide on its most momentous step since its formation. It would take the existing European Monetary System – in which governments agreed to keep their currencies roughly in line – into a full currency union by the end of the century, embracing eleven of its members (later twelve). For Germany this was a difficult step, meaning the death of the Deutschmark, talisman of its post-war prosperity. The compensation was an overvalued euro and the lack of any tool of internal economic equilibrium, much to Germany's advantage. The euro finally replaced national currencies in 2002, wiping away such ancient symbols of national pride as the franc, the lira, the drachma, the peseta and the escudo.

The eurozone's significance was more than symbolic. It implied the gradual synchronization of its members' economies, including monetary policy, national investment and transfers between rich and poor regions. For northern Europe the euro bound Germany into ever closer union. For Spain, Italy and Greece, it was a double-edged sword. It signified merger with Europe's most sophisticated economies, but also economic adjustments for which these countries were by no means ready. Britain had joined the Exchange Rate Mechanism, but dropped out with the pound under extreme pressure on 'black Wednesday' in 1992. The Major government declined to join the euro. It also 'opted out' of Maastricht's 'Social Chapter', which covered areas such as employment rights.

The EEC now became the European Union (EU), the word economic being significantly dropped and 'union' left to imply anything and everything. Britain's semi-detachment from it meant that Germany stood alone as its most potent member. Its bankers headed the eurozone's financial regime, with a whip hand over the terms of Europe's trade. Germans seemed to accept their new economic hegemony. In particular, they eagerly invited the former Soviet bloc nations to join the EU. First in line stood Poland, Hungary and the Czech Republic, Czechoslovakia having split into this and Slovakia in 1993.

To Germany these states, also now members of NATO, would form a buffer between it and any emergent Russia, under the continuing security shield of the American deterrent. The EU insisted that the states 'satisfy the union's political and economic conditions', including political freedom and action against corruption. This insistence proved lax in the extreme. Sweden, Finland and Austria also left EFTA and in 1995 joined the EU, with Bulgaria and Romania to follow. Apart from Norway, Switzerland and some mini-states, the EU was now all of Europe other than the Russian federation. A sort of dream had been realized.

The rise of Putin

Yeltsin had warned NATO of the flames that might accompany a tilt in the balance of European power. The first ignition appeared in the one communist state that had stayed outside Moscow's orbit,

Yugoslavia. In June 1991 the Yugoslav province of Slovenia had declared independence of Belgrade and been left in peace after a brief conflict. When it was followed by Croatia, and Bosnia, and then by a separatist rising in Kosovo, the largest province, Serbia, took military action to prevent secession. Both the EU and the UN were powerless to halt the resulting conflict, which lasted from 1991 to 1999. It was left to NATO to overstep its defensive remit and intervene. By 1999 NATO had found itself compelled to guarantee Bosnian and Kosovan independence. It thus legitimized the break-up of a European state.

A light-headedness now crept into discussion of European defence policy. The Soviet Union, the great enemy, had vanished and its Red Army was shrinking. The Russian component of the old Soviet arms budget plummeted from \$33 billion in 1988 to just \$14 billion in 1994. Common sense might suggest that Europe's defence should now transfer to the 'ever closer' EU. It was perhaps time for the American umbrella to be replaced by a European deterrent, even for NATO in its current form to be wound up.

Russia under Yeltsin was at this point experiencing extremes of humiliation and paranoia. It had a wrecked economy and a triumphant western alliance advancing towards its doorstep. Negotiations now began for Estonia, Latvia, Lithuania, Bulgaria and Romania also to join NATO, turning the earlier necklace of former communist states into what looked to Moscow more like a noose. But Yeltsin had other worries. He decided not to move Russia gradually towards capitalism, by ensuring currency control and strict financial policing. Instead he went full speed ahead. He curbed public spending, cut subsidies, freed prices and gave the ownership of factories and utilities to Russian citizens in the form of share vouchers. These grossly undervalued vouchers were swiftly bought up by middlemen and sold on to a network of oligarchs, who became sensationally rich before vanishing abroad. A Siberian oil well was swiftly converted into a Knightsbridge mansion.

The value of Russia's copious natural resources was thus invested in London, Cyprus, the Middle East and other boltholes in what became one of Europe's most systematic acts of kleptomania. (William the Conqueror's plunder of England in the eleventh century at least remained largely in situ.) By the end of the nineties, Russia's national product had halved and the rouble collapsed. Millions lost their savings and, in some parts of the country, there was a cry for a return to communism. This in turn led to attempts to unseat Yeltsin. If Gorbachev had lost control over the demise of communism, Yeltsin lost it over the rise of capitalism.

In 1999 the ailing Yeltsin anointed a former Leningrad KGB boss, Vladimir Putin, as his successor. The contrast was total. Putin was the epitome of a tough, communist-era apparatchik. The ex-intelligence officer had no time for the niceties of democracy, but a keen sense of the need to restore Russian pride. He would issue pictures of himself hunting and bare-chested on horseback. His court of oligarchs made sure he secured as much overseas wealth as they had. Putin's politics, endorsed at increasingly rigged elections, made no mention of civil rights or market economics. He was a populist and a nationalist, his pledge merely to restore Russia's integrity and self-confidence. Opponents were bribed, imprisoned or killed. The west might have felt able to humour and torment Yeltsin. It now faced the pastiche tsar of a macho state. That Russia's economy was debilitated was irrelevant. Dictatorship thrives on poverty.

The credit crunch

The European Union had by the end of the century expanded to twenty-eight very different members, with a constitution designed for six like-minded ones. As recognized in America's federalist debates in the 1780s, the constitutional relationship between a central state and its component members is crucial to its stability. America's constitution had flaws, but it proved astonishingly robust. Europe's at the end of the twentieth century was fragile. It sought to govern not a mostly homogeneous set of commonwealth states, but countries with distinct personalities, cultures and vulnerabilities. Few were ready to submerge them in a continental whole, as fashioned by the champions of ever closer union in Brussels.

The European Commission and Parliament had both become unwieldy. The former's bureaucratic expansion into everything from building regulations to food sizing and bat control was ridiculed. The impending eurozone was a gamble. Lacking the safety valve of internal devaluation or other adjustments, it would involve a severe loss of sovereignty for its member governments. The European Parliament was a paper tiger, given over to lobbying for domestic projects. Election turnouts fell steadily from sixty-two per cent in 1979 to forty-three per cent in 2009.

Undaunted, the Brussels establishment continued to pursue unification. By 2005 it had sought to adopt a new constitution, overseen by the veteran French politician Valéry Giscard d'Estaing. This awarded the EU a third presidency (now of the European Council as well as its Commission and Parliament), and further extended majority voting in the European Council. This ran into immediate trouble. Rarely in the EU's history were the peoples of Europe directly consulted on its powers, or even its existence. Decisions were taken by elected governments. The Giscard constitution was rejected in French and Dutch referendums, and the final treaty by the Irish. These votes were either rerun or ignored. The final Treaty of Lisbon was signed in 2007, with virtually no concessions to subsidiary nationalism, its authors blind to any incipient resentment it might breed.

A year later, Europe and America experienced the most traumatic financial crash since 1929. In Europe the chief impact was on the weaker states of the EU, notably those of southern Europe. The eurozone's

German-controlled European Central Bank (ECB) looked immediately to the security of Germany's overseas loans, including those to the zone's weaker members. Though the ECB was impressively ready to print money – there was no repetition of the squeeze of 1929 – the liquidity went to German (and other) banks rather than to member states or their citizens. Extreme austerity was forced on Greece, Spain and Italy, with levels of unemployment that rose to twenty-five per cent of the working population. In Spain, half of all young people became unemployed. Nothing could have more boosted a re-emergent European nationalism, or more damaged the cause of closer union.

Russia resurgent

In 2004 the Baltic states, Bulgaria and Romania formally joined NATO, as did Slovakia and Slovenia. Soon afterwards, the American president, George W. Bush (2001–9), openly mooted Ukraine and Georgia also joining, which would advance NATO to Russia's southern frontier. Both Germany and France challenged the wisdom of such blatant provocation. Putin repeated Yeltsin's warning that any NATO advance to the frontier 'would be taken in Russia as a direct threat to the security of our country'. In the summer of 2008 he reacted by invading Georgia's Russian-speaking northern provinces of South Ossetia and Abkhazia. Europe's only response was for France's president, Nicolas Sarkozy, to negotiate a ceasefire.

In 2010 the pro-Russian leader of Ukraine, Viktor Yanukovych, opposed any move to take the country closer to NATO or the EU, but within four years he was ousted by pro-western parties in Kiev, precipitating an open civil war in Ukraine's Russian-speaking eastern provinces, the latter supported by Moscow. Tension was further increased when in 2014 Putin annexed the formerly Russian territory of Crimea, granted to Ukraine in the 1950s. Europe replied with a barrage of economic sanctions, which had no political effect beyond entrenching Russia's siege economy and bringing Putin closer to his oligarchic associates. The economy switched to import substitution, including the manufacture of domestic mozzarella and camembert. NATO reopened its invitation to Ukraine and conducted military exercises in the Baltic countries. Russia did likewise. Europe slid back into brinkmanship mode.

Misjudging Moscow had long been the occupational disease of European diplomacy. It cursed alike Swedes, Poles, Napoleon and Hitler. It now blighted a western alliance divided on how to respond to this newly aggressive Russia. The EU had no military arm, though it often toyed with the idea of one. There had been a European 'defence community', a Eurocorps, a rapid reaction force, a 'military action plan' and even a joint operational headquarters. For good measure, Britain's prime minister Tony Blair had in a speech in Chicago in 1999 suggested that a concept of 'humanitarian intervention' be seen as valid wherever democracy and human rights were under threat. To him, there could be no limit to NATO's responsibility. But who should define threats and responsibilities?

After New York's 9/11 atrocity in 2001 at the hands of Al Qaeda, NATO found itself expected to intervene wherever Washington's rulers ordained. Armies from virtually all Europe's states were summoned to fight with varying degrees of enthusiasm and engagement in Afghanistan, Iraq, Syria and Libya. As America tested its hegemonic muscles, obedience was the price for the continuance of the nuclear umbrella. No one asked, let alone answered, the question of who should police the ever-expanding borders of democratic Europe.

In 2017 a new American president, Donald Trump, directly called Europe's bluff. His two immediate predecessors, George W. Bush and Barack Obama (2009–17), had both indicated a desire to withdraw from the role of policing Europe. While Bush was consumed by the Middle East, Obama 'pivoted' towards Asia-Pacific. Trump dismissed NATO as 'obsolete' and suggested Europe was now rich enough to defend itself. At a rally in December 2017 he said he had told the people of Europe 'they've been delinquent. They haven't been paying . . . I guess I implied you don't pay, we're out of there.' He was also avowedly a friend, if not an ally, of Putin.

Russia was now becoming a dominant factor in European diplomacy. It had copious natural resources, a large army, a nuclear arsenal and a reckless capacity for mischief-making, cyber attacks and overseas assassination. As Churchill had said in 1939, Russia might always be 'a riddle wrapped in a mystery inside an enigma', but on one matter Putin was crystal clear. He did not like NATO's encirclement of his borders or meddling within his 'sphere of interest'. In this he had an increasingly sympathetic ear from Germany's Angela Merkel and from some former Warsaw Pact leaders. Geography mattered. It was easy for Britain and France to play belligerence with Moscow. It was less easy for Germany and the still ingénue democracies to its east.

Old troubles reborn

As Europe struggled to recover from recession, in 2015 the British prime minister David Cameron tossed Brussels a grenade. He said he would hold a referendum on the UK's continued EU membership the following year. The torch of British Euroscepticism had passed from left to right. It was now Conservatives rather than Labour who were most anti-European. Cameron's attempts to appease his 'leave' voters by negotiating reforms to the EU were dismissed by the ever cautious Merkel and, in June 2016, to Cameron's surprise and dismay, the British electorate voted narrowly to leave the EU. The vote was taken as binding by the government. The date decided by Parliament for departure was March 2019.

Britain's departure could not lightly be dismissed. Its economy was second only to Germany's in size, and contributed twenty per cent of the EU budget. The UK might long have been half-hearted in its commitment to European union, but now it was not alone. A Pew survey in mid-2016 was one of many showing disapproval of the EU as high in Germany and the Netherlands as in Britain, and higher in France and Spain. Few governments dared imitate Britain and hold an open vote on continued membership. Union might be popular but the EU was not.

European democracy now entered a period of trauma. As of old, regional identities and grievances came to the fore. Separatist movements gained momentum in Scotland, Catalonia and parts of France, Romania and Italy, wherever clashes between central and local government turned critical. A virulent nationalism began to emerge in the so-called Visegrád-4 countries of Poland, Hungary, Slovakia and the Czech Republic. Right-wing parties thrived in Austria, the Netherlands, France and Italy. At the core of their appeal was the oldest of emotions, a desire to protect the character and integrity of established communities from assault by globalization and immigration.

The federalist adventure, so assured in its idealism, had always required the honouring of Rousseau's social contract, a consensual relationship between the state and the citizen. Europe's diverse peoples would support union, but only insofar as it did not infringe their perceived character and way of life. Europe's booming cities might be able to absorb change, but this was not true of formerly industrial provinces, rural areas and ageing populations. Britain's pro-Brexit voters – heavily provincial, rural and older – reflected this divide. Parties variously labelled right-wing, nationalist or populist gained strength in most if not all European states, responding to a call for voters to 'take back control' of their political and social environment. Most alarmingly, the 2016 World Values Survey reported that 'fewer than half' of respondents born in the seventies and eighties believed it was 'essential to live in a country that is governed democratically'. In Germany, Spain, Japan and America, between twenty and forty per cent would prefer 'a strong leader who does not have to bother with parliaments or elections'.

In 2015 Merkel in Germany made a radical gesture. After the failure of an EU plan to absorb refugees from the Syrian civil war flowing into Greece, she decided to offer them sanctuary in Germany. Over a million accepted. The reaction was fierce. An unashamedly right-wing group, Alternative for Germany, emerged in the 2018 German elections as the third largest party, strongest in the former East German provinces. Merkel, so long the queen of Europe, was almost toppled. A charismatic French president, Emmanuel Macron, elected in 2017, swiftly moved into lead position in the EU and promptly initiated yet another attempt to concentrate and reform the eurozone. Germany disagreed. Europe looked ever more divided and confused.

Darker clouds were gathering to the east. In 2018 Hungary's quasi-autocratic leader, Viktor Orbán, was overwhelmingly returned to power under the slogan 'Sovereignty, independence, freedom, God, homeland and security.' He did not mention Europe, and dismissed the EU as 'liberal babble'. Opposition, the free press and the rule of law were suppressed. Politicians in Poland, Slovakia, Austria and Serbia were equally out of tune with the liberal ethos of the EU. In a 2018 poll, just twenty-one per cent of Slovaks said they 'belonged' to the west. Most were reluctant to enforce tighter western sanctions on Russia and were fiercely anti-immigrant. The old ideological fault-line between east and west was re-emerging, while a gulf was also widening between rich north and poor south.

To these challenges to the values that had fashioned post-war Europe, the EU offered little response. A constitution intended to curb Germany and avoid the emergence of a pre-eminent state now suffered from the lack of just such leadership. Russia was bruised and angry, America unclear on where it stood. There loomed over Europe the same divisions and uncertainties as of old.

24
Epilogue

My story began with a bull. It ends with a lion. Outside the gates of the Arsenal in Venice stands a marble beast, symbol of the city that once commanded Europe's greatest commercial empire. It was carved in the fourth century BC and looted from Piraeus in Greece by a seventeenth-century Venetian, Francesco Morosini, who also blew up the Parthenon. The lion sits on its haunches with strange characters scratched into its surface. For centuries they were a mystery, but they have recently been deciphered as eleventh-century Norse runes, by one 'Asmund' on the orders of 'Harold the Tall'. Harold was a Viking mercenary employed by the emperors of Constantinople.

The story of the Piraeus lion thus encircles Europe. It embraces the temples of Athens and the fjords of Scandinavia, the walls of Byzantium and the merchants of Venice. It bids us free ourselves from our own place in history and see the past as a distant land, one through which we must travel with eyes and minds open, free of preconception and hindsight but aware of the constant interconnectedness of events.

At the end of this journey, I see the themes I noted at the start as vivid as ever. Geography remains godparent to Europe's history. France, Germany and the Low Countries, the core of Charlemagne's domain, dominate the European conversation as they have always done. Europe's Mediterranean border, of Greece, Italy and Spain, is trapped by the eurozone, and held apart from the prosperity of the north, as it has been since the seventeenth century. Britain remains aloof. Russia remains enigmatic, and its relations with its neighbours fraught. Little seems to change.

Into the pint pot of Europe's geography has been tipped the quart of migration, in early times from Asia and more recently from all corners of the globe. This kaleidoscope has produced a diversity of peoples and languages that is so vivid a feature of the modern continent. Whether or not this diversity, traced back to the earliest tribal settlements, holds the key to the disparate strands of Europe's history is the source of ceaseless controversy.

Most obvious to historians is the part tribal and later communal differences have played in the violent conflicts that have been Europe's default setting. These conflicts emerged from the Middle Ages as an ingrained, almost ritualized, addiction to war, practised by youths mostly still in their teens and twenties, men such as Clovis, Frederick II of Germany, Edward III of England, Charles V of Spain, Louis XIV and Napoleon. At this level, Europe's story has been a tragedy of competing virilities.

Each of the treaties that have waymarked history – Augsburg, Westphalia, Utrecht, Vienna, Versailles – has struggled to keep the peace but has done so for little more than two generations before war resumed. Even Potsdam in 1945 lasted only until the fall of the Soviet Union in 1989. Now the conspicuous lack of a post-cold-war settlement is putting Europe's diplomacy under renewed strain. The continent's DNA seems to allow people to live calmly with each other only as long as the memory of the last bout of bloodletting survives. A note of wisdom from the past might be that of the dying Louis XIV, 'Above all, remain at peace with your neighbours. I loved war too much.'

Whether Europe's belligerence can be attributed to the fractiousness of its original tribes I cannot tell. Perhaps more fruitful is to see in diversity the roots of the competitive energy that has underpinned Europe's more positive achievements. I believe this energy emerged from the tension between its land-based and its sea-based early settlers. Seafaring fostered enterprise, curiosity, contact and innovation. It involved rivalry between individuals and groups, and a readiness to engage with strangers. The early maritime city states gave rise to Athens and the Aegean diaspora. The necessity of expansion produced Scandinavia's explorers and adventurers. The spirit of the sea created the trading cultures of the Mediterranean, the Baltic, the North Sea and eventually the Atlantic. In contrast, land-based peoples reaching Europe from Anatolia and the Russian steppes might put down roots, amass wealth and control territory, but they were constantly in contention with the peoples of the sea.

I view what are called European values as being forged from this contentiousness, expressed by Machiavelli as a 'multiplicity of states encouraging . . . the capacity for action, and the creative energy of the individual'. Europe's faith, Christianity, did not always contribute to this energy. Some historians blame a schismatic Christian church for Europe's intellectual lethargy in the millennium after Christ, while others see virtue in the church's encouragement of education and its complex theology of sin, love and redemption. The church was certainly a divisive and often violent force. But this did not prevent, and perhaps stimulated, the revolutions that fashioned the Europe we know today, those of Renaissance, Reformation and Enlightenment.

Both classicism and Christianity can claim parenthood over the values so often ascribed to European civilization. They are values of tolerance, equality before the law, freedom of speech, human and civil rights and consent to rule. The application of these values was often partial and hypocritical, as in autocracy, slavery and the craving for empire. But both the US constitution and the Charter of the United Nations were based on ideals adumbrated by Plato and Aristotle, reflected in Magna Carta and disseminated by the Enlightenment.

Europe's mix of regulated capitalism and social welfare has long been the ambition of the world's economic and political reformers. They still lie at the ideological heart of the European Union. The continent is home to ten per cent of the world's population, yet it consumes half the world's spending on welfare. For all their flaws, the EU's treaties of Rome, Maastricht and Lisbon have presided over half a century not just of peace but also of prosperity. As a result the continent is, with its offspring America, the desired destination of the world's most youthful and enterprising migrants.

Europe's universities are celebrated, its museums crowded, its artistic legacy honoured. When I enter a concert hall in Los Angeles, Tokyo, Shanghai or Dubai, it is the music of Mozart and Beethoven that floats in the air. The English language is that of global communication. Europe's battered cities remain the most magnetic to tourists. Their cultural legacy is such that what Burke said at the turn of the nineteenth century is even truer of the twenty-first, that 'no European can be a complete exile in any part of Europe'. This does not detract from what I find exhilarating about other continents and cultures. But to this European, the continent's qualities remain supreme.

All that said, as I write, clouds are appearing on the horizon. Europe's euphoria at the end of the cold war – reminiscent of that of the 1890s – is wearing thin. Its democratic practices are no longer seen as inevitable to people of all other continents. As we saw in the last chapter, faith in Europe's institutions is limited. The expectation at the turn of the twenty-first century was that 'western values' had won the argument and would take over the world. That no longer looks plausible. The rise of an authoritarian China, the relapse of Russia and the struggle for reform within Islam have left Europe's liberal qualities looking more peculiar to Europe than a beacon of hope to the world.

One reason could be that Europe is losing its ideological

homogeneity. The EU's political structure, fashioned by the cold war, has become cumbersome and retrospective, gripped by a democratic deficit which no one has been able to bridge. It lacks a constitution to which its multitudinous subjects can give wholehearted assent. Europe's leaders have been unable to achieve the balance so vital to regional stability, between state and superstate, locality and centre, the citizenship of a nation and the citizenship of Europe. Fifty years of centripetalism have given way to centrifugalism.

All eyes have turned, yet again, towards Germany, but Germany's leadership of Europe is uncertain and widely questioned. Europe's second-biggest economy, that of the United Kingdom, has lost patience and resumed its historical detachment. Following such fractured leadership, Europe's oldest dividing line, roughly east and west of the Elbe/Danube, is re-emerging. The nations to its east are drifting away from the liberal values entrenched in half a century of union, and are moving in the direction of nationalism and autocracy. Relations with Putin's Russia have reverted to the belligerence and rhetoric of the cold war. It seems Europe never learns.

The reality is that, since the fall of Rome, no power has come near to ruling this continent. Charlemagne did not do so, nor did the Habsburg Holy Roman Emperors, nor France's Napoleon, nor Germany's Hitler, nor yet the commissioners of the European Union. If history teaches anything, it is that all attempts to straighten Kant's 'crooked timber of humanity' will fail. Europe's peoples will not be put in bondage to a superior state, however liberal its intentions.

The EU arose from an eagerness to merge Europe's economies into one trading bloc. I have no doubt that if the EU did not exist, Europe's statesmen would be currently circling its capitals trying to invent it. But such integration needs policing, and policing needs government. Such government has, throughout history, failed when shorn of consent. The EU has sought ever more power without consent. It can now only decay if it does not repatriate that power to its members. This currently includes control of borders and immigration, and thus a role, as members see it, in the evolving character of their societies.

I have come through this story under no illusion that peace in Europe can be taken for granted, let alone that we are at 'the end of history'. But I do remain intrigued by a final question, whether anything in the past half-century might indicate that Europe has seen the philosopher's stone of peace. This melting pot of peoples has spent two thousand years feuding, fighting and expanding to dominate, or at least influence, much of the world. Is it conceivable that they have found, through the mechanism of an imperfect trading bloc, the means to live in harmony with themselves and their neighbours?

In time, I believe, this could happen through the EU evolving into a multi-tiered, multi-valent confederacy. There will be zones within zones, each with a bespoke relationship with the rest. Relations with Russia and its neighbours will always be vexed, but not necessarily aggressive. Britain will always be Janus-faced, but at least half-committed. The continent will be messy, rather as the Holy Roman Empire was messy. But that empire did not set too bad an example. Europe might live more comfortably with messiness than with centralism.

I have travelled the length and breadth of Europe. I have journeyed from Portugal's Algarve to the quaysides of St Petersburg, from Galway's Aran Islands to the beaches of Minoan Crete. I have walked the streets of Europe's cities, from London to Paris, Berlin, Moscow, Athens, Rome, Lisbon and Madrid. I love them all. And I can sense the ghosts of the past, gazing down on them as from a Tiepolo ceiling. I see Augustus and Charlemagne, Charles V and Catherine the Great, Talleyrand and Bismarck, nodding in recognition of today's continent. But I hear them say to each other, 'How familiar – and how very fragile.' Then I glimpse the Piraeus lion, who has seen it all before, and he gives me an enigmatic smile.

A Timeline of European History

955	Otto defeats Magyars at Lechfeld
988	Vladimir brings Russia into the Byzantine church
1015–17	Cnut occupies England
1054	Great Schism between Rome and Byzantium
1066	Normans conquer England
1077	Penitent Henry IV, Holy Roman Emperor, walks to Canossa
1099	First crusade occupies Jerusalem
1147	Second crusade
1170	Murder of Becket at Canterbury
1204	Fourth crusade sacks Constantinople
1215	Magna Carta in England
1216	Innocent III's Fourth Lateran Council decrees promulgated
1241	Golden Horde reaches Hungary
1265	De Montfort's parliament
1309	Philip of France establishes Avignon papacy
1337	Outbreak of Hundred Years War
1346	Battle of Crécy
1347–51	Black Death ravages Europe
1378	Divided papacy causes western schism
1402	Jan Hus preaches Wycliffe's teachings in Prague
1415	Council of Constance, burning of Hus
1417	End of Western Schism
1453	Battle of Castillon ends Hundred Years War
	Fall of Constantinople to Ottomans
1455	Gutenberg prints Bible
1456	Sailors sent by Henry the Navigator reach Cape Verde Islands
1480	Ivan the Great drives out Tartars
1483	Torquemada heads Spanish Inquisition

1492	Fall of Moorish Granada
	Columbus lands in the Caribbean
1494–8	Savonarola in Florence
1517	Luther publishes theses against Rome
1519	Charles V becomes Holy Roman Emperor
1520	Francis I and Henry VIII meet at the Field of the Cloth of Gold
1526	Suleiman the Magnificent defeats Hungarians at Mohács
1530	Diet of Augsburg hears Protestant confession
1545	Council of Trent hears Catholic rebuttal
1555	Peace of Augsburg compromises on *cuius regio, eius religio*
1571	Catholics defeat Ottomans at Lepanto
1572	St Bartholomew's Day massacre
1588	Defeat of Spanish Armada
1598	Henry IV passes Edict of Nantes tolerating Protestant Huguenots
1618	Defenestration of Prague begins Thirty Years War
1648	Peace of Westphalia
1649	Execution of Charles I initiates Cromwellian commonwealth
1660	Restoration of Charles II to English throne
1661	Louis XIV begins personal rule
1672–8	Franco–Dutch War
1685	Louis revokes Edict of Nantes, expels Huguenots
1688	William of Orange invades England, James II flees to France
1688–97	Nine Years War
1701–14	War of Spanish Succession
1713	Treaty of Utrecht

1740–48	War of Austrian Succession
	Frederick of Prussia invades Silesia
1756–63	Seven Years War
1762	Catherine the Great seizes throne of Russia
1763	Treaty of Paris concludes Seven Years War
1773	Boston Tea Party
1775–83	American War of Independence
1789	French Revolution starts
1793	Robespierre's Terror
1804	Napoleon crowns himself French emperor
1805	Battles of Trafalgar and Austerlitz
1806	Dissolution of the Holy Roman Empire
1812	Napoleon's retreat from Moscow
1815	Battle of Waterloo and fall of Napoleon
1830	Greek independence
	First year of abortive revolutions
1832	British Reform Act abolishes rotten boroughs
1848	Second year of abortive revolutions
1853–6	Crimean War
1861	Unification of Italy
1866	Bismarck defeats Austria
1871	Bismarck defeats France
1885	Second Congress of Berlin defines Europe's empires
1914–18	Great War
1917	Russian revolution
1919	Treaty of Versailles
1925	Treaty of Locarno
1929	Start of Great Depression
1939	Hitler invades Poland, start of Second World War
1941	America enters war following Pearl Harbor
1945	Yalta and Potsdam conferences; war ends
1948–9	Blockade of Berlin

A Timeline of European History

1949	Foundation of NATO
1957	Treaty of Rome sets up EEC
1962	Cuban missile crisis
1989	Fall of Berlin Wall
1991	Dissolution of Soviet Union
1999	Putin assumes power in Moscow
2002	Euro becomes pan-European currency
2016	United Kingdom votes to leave EU

Author's Note

This book follows the pattern of my *Short History of England* (Profile, 2011). It seeks to give a straightforward narrative of Europe, its politics and its people, seen from the standpoint of the continent as a whole. Any short history must rely on secondary sources, which are chiefly those mentioned in the Further Reading section. Most are histories of Europe in general, as that is the theme of this book. Most reliable has been the Penguin History of Europe series. Of modern books, those of Norman Davies and J. M. Roberts are masterly. A useful narrower focus comes from Daniel Boorstin's *The Discoverers* and Peter Wilson's study of the Holy Roman Empire. Of the classics, I found Edward Gibbon and H. A. L. Fisher always elegant and enjoyable.

Modern scholarship is challenging many customary interpretations of Europe's past, questioning reputations and the significance of well-known events. In the earlier chapters even dates and quotations tend to be the subject of debate. For the most part, I have had to resist the temptation to burrow down into controversy and have gone with the conventional wisdom. I have in large part used the anglicized spellings of foreign places and people. Dates after the names of rulers are those of their period in power, unless otherwise stated. I of course welcome any comments and corrections.

I must thank those who have read and commented on the text. They include Jeremy Black, Peter Furtado, Mark Greengrass, Elina Screen, Chris Wickham, my brother, Tom Jenkins, and my wife, Hannah. Since I have mostly but not always accepted their advice, I must exonerate them from any responsibility for errors of fact or analysis. I also thank at Penguin my editor, Daniel Crewe, who first induced me to undertake this awesome task, Natalie Wall for managing the editorial process, Connor Brown, Mike Davis for maps, Cecilia Mackay for researching and supplying the illustrations, Trevor Horwood for copy-editing and Ruth Killick for publicity.

Further Reading

The following books are either cited in the text or have been used as sources of reference:

Abulafia, David, *The Great Sea*, 2011
Beard, Mary, *SPQR*, 2015
Black, Jeremy, *What If?*, 2008
Blanning, Tim, *The Pursuit of Glory*, 2007
Boorstin, Daniel, *The Discoverers*, 1985
Bradford, Ernle, *Mediterranean*, 1971
Clark, Christopher, *The Sleepwalkers*, 2012
Davies, Norman, *Europe, a History*, 1996
———, *Vanished Kingdoms*, 2011
Evans, Richard J., *The Pursuit of Power*, 2016
Fisher, H. A. L., *A History of Europe*, 1938
Frankopan, Peter, *The Silk Roads*, 2015
Gaddis, John Lewis, *The Cold War*, 2005
Gibbon, Edward, *The History of the Decline and Fall of the Roman Empire* (3 vols.), ed. David Womersley, 1994
Greengrass, Mark, *Christendom Destroyed*, 2014
Hawes, James, *The Shortest History of Germany*, 2017
Herrin, Judith, *The Formation of Christendom*, 1987
Hitchcock, William, *The Struggle for Europe*, 2003
Hughes, Bettany, *Istanbul*, 2017
Judt, Tony, *Postwar*, 2005
Kershaw, Ian, *To Hell and Back*, 2015
MacCulloch, Diarmaid, *A History of Christianity*, 2009

Further Reading

MacMillan, Margaret, *The War That Ended Peace*, 2013
Morris, Ian, *The Measure of Civilisation*, 2013
Nixey, Catherine, *The Darkening Age*, 2017
Norwich, John Julius, *The Popes*, 2012
————, *Four Princes*, 2016
Robb, Graham, *The Discovery of France*, 2007
Roberts, J. M., *A History of Europe*, 1996
Runciman, Steven, *Byzantine Civilisation*, 1933
Siedentop, Larry, *Inventing the Individual*, 2014
Simms, Brendan, *Europe, The Struggle for Supremacy*, 2013
Vincent, John, *An Intelligent Person's Guide to History*, 1995
Wedgwood, Veronica, *The Thirty Years War*, 1938
Wickham, Chris, *The Inheritance of Rome*, 2009
Wilson, Peter, *The Holy Roman Empire*, 2016
Winder, Simon, *Germania*, 2010
Zamoyski, Adam, *Holy Madness*, 1999

Index

Aachen (Germany) 54, 55, 56

Abbasids 52

Aberdeen, George Hamilton-Gordon, 4th Earl of 217

Abkhazia 295

Achaeans 9–10

Acheson, Dean 278

Achilles (mythological figure) 17

Acre, Siege of (1191) 74

Act of Settlement (England; 1701) 147–8

Act of Supremacy (England; 1534) 122

Actium, Battle of (31 BC) 27

Adam, Robert 34

Adenauer, Konrad 274–5

Aeschylus 15

Aethelbert, King of Kent 49

Aetius, Flavius (Roman general) 41–2

Afghanistan 231, 296; Soviet invasion (1979) 281

Afonso I, King of Portugal 72

Africa: Roman era 22, 25, 33; Vandal rule 40, 44, 46; Byzantine era 47, 50, 52; 15th-century colonial expansion 107, 109; slave trade 127, 153, 199; 19th-century colonial expansion 230; Second World War campaigns 262, 265; see also Algeria; Egypt; Ethiopia; Libya; Morocco; South Africa; Tunisia

Agincourt, Battle of (1415) 97, 98, 119

Agrigentum (Sicily) 11

Agrippa (Roman statesman) 28

Al Qaeda (Islamist militant organization) 296

Al-Hakam II, Caliph of Cordoba 53

Alaric, King of the Visigoths 39–40, 42

Alaska 230–31

Albert, Prince consort 206, 212, 216

Alberti, Leon Battista 100

Albrecht of Brandenburg, Elector of Mainz 113

Alcuin of York 55

Alexander I, Russian tsar 187, 190, 193, 199, 203

Alexander II, Pope 65

Alexander II, Russian tsar 218, 227, 228

Alexander V, Anti-pope 95

Alexander VI, Pope 110

Alexander the Great 18–19

Alexandria (Egypt) 34, 38, 50, 51; library 18, 19, 22, 100

Alexios Komnenos, Byzantine emperor 69, 70

Alfred, King of Wessex 58

Algeria 40, 277

317

He just wanted a decent book to read ...

Not too much to ask, is it? It was in 1935 when Allen Lane, Managing Director of Bodley Head Publishers, stood on a platform at Exeter railway station looking for something good to read on his journey back to London. His choice was limited to popular magazines and poor-quality paperbacks – the same choice faced every day by the vast majority of readers, few of whom could afford hardbacks. Lane's disappointment and subsequent anger at the range of books generally available led him to found a company – and change the world.

'We believed in the existence in this country of a vast reading public for intelligent books at a low price, and staked everything on it'
Sir Allen Lane, 1902–1970, founder of Penguin Books

The quality paperback had arrived – and not just in bookshops. Lane was adamant that his Penguins should appear in chain stores and tobacconists, and should cost no more than a packet of cigarettes.

Reading habits (and cigarette prices) have changed since 1935, but Penguin still believes in publishing the best books for everybody to enjoy. We still believe that good design costs no more than bad design, and we still believe that quality books published passionately and responsibly make the world a better place.

So wherever you see the little bird – whether it's on a piece of prize-winning literary fiction or a celebrity autobiography, political tour de force or historical masterpiece, a serial-killer thriller, reference book, world classic or a piece of pure escapism – you can bet that it represents the very best that the genre has to offer.

Whatever you like to read – trust Penguin.

read more
www.penguin.co.uk